W9-CPB-654

Black Dahlia™

Prima's

Official

Strategy

Guide

Mel Odom

PRIMA PUBLISHING
Rocklin, California
(916) 632-4400
www.primagames.com

PRIMA'S SECRETS ® is a registered trademark of Prima Publishing, a division of Prima Communications, Inc.

P

PRIMA ® and Prima Publishing® are registered trademarks of Prima Communications, Inc.

© 1998 by Prima Publishing. All rights reserved. No part of this book may be reproduced or transmitted in any form or by any means, electronic or mechanical, including photocopying, recording, or by any information storage or retrieval system without written permission from Prima Publishing, except for the inclusion of quotations in a review.

Project Editor: Richard Dal Porto
Original Icon Illustrations by Susie Bell

The Black Dahlia game © 1997 by Take 2 Interactive Software, Inc. All rights reserved. Original characters are copyrighted characters of Take 2 Interactive Software. The trademark "Black Dahlia" is owned by Take 2 Interactive Software. Unauthorized use is prohibited.

No part of this book may be reproduced or transmitted in any form or by any means, electronic or mechanical, including photocopying, recording, or by any information storage or retrieval system without written permission from Prima Publishing, except for the inclusion of quotations in a review.
All products and characters mentioned in this book are trademarks of their respective companies.

Important:
Prima Publishing has made every effort to determine that the information contained in this book is accurate. However, the publisher makes no warranty, either expressed or implied, as to the accuracy, effectiveness, or completeness of the material in this book; nor does the publisher assume liability for damages, either incidental or consequential, that may result from using the information in this book. The publisher cannot provide information regarding game play, hints and strategies, or problems with hardware or software. Questions should be directed to the support numbers provided by the game and device manufacturers in their documentation. Some game tricks require precise timing and may require repeated attempts before the desired result is achieved.

ISBN: 7615-1213-6
Library of Congress Catalog Card Number: 97-68842
Printed in the United States of America

98 99 00 01 DD 10 9 8 7 6 5 4 3 2 1

Contents

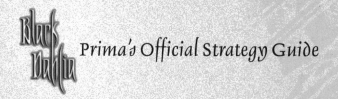
Introduction

Behind Black Dahlia

The time is the 1940s. The streets are mean, and they wind through Cleveland, Ohio, Germany, and finally Los Angeles. The world is at war for the second time. The Nazis are bigger, stronger, and bolder than ever before, and the whole free world is at stake. Throw in a quest for mythological powers and some psychic phenomena, and you're off on one of the grandest adventures ever to pulse through your computer.

Take 2 Interactive Software has created a game with arcane and intricate puzzles to bedevil you to no end. *Black Dahlia: Prima's Official Strategy Guide* was designed to help you through some of the rough spots by offering insights into those puzzles and showing you how all the threads tie together.

But even more intriguing is the pursuit of the madman who has tortured and killed so many innocents. The story presented within the framework of the game is at once intense and compelling. As you pursue the clues and the action, you will become Agent Jim Pearson, knowing that only you can stop the butcher before he strikes again.

The world that has been created for the game is realistic. From the music to the language, to the actual events of the murders, care has been taken to make the player feel at home and experience the desire to solve the crimes and nail the murderer.

The video sequences were filmed and carefully placed within the gameplay. Dennis Hopper and Teri Garr star in the game, and Darren Eliker turns in a great performance as Jim Pearson. The texture, mood, and props of the game are dead-bang on.

Much attention was given to Pearson and his world as well. Watch how the World Map screen changes throughout the game. That World Map screen reflects the lengths Pearson goes to in order to trap the killer. And it shows how that world steadily erodes, leading to the dynamic conclusion of the game.

There is so much that you're going to enjoy about the game, but let us turn our attention for a moment on the impetus of the project.

On January 14, 1947, Elizabeth Short was a 22-year-old woman with dreams of breaking into the film world of Hollywood and capturing attention, possibly even fame. As far as anyone knows, she never even made it to a screen test.

But on January 15, 1947, she became famous. That day, her body, cut in half and brutalized, was found in a vacant lot on 39th and Norton. One of the witnesses later interviewed by journalists gave her the nickname she became known by: The Black Dahlia. The witness told the newshounds that Miss Short had an affinity for black clothing. She was also beautiful, so the nickname fit: a black flower.

So, who actually killed the Black Dahlia? We may never know the true answer. Michael Newton, a noted true crime journalist, whose work has been used in FBI databases regarding serial killers, wrote the non-fiction book, *Daddy was the Black Dahlia Killer*. In the book, Newton and his co-author, Janice Knowlton, delineated a solution to the crime that the LAPD still refuse to acknowledge.

Detective John St. John of the LA Police Department, also known as Jigsaw John, was one of the top homicide investigators in his field. Over his career, Jigsaw John managed to solve an incredible 98–99 percent of his cases, but he never solved the mystery of the Black Dahlia. At least, not officially.

Another resource for *Black Dahlia* was the serial killer known both as the Torso Killer and the Mad Butcher of Kingsbury Row. The investigating officer on that case was Eliot Ness, of the Untouchables fame. The Torso Killer murdered in the same fashion as the person who killed the Black Dahlia. Those murders also remain unsolved to this day.

Using the background of World War II, Take 2 presents a complete mystery involving the Dahlia and a solution for who killed her and why. That solution incorporates the known interest by Hitler's military to revive the old Norse mythos and their search for supernatural objects that would give them power to take on a world and win.

In the first part of the game, Pearson is an investigator drawn into the macabre web surrounding the Black Dahlia (which first began as something other than a nickname for Elizabeth Short). Midway through the game, we journey with Pearson to plunder the remains of a ravaged monastery that still contains secrets, taking on puzzles and dangers that would challenge even the greatest adventurer. The world of wonderment expands, letting you know that the solution is going to be much more twisted than you were expecting.

And time is running out as the chase leads you back to Los Angeles, to a meeting with warped destiny on January 15, 1947. Enjoy the mystery, the puzzles, the suspense, and the chase. Take 2 has delivered a game that will satisfy for hours and linger in your mind even longer.

How To Use This Book

The strategy guide is divided into two sections. If you want a blow-by-blow account of how to figure out the mystery and all the puzzles you encounter, stay with the first 16 chapters. In those chapters you'll find documentation and logical thinking that will help you solve some of the puzzles you may have gotten stuck on during your own play.

The step-by-step solution to the puzzles will be found in tips in the part of the walkthrough where the puzzles appear. The main text in these areas contain hints and clues that may help you reach a conclusion that you had missed on your own. That way you still have the satisfaction of knowing you solved the problems with only a little nudge in the right direction.

If you've gotten frustrated with a puzzle and simply want to get through it, the tips are definitely the way to go.

Now, if you're looking for the down-and-dirty-get-me-there-quick-'cause-I'm-screaming-all-the-way guide, turn to Chapter 17. There, you'll find a Quick Trip walkthrough, which—except for the major puzzles—gives you a click-by-click account of where to go in the game. For the major puzzles, you'll have to refer back to the chapters where the solutions are given.

Playing the Game

Black Dahlia play is very uncomplicated: your mouse operates almost all of the play. There are a couple instances where you need the (Esc) key, and you'll need to type in a name or two here and there.

Left-clicking on an individual will bring up a list of topics you can discuss with that person at that time. You know you are done talking to someone when left-clicking on them no longer brings up any options. Coming back to different characters in the game after different events have happened often will reveal new topics you need to discuss.

Left-clicking on the directional arrows that appear will allow you to go in that direction. Left-clicking on objects when the cursor rune becomes interactive (changes into a revolving arrow shape) will let you manipulate those objects.

Right-clicking at any time during gameplay pulls up the Supplemental List, allowing you a choice of: Options, Inventory, World Map, Notebook, Help, Restore, Save, and Exit. Options lets you adjust settings to the game. Inventory takes you to the list of items you've discovered during your investigations and allows you to interact with them there. Use the World Map to change locations in your pursuit. The Notebook function gives you a means to check through the pertinent details of your case (and provides clues for you to know what details are pertinent). The Help function assists with any gameplay problems. The Restore function enables you to restart a Saved game. The Save function saves your games when you have to quit for the moment or the night. And the Exit function allows you to quit *Black Dahlia*, a function you'll be loathe to use.

The Pen
Quest

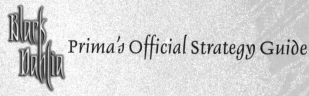
Mr. Sullivan

You're going to hit the ground running in this one, so don't worry about keeping those crisp lines in the old trench coat or that neat bend in the fedora. In the tradition of true *film noir*, things are not going to be as they appear to be.

Perhaps not even at the end of the hunt set before you.

Mr. Sullivan, the head of the Cleveland branch of the COI, is a gruff, brusque man.

Any information you get from Sullivan will require a certain investment of shoe leather and thinking on your part. He won't answer just any question you may pose. As you uncover more information during your investigation, you'll find that you can return to his office and ask new questions that will help streamline the search you've been assigned.

As you first enter Sullivan's office, notice the *Cleveland Times*—especially the glaring headline he's reading: SEVENTH TORSO VICTIM FOUND; Mad Butcher Still on the Loose.

Sullivan briefly introduces himself and immediately hands over your agency ID and a complaint file passed on by a Cleveland city detective. According to Sullivan, the complaint should be straightforward and handled as quickly as possible. He informs you that his door is always open in case you have any questions.

Then he tells you that your office is across the hall. He asks that you forgive the mess in your new office. Your predecessor left unexpectedly, and no one has had time to clean the office.

When you stand there a little too long, he says he hopes that you can handle things on your own, letting you know he's not going to be there to nursemaid you. It's something you're going to have to get used to in the COI.

Agent Pensky's Aberrations

When you get to your new office, the impression that things may not run as smoothly as you had hoped begins to settle in. The office is a mess, indicating to you that the person had lax organizational skills. Books and file cabinet drawers are scattered across the desk, and the bookcase on the left is stuffed haphazardly with volumes.

Turn to the right and flip on the light switch. The illumination is dim, but it does help.

Closer inspection of the contents of the bookshelves leads you to believe that the previous agent in this office had peculiar interests.

NOTE

As mentioned in the introduction, Black Dahlia *is mouse-driven and user-friendly. When the arrow flattens out in a particular direction, you can walk in that direction. When the ⊗ changes into a spinning arrow you can interact with that person or object.*

For the moment, take a look at the books and objects on the shelves. They will pique your interest. We'll get around to the other things as they come up during the natural progression of the story.

From the casebook of COI Agent James R. Pearson:

President Roosevelt had just authorized the formation of the COI that summer. They were supposed to be the outfit that handled the real spy stuff overseas. It was the place to be if you wanted real adventure.

At least, that was the bill of goods the recruiters for the COI sold me.

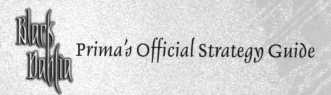
And here I was: stuck in a crummy old office. In Cleveland of all places, as far away from any real action as I could imagine.

The books and objects scattered across the shelves to the left immediately draw your attention. But so does the locked cabinet. For the moment, opening it is impossible.

Other points of intense interest will be the skull on the center shelf...

...the vase on the lower right shelf...

...the cylinder on the upper left shelf, and the selection of books on the shelves.

Whoever had this office before you certainly had eclectic reading habits. Histories are side by side with books on mathematics. Ancient novels balance books on geography. Romance novels and poetry occupy the same level of importance as political trea-

tises and dictionaries.

Curious about who was in this office before you? Well, curiosity should be in your nature. Time to see about settling part of it.

Sullivan handed over an ID case and the file, right? Part of any good ego stroke in the field of investigation

is seeing what kind of buzzer they give you. I mean, you get a small shield; chances are, when you flash it in someone's face, they may not be as impressed. COI hasn't been around long, so not many people know of it.

Take the Badge out and take a look at it.

TIP

To access any items in your Inventory, right-click the mouse to pull up the supplemental list and then select Inventory. For the moment, there are only two items in the Inventory: the Badge and the Case File. Left-click on Badge in the Inventory list and then left-click on the Badge itself.

Hey, not bad. The Badge fills up one whole side of the ID case. Nice to know that President Roosevelt feels that the COI deserves the attention. Throw that buzzer in somebody's face, and they're going to sit up and take notice, brother.

Hold up a minute, shamus! Don't put that ID case away yet. Didn't you notice something over on the left, in the pocket behind the ID card?

Yeah, a silver disk. Take it out and look at it.

TIP

Again, getting the St. Christopher's medal out is easily accomplished by left-clicking the rune on it.

To get out of the Inventory list, left-click on Exit.

A St. Christopher's medal? It's yours, brother—been yours for a long time. You carry it as a good luck charm. And maybe you need some good luck, because in this office you start wondering what happened to the Joe that was here before you.

Sullivan seemed intent on remaining vague about who the guy was and what happened to him. Did he just get fed up and quit? Or did he get bounced? The most uncomfortable thought that races around in the back of your brain (that's kept you alive in one scrape after another) is that the other agent is dead, killed somewhere in the line of duty.

But maybe no one knows what happened to the guy at all. Now there's a creepy thought.

Okay, enough dwelling on that. You got your investigator's radar kicked on, and that's the main point. Time to dig in and take a look at everything else you've been given to work on.

Instead of getting to that case file immediately, though, why not toss the room? If the ID case and buzzer did belong to the agent who held this office, and nobody at Cleveland COI has made an effort to clean up things, maybe there'll be some clues lying around the room. You can get the skinny on the guy all by yourself.

Like that, huh? Take a seat behind the desk and let's get started. Nothing like casing a joint, is there?

TIP

Left-click and drag the cursor down to the desk drawers.
Left-click on the desk drawers to open and close them.

FDR Creates New Intelligence Service

Nothing on the desk seems to have anything interesting in it. Try the center desk drawer. Look, there's a newspaper article: FDR Creates New Intelligence Service.

Well, that's certainly old news. Since you were hired for the Office of the Coordinator of Information, you know all about the COI and the fact that the agency is supposed "to collect and analyze all information and data which may bear upon national security, to correlate such information and data and make the same available to the President and to such departments and officials of the Government as the President may determine, and to carry out when requested by the President such supplementary activities as may facilitate the securing of information important for national security not now available to the Government."

Of course, the newspaper reporter goes on to dish out some negatives about the COI's formation and says that the agency is going to be a new American Gestapo as Hitler's boys are setting up in Europe these days. And old J. Edgar Hoover of the FBI damn sure isn't happy about the COI. The United States has always been J. Edgar's stomping grounds, and he considers the COI an infringement on his territory.

Tough. America has a lot of enemies, and you're just doing your bit to protect the grand old lady, right?

There's a report in the folder next to the newspaper article. *The "Magic" Chink in Hitler's Armor: A Preliminary Report.*

Now that sounds like some heavy reading. But you flip through it anyway, because you know only the guy willing to dig through everything is going to find

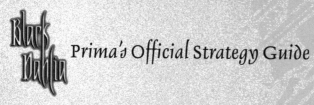

everything. The report goes on to document how interested the Nazi Führer and his closest supporters are in mysticism and occult studies. It also recounts how Rudolph Hess, one of Hitler's main people, was captured after British intelligence tricked him through astrological forecasts that he believed in.

Part of the report also provides details on Heinrich Himmler, who has reportedly refurbished an ancient monastery in Wevelsburg. He turned it back into a version of a knight's castle and meets there with his council of Black Knights who are high ranking SS officers. They've even had seances there, and ain't that a kick in the pants thinking about one of Hitler's finest sitting around a table trying to contact long dead Aryan heroes?

You've got to wonder who penned such a fantastic report and what the press would do if they got their hands on it.

Still, as a COI agent, you've been told to expect all kinds of strange rumors. It's your job to check them out. Evidently, the agent who last had this office had yet to get around to this one. Or maybe he was working on it when he "disappeared"? Definitely something to think about.

Look down on the right side of the desk where there's another drawer. Pull it open and give it a whirl.

TIP *In case you haven't noticed yet, to look up or down, simply drag the mouse through the top or bottom of the screen to change perspectives.*

The last agent in this office may not have been organized, brother, but his heart was in the right place. He left a "Things To Do" list on the notepad you find here.

- ✔ Return library books
- ✔ Withdraw money
- ✔ Phone Cassie
- ✔ Contact jeweler
- ✔ Check post office box
- ✔ Get a good stiff drink
- ✔ Get new boots

✔ Change bulb in ceiling light

Check back with Professor Strauss

Clean office!

So okay, the guy wasn't perfect, and he didn't quite get around to everything on the list. But he was thorough enough to figure in some personal time. Phoning Cassie, getting a good stiff drink, and getting some new boots—sounds like a guy who's got more going on than only the job. That doesn't sound like somebody who'd be suicidal, does it?

Yeah. So where did that happy little thought come from? I know. I don't like mysteries myself, and the other agent is really pressing on your brain. Sitting here in this quiet, cluttered little office, it's hard to keep your mind focused on anything else.

Not for the first time, you have your doubts about all the great things you were planning to do while on the COI's payroll.

And hey, what's this little number? Take a look under the notepad.

TIP

To look under the notebook, put the cursor over it, press the left-click mouse button down and slide the notebook up. Once the notebook is clear, left-click on the pistol to add it to your Inventory.

Armed and Dangerous

That's a snub-nosed .38. Not as big as the .45 you're packing, but a handful of knockdown firepower all the same. You drop it in your pocket. A little backup insurance isn't going to hurt you at all.

Close the drawer and inspect the file cabinet to the right of the desk.

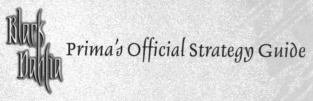
The books on top of the filing cabinet yield a COI propaganda publication called *Fifth Column Lessons for America*. Quickly flipping through it, you discover that it's quite similar to the other COI information shown by the recruiters who signed you. With Nazi Germany storming through the European theater, it makes good sense for the American people to be on the lookout for saboteurs in their own cities. After all, the US didn't exactly sit out the Great War the way some thought it would. An opening strike against the US wouldn't be completely unexpected.

Opening the top drawer of the filing cabinet, you find a report dated September 12, 1941. Only a short time ago. Reading through it, you see that the first page and a half talks about fantastical stories and marks and runes. Maybe the writer was thinking about submitting a story to one of the pulp magazines that are all the rage these days. You've even read an *Operator 5*, *Phantom Detective*, *Shadow*, and *Doc Savage* yourself. This kind of stuff seems as though it would fit right into one of those magazines.

There are other passages; these are dated September 22, October 8, and October 30—relatively new additions. All of them center on a ritual that you don't grasp at the moment.

Nor is there any indication of who authored the document. But it is typewritten, suggesting that it may have been written by the agent who held this office.

Sitting back in the desk chair and contemplating everything that you have uncovered—thinking about the last guy with his butt parked in this seat behind this desk—leaves you uneasy. It makes you wonder if the guy was a few bricks shy of a full load.

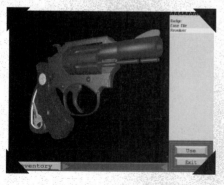

So you think about that .38 you picked up and examined so casually. Was it fully loaded? Or was the guy packing gumdrops in the cylinder instead of lead? Take it out and give it another examination.

Well, it's loaded all right. And the bullets all look in good condition. Everything's jake. The grips, however, seem a little loose. Maybe you should tighten them.

Wait, they're not loose...there's something rattling around inside them. Give the grips a push and see if they'll give. Jumping Jehosaphat—that's a key someone's hidden away inside there!

TIP

To get the key to the locked bookcase cabinet door, right-click the mouse to get the supplemental list, left-click on the Inventory, and left-click on Revolver in the list. Once you have the Revolver, left-click and hold on the bottom of the grip. Pull the grip forward to the right. When it opens, the key will be revealed.

Left-click on the key to add it to the Inventory list.

What kind of squirrel would hide a key in a gunbutt?

Yeah, well, that's the kind of question you have to ask yourself in a situation like this. The guy wasn't dealing from any kind of deck you're familiar with.

Still, you have a key and a locked cabinet on the bookcase. I don't think you'll be betting against the house odds if you get the idea that two plus two equals four. Get up and try the key in the locked cabinet.

TIP

To use the Gun Key to open the cabinet, walk over to the cabinet and then right-click the mouse to bring up the supplemental list. Left-click on the Gun Key and then left-click on Use. The cabinet opens right away and puts you back in the gameplay mode.

All right! Now you're cooking with gas. Let's take a look at what treasures you've just found.

Spies, Codes, and Artifacts

There's a message at the top of the stack of books on the left.

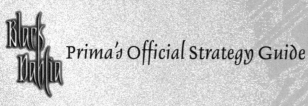

Mr. Pensky,

I am very intrigued by your message and am indeed interested in examining the artifacts that you describe. Please call me as soon as possible! I feel that these items may be of CRITICAL importance to your investigation.

—Dr. Strauss

Dr. Strauss, eh? He was mentioned in the "Things To Do" list on the desk, and the note is addressed to Mr. Pensky. Maybe Pensky was the last agent, the one you're taking over for.

But that bit of information also brings up new questions. From the "Things To Do" list, you know that Dr. Strauss is actually a professor. But professor of what?

And what are the artifacts that the message is talking about? The skull you found on the bookshelves? The vase? Or something else entirely?

Further searching turns up another note.

August 6, 1941

Walt,

We've finally received the "List" from the FBI, but of course, there's an encrypted number associated with each of the names. Keep it under your hat, but I want you to see what you can do about cracking their code. They may be keeping important information from us.

Sullivan

The note's from Sullivan. It suggests that Walt may have been Pensky's first name. Below is a list of numbers and letters with a lot of Xs drawn through notations made to the right, as if someone were trying to make sense of them.

Another interesting facet is that Sullivan acquired this "List" from the FBI, but he doesn't trust them to have been entirely truthful with him. It isn't the first time that you've heard of old J. Edgar playing fast and loose with inter-agency cooperation.

What was Pensky working on? And what did it have to do with his "unexpected" departure from the COI?

Stymied by the lack of answers, turn your attention back to the case file Sullivan gave you earlier. After all, this is the snooping you're drawing a paycheck for.

TIP

Get the Case File from your Inventory by right-clicking the mouse and then left-clicking on Inventory. Left-click again on the Case File. Left-clicking on the pages of the report turns them.

When you're finished, left-click on Exit.

The Case File

The first page appears to be an Initial Crime Report.

The victim is listed as Henry Finster, evidently the owner of Finster Munitions Plant where the crime was committed on November 12, 1941, at 3:30 p.m. The perpetrator's name must not have been known because all that is listed on the bottom portion of the sheet is a description.

The crime was harassment—not a big one, but you start wondering what the angle is if it involves the COI. Of course, with the victim being the probable owner of a munitions plant when Hitler is running rampant over all of Europe—that may be cause enough.

TIP

To move the pages (or objects) up in the Inventory section, left-click and hold down the button; then scoot them up.

At the bottom of the sheet, there is the following additional information:

```
H. Finster files complaint regarding alleged Nazi
recruitment.
```

Bingo! Now there's a reason for the COI to get involved. Keep reading.

```
Cause of complaint is a flyer passed out at Finster
munitions plant by unknown messenger. After review of
flyer and interrogation of plaintiff, Nazi recruitment
deemed unlikely and case given low priority. Plaintiff
became verbally abusive when informed of such.
Forwarding complaint to COI office.
```

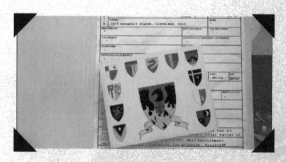

The signature at the bottom of the page belonged to Peter Merylo. Judging from the form, Merylo was probably the investigating detective from the Cleveland police department. The PD's interest wouldn't have covered Nazi sympathizers.

The second sheet catches your eye with all of the fantastic colors and designs. Twelve shields cover the page. They make you think of family heralds, but there aren't any notations that offer clues as to what they actually represent.

Inside is the text of the flyer that must have been handed out at the munitions plant. Revolutionary stuff, all right, and plenty enough for Finster to get sore about.

> The time of struggle is now at hand. No longer will parliaments determine the fate of the people. In their place will rule wise priest-kings, masters of ariosophical mysticism and leaders of chivalrous and spiritual orders. As long as we hold to the three, the Brotherhood of Thule shall rule. The black eagle is the symbol of the Thule. The black eagle rises from a blanket of flames , which warns us that we must die in order to live.
>
> Our Order is a Teutonic Order; loyalty is also Teutonic. Our way is the way of the trinity: Wotan, Wili, We is the unity of the Trinity. Their power is contained in the three.
>
> The Order is your Heritage; your Heritage is Teutonic; your loyalty is Teutonic. The old Order shall be restored, and the trinity shall rise like the black eagle. Reclaim your Heritage; rejoice in the time of Thule; rise with the black eagle

Thule Awakens

```
The time of struggle is now at hand. No longer will
parliaments determine the fate of the people. In their
```

```
place will rule wise priest-kings, master of
ariosophical mysticism and leaders of chivalrous and
spiritual orders. As long as we hold to the three, the
Brotherhood of Thule shall rule. The black eagle is the
symbol of the Thule. The black eagle rises from a
blanket of flames, which warns us that we must die in
order to live. Our Order is a Teutonic Order; loyalty is
also Teutonic. Our way is the way of the trinity: Wotan,
Wili, We is the unity of the Trinity. Their power is
contained in the three.
     The Order is your Heritage; your Heritage is Teutonic;
your loyalty is Teutonic. The old Order shall be
restored, and the trinity shall rise like the black
eagle. Reclaim your Heritage; rejoice in the time of
Thule; rise with the black eagle.
     The messenger shall receive your word.
```

Now that you've had a gander at the case file Sullivan gave you, it's time to hoist those dogs off the desk and start earning your keep. Investigators investigate, and history lessons haven't been a real interest of yours anyway. Let's go see what else Sullivan knows since he was so kind to offer his ear any time you needed it.

And, if you play your cards right, maybe you can drum up some more information on the missing Pensky. That guy's turning out to be as big a mystery as any you've ever gotten your mitts on.

TIP

To get to Sullivan's office, right-click on the mouse. Choose World Map. Anytime a destination is open to you, a photograph representing it appears in this section. To go to your desired destination, left-click on it.

As you progress through the game, different destinations will appear while old ones disappear. Their availability depends on your gameplay. If you've gotten stuck while playing the game on your own, this strategy guide will help you through the game's interior logic.

And the old black and white photographs are a nice touch, don't you think?

NOTE

You may also access the World Map at any time by left-clicking on the Exit Doorway of your current location.

Back in Sullivan's office, a number of questions immediately come to mind.

TIP

To get the list of questions to appear on the screen, left-click on Mr. Sullivan. At this point, you do have questions for him. When you happen to pass through at a later time in the game, however, the cursor may not turn into an arrow, signaling that you cannot ask Sullivan questions at that time.

When you open the case file, put the cursor first on Henry Finster's name and then on Peter Merylo. This causes Sullivan to give you more information about Finster and Merylo and allows the World Map to include their location next time you access it.

For the moment, avoid asking about Pensky. Let's go to the case file.

Ask about Henry Finster first by left-clicking on his name on the initial crime report.

Sullivan says that Finster is an important man in the government's scheme of things, but that he is considered to be somewhat of a pain in the butt because he always sees Nazis and Communists lurking around every corner. But, Sullivan says, Finster may have something this time. He tells you to take a look at the invitation and then asks you your opinion of it.

After having read it, your only opinion is that it looks like fascist propaganda.

Readily agreeing, Sullivan also offers the caveat that it may not be of Nazi origin. He goes on to say that it appears primarily directed at people of wealth, which means you're going to have to keep the kid gloves on while you poke around.

Next, ask about Merylo.

The detective, Sullivan replies, is the one who passed the complaint file along. Merylo also has his hands full these days, as he's the top dog chasing after the Torso Killer, the murderer who's chopping up people all across the city.

After dealing with the business at hand and finding Sullivan easy to get along with, you ask about your predecessor.

Walter Pensky, Sullivan explains, once was a good agent and a good man. But the job got the better of him. The COI chief doesn't elaborate on his cryptic statement, but he does admonish you to remember that your job with the agency doesn't allow for personal crusades.

Seeing no openings for further questions about either the case or Pensky, take your leave. Since you're following up on the case file, you figure it's best to get a little more information on the case before confronting Henry Finster in his den.

And the best place to get that is from Detective Peter Merylo of the Cleveland PD.

 **TIP**

To get to Merylo's office, right-click the mouse to bring up the supplemental list and then left-click on the World Map. Left-click again on the photograph of Detective Merylo's Office.

2

Get a Clue, Get a Bigger Puzzle

Mugshot at the 15th Precinct

After dusting your knuckles on the frosted glass of Detective Merylo's office door, a deep voice growls for you to come in.

Detective Peter Merylo is a bull-dog of a man seated behind his desk. He doesn't seem happy at all to see you throwing a shadow into his office. Over his left shoulder, you see a bulletin board filled with black and white photographs. Tagging them in your mind, you count them and come up with 11. Is that how many victims the Torso Killer has claimed?

Something stirs in the back of your mind, and you'd like to give it your full attention, but Merylo isn't the kind of guy you can keep waiting. So leave that unconscious itch on the back burner till you can get back to it.

Telling Merylo that you're from the COI and that you're there to investigate Finster's complaint doesn't make him feel any more charitable toward you.

He nearly explodes like an old steam radiator in a flophouse. He tells you that, whatever you've got to say, it better be good because he's up to his ears in bodies.

Wanting to win him over to your side somewhat, ask him about the Torso Murders.

Merylo waxes eloquent on the subject, telling you that the Torso Killer drains the blood of his victims, washes them clean, and then wraps them up all nice and neat. Apparently, the killer has some familiarity with medical knowledge. The murderer leaves little behind and seems to concentrate on homeless people and prostitutes—victims who won't be missed much by society.

When asked if the FBI is helping with the murders, Merylo almost blows a gasket. Eliot Ness has assigned a junior G-Man, named Winslow, who doesn't know anything about investigations. He only works at looking good in his expensive suits for all the photographers attracted to the case, while he says he's the one who'll catch the Torso Killer.

Throwing caution to the wind, ask him about Finster's complaint.

Merylo definitely has a very low opinion of Finster and the federal agents. He's convinced that the public line that the federal agencies have taken with US citizens has *created* an overflow of sightings of Nazi spies and traitors everywhere. Dozens of people have been in his office filing complaints, but none of them have panned out. He's more interested in catching the Torso Killer, who's more real than any Nazi spy he's heard about.

But, he adds, Finster was in his office and claims to have identified the man who was handing out the flyers at the munitions plant in the mug book. Merylo says that you're welcome to take a look if you want. (Beneath that gruff exterior and short temper is a dedicated working stiff, who, you figure, is good at his job.)

Take a look at the mug book. It's on the corner of the desk to your left.

TIP *To locate the mug book, drag the cursor to the bottom of the screen on the left. It's the closed black book. When you place the arrow cursor spinning over it, left-click on it to open it. Continue left-clicking on it to turn the pages.*

There's little chance of your finding the person Finster identified without knowing what the guy looks like. But do it to humor Merylo and to show that you're willing to take some direction. You can play the hard guy when it comes to *that*, but there's an amount of finesse that comes with this job, too.

When you open the mug book, the first noticeable thing is the sheet of Finster Corp stationery. It looks blank, but you're investigating spies, right? There could be any number of secret messages written on that single sheet of paper.

When Merylo's not watching, slip the paper into your coat.

TIP *To add the stationery to your Inventory, left-click the spinning arrow cursor on it. The paper automatically goes into the Inventory.*

Left-click on Finster Stationery to take a look at it in the Inventory.

Diligent and eagle-eyed as you are, you're not going to find a guy in this book until you know more about who you're looking for.

Thank Merylo for his time and leave his office. Out of his sight, take a closer look at the piece of stationery you just swiped. (This can be done by simply accessing the Inventory with a right-click of the mouse.)

Hey, eagle-eye, doesn't that coat of arms at the top of the page look familiar? Open up the case file to take another look at the invitation.

There it is! The second coat of arms from the left on the top row is an exact duplicate of the one on Finster's stationery.

What does it mean? Beats me, brother—you're the sleuth. But if something comes to mind, I'll definitely let you know. It kind of gives you an idea that maybe Finster has more going on than he's willing to admit, doesn't it?

Well, get the dogs in gear, shamus; you've got a case to solve. Get over to Finster's office.

TIP

Right-click to pull up the supplemental list and then left-click on the World Map. Left-click on Finster's Office to go there.

One Suspicious Corporate Mogul

Finster's not a pleasant guy, and that's the most pleasant way you can put it. When you introduce yourself, he jumps all over you for not being there sooner. While he's jawing at you, take a look over his shoulder at the coat of arms with crossed swords on the wall behind him. That's definitely a copy of the one on the stationery and the invitation in the case file.

TIP

To initiate a conversation with Finster, left-click on him.

Ask him about the man who gave him the invitation first.

Finster doesn't remember the guy at all. His explanation becomes confusing, but he finally says that George Hansen is the man who worked for him, who invited the Nazi into the munitions plant. Finster fired Hansen on the spot.

Finster doesn't remember the man's name, telling you that the guy said he was just a messenger.

When you ask for the messenger's description, Finster grows even more belligerent. He already gave the description to Merylo and picked him out of the mug book. Further questioning elicits a description, but it's not going to help you nail down anything worthwhile at this point.

Finster has no idea where to find the messenger, but he tells you that George Hansen frequents a saloon on the Roaring Third called McGinty's.

Okay, that's a solid lead. See if you can get around that.

Oh, got that stubborn streak working, do you? Got to push the envelope on this one and ask about the Brotherhood of Thule because of that coat of arms, right?

Well, Finster blows his stack at that one. He lets you know, in no uncertain terms, that the Brotherhood of Thule is a Nazi conspiracy.

(Yeah, that's right—stay with it until you get him to blow.)

When you ask him about the symbols and signs, Finster says that he has seen them all over Germany. Then he goes off on a tear to point out that many good families have come from Germany and, in fact, still live there. He still has relatives in Germany.

You're wondering about those relatives, aren't you, sleuth? You do have a suspicious nature—maybe it'll help keep you alive a bit longer.

For the moment, follow the trail to McGinty's down on the Roaring Third.

TIP

Reach McGinty's by right-clicking on the mouse to bring up the supplemental list and then left-clicking on the World Map. Another left-click on McGinty's Bar places you at its door.

Stakeout

Music greets you even before you step down to the small tavern set off from the street. Inside the bar, a radio announcer gives the latest story about the Torso Killer, who has claimed his seventh victim.

The bartender concentrates on wiping glasses clean. Two tough looking customers sit at a table to your left. Neither of them has a beard, so unless the messenger got a shave, neither guy is the one you're looking for.

Maybe the two guys are regulars. Maybe not. But it stands to reason that the bartender puts in a lot of time in the saloon. Go ask him about George Hansen.

The bartender is quick to tell you that he doesn't know anyone or anything. He lets you know, in no uncertain terms, that he doesn't think highly of Feds. Then he points to your right, telling you to take the guy he's pointing at with you.

As you turn slowly, you spot the guy the bartender was talking about. This guy sticks out like a sore thumb in present company. He's nattily dressed, and attitude oozes from him.

Cross over to the guy and show him your buzzer to identify yourself. Most people tend to come across pretty quick when they get a flash of the tin. When asked, he has no idea who George Hansen is. Ask him who he is.

He gets friendly fast, giving his name as Dick Winslow. Two Winslows in one day and both of them dressed to the nines—it isn't a great leap in logic to guess that this is Merylo's FBI agent.

Winslow admits that he's an FBI agent and that he's there to stake out the bar to find the Torso Killer. He hasn't had much luck, though.

He goes on to mention that, if you're looking for a team of German subversives, you should check for names on the Blacklist, a list of suspicious

Americans of German descent. The FBI has shared this information with other agencies, and your chief should have the list, too.

When you thank him for his time, he also says you should drop by his office if you need anything else.

Having no other options to explore on your own at this point, return to Sullivan's office to see the Blacklist Sullivan supposedly has.

TIP

Right-click on the mouse to bring up the supplemental list and then left-click on the World Map. Left-click again on Sullivan's Office.

Blacklisted

Face to face with Sullivan again, ask him about the Blacklist.

Sullivan demands to know who you've been talking to. Rather than give up the fact that you have managed to get into Pensky's locked cabinet and found the letter, you drop Winslow's name.

Your chief develops a lemony grimace and then states that there is such a list. He relates how J. Edgar Hoover justified and rationalized to the federal government putting together this Blacklist.

Sullivan reluctantly hands the list over, telling you that it is possible that many of the men on the Blacklist are hard-working men with no interest in Nazi Germany.

Take the Blacklist and return to your office.

TIP

Right-click on the mouse to bring up the supplemental list and then left-click on the World Map. Left-click again to go to your office.

Cracking the Code

Take out the Blacklist and give it a scan, shamus. The names are on the left side of the page, followed by their location by bureau and then by the case numbers.

The case numbers remind you of the numbers you found on the note Sullivan wrote to Pensky. Take out the cabinet key and go take another look.

Score one for the whippersnapper! See the X-ed out portion that reads CLV 21-84-11? Judging from the notations to the left of the code, Pensky figured out these numbers were encrypted to hide phone numbers, not birthdays or addresses.

Using the column on the left, Pensky was able to deduce that CLV 21-84-11 was actually CLV 3-12-2. The code was so simple it made itself confusing. 21 becomes 3 through addition (2+1); 84 becomes 12 (8+4); and, 11 becomes 2 (1+1).

Given that, you can now crack any encryption on the Blacklist and get a phone number—who're you gonna call?

Ah, here's one you know: Henry Finster at the top of the second page. His encryption number is CLV-21-84-11, the same number Pensky was working with. Finster's phone number was probably the one that helped Pensky crack the code.

Let's verify your findings before you start getting too excited. There's nothing worse than a guy who goes off half-cocked.

According to Pensky's and your figuring, Finster's real phone number should be CLV-3122. But that can't be right. Phone numbers have only three digits after the exchange. Check that number against the piece of stationery you took from the mug book in Merylo's office.

Damn! You're right; it's wrong.

Finster's number is 140. So how does 21-84-11 equal 140?

C'mon, sleuth, the answer's as plain as the nose on your face. You don't ADD the numbers; you subtract them. Look: 2–1 = 1, 8–4 = 4, and 1–1 = 0.

140. And, for the exchange, follow the "0+1-1" rule. Thus, "CLV" becomes "CMR" just like on Finster's Stationery.

That's Finster's number.

Okay, maybe you're more clever than Pensky was. Or at least, you think you are at the moment. Remember, Pensky's no longer around—one way or another.

Nothing like a shot of cold water down your back, is there?

Besides Finster, is there anyone else on the Blacklist you may be interested in calling? You search the list of names diligently, drawing one steady blank after another, until you reach the third name from the bottom.

DR. KARL STRAUSS.

Left-click the mouse button on the first page of the Blacklist and hold it down. Scoot the list up until you reach the bottom of the page.

Remember Dr. Strauss, don't you? Sure you do. That's the guy Pensky was going to get in contact with, the guy who wrote the note to Pensky wanting to see the artifacts that Pensky had.

Until now, you didn't have a way of getting in touch with this Dr. Strauss. Now, though, you have his phone number. At least you will have one once you break the encryption.

CMR is the exchange. Doing the math, 51-22-40 quickly becomes CLV-404. And there's a phone on your desk. Make the call.

Take a look at the phone dial. You'll find the "C" becomes "2," "M" becomes "6," and "R" becomes "7," giving you the whole number as 267-404.

At this time in Ma Bell's history, all exchanges were called out by name rather than a three-digit number. Back then, one exchange name could cover all the phones.

To use the phone, put the cursor on each number in turn and left-click on it.

An old man's voice answers at the other end of the connection, letting you know that you have reached the Cleveland Museum of Natural History. The

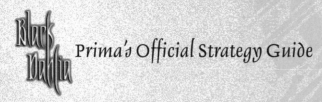

man tells you that Professor Strauss is not in, but that a message can be left for Strauss. You leave a message, asking that Strauss call you.

Now what? The sleuthing appears to be all done. Now it's just a waiting game. But you don't sit well, do you? And you have learned that, once an investigation seems to have hit the skids, there's nothing to do except to make the rounds again. When there's no stone left unturned, go back and kick some of the old ones over again.

TIP

Right-click on the mouse to bring up the supplemental list. Left-click on the World Map and then left-click on Detective Merylo's Office to return there.

While you're talking to Merylo, tell him about Special Agent Winslow. Since you're about as impressed with Winslow as Merylo is, he takes a shine to you. Unfortunately, that's about all you have to talk about for the moment.

TIP

Right-click the mouse to bring up the supplemental list. Left-click on the World Map and left-click on your office.

When you get back to your office, there's a note waiting for you.

MESSAGES

Miss Helen Strauss called to say that her father is out of the country for the next several weeks, but she would be glad to have a look at your artifacts herself if you would like. Feel free to call on her at the Cleveland Museum of Natural History.

A skirt, huh? Well, after all the ugly mugs you've looked at today, things are sure looking up. Don't just stand there grinning, you big lug. Put that spiffy crease back in that fedora and go see the lady.

TIP   *Left-click on the Message to read it.*

NOTE   *Change to Disk #2.*

3

Puzzling Encounters

The Professor's Daughter

Don't know what you were expecting when you got here, ace, but the little redheaded number behind the big desk is a welcome sight. Kind of prim and proper in her skirt suit, but she quickly takes off her glasses and introduces you to the fire in her eyes.

She quickly tells you that her father isn't in, but she'd be more than happy to help you if she can.

You figure breezing with the dame can't hurt, and besides, it would be a welcome relief from talking with people who are only interested in telling you how to do your job and asking you why you haven't finished with it sooner.

TIP

Put the cursor on Helen Strauss and left-click on her to bring up the list of questions you can ask her.

Ask Helen about her field of experience. Maybe she can't help you with what you're working on, but at least—perhaps—you'll find some common ground.

She tells you that she's a graduate intern student with hopes of running the museum one day. Her specialty is in Central European studies; the museum presently has quite a display on the subject.

Ask Helen about her father, the professor.

According to Helen, Walter Pensky had been talking to her father about several artifacts he had found in one of his investigations. Pensky and the professor never got together, though, so neither she nor her father have seen any of the artifacts that Pensky was so excited about.

Meaning what? Put it together. I can hear those two little marbles inside your head grinding against each other.

If Pensky never brought the artifacts in, that means he kept them. So, did he stash them? Or did he take them?

Taking them means that Pensky got out of this business with a whole skin, but you don't have any proof of that yet. The man didn't even get a chance to clean out his office before he left, didn't even get the chance to finish his "Things To Do" list.

And Pensky was one for hiding things, wasn't he? He hid the files in the bookcase cabinet and then hid its key in the butt of his gun. And, by the way, Pensky not having a gun wherever he ended up is kind of unsettling, isn't it?

Given that Pensky had time to hide whatever these artifacts were, where did he hide them? He didn't have access to many places. In fact, the place he seemed to keep most of the things he was working on was his office.

If you ask me, I think it's time you got back to the office and gave it the old once-over again—this time with an eye more toward completing what you started earlier.

Tell Helen that you'll be seeing her around and then return to the office.

TIP *Right-click on the mouse to bring up the supplemental list. Left-click on the World Map and then left-click on your office to return to it.*

The Hiding Place

Okay, you've been through the shelves. You've been through the desk. You've been through the filing cabinet and through the locked bookcase cabinet.

Where haven't you looked?

Jeez, still seems a little dim in here, doesn't it? What's wrong with that stupid light, anyway? Maybe you should crawl up there and take a closer look.

Hey, take a gander at that dark spot inside the lamp. That's not supposed to be there. Take the object out to see what it is.

TIP

Climb up to the light fixture by dragging the cursor up toward the top of the screen. Click the rune cursor on the light fixture itself to retrieve the object inside. When you have the bag, it automatically is added to your Inventory. To study it, simply go to the Inventory and click on the objects you want to look at. Clicking on the Bag of Runes opens the bag to let you look at the pieces.

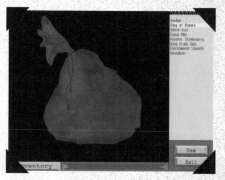

Looks like an average velvet bag on the outside, but it's making some interesting clacking noises inside. Reaching into the bag, you discover some folded papers.

The papers feel old. When you open them up, the writing on it is confusing to you—nothing you can read. It does, however, remind you of the symbols on the Brotherhood of Thule flyer in the Finster case file, doesn't it?

At the top of one of the pages are the words NINE GIFTS TO ODIN. Maybe Pensky took notes. But you're only guessing at that. Still, a working hypothesis is there to give you something to disprove. Do that and you'll be closer to the answers you're looking for.

The strangely shaped black ceramic tiles you find in the bag have the same symbols on them. In fact, three of them are exact replicas of the symbols at the top of the flyer.

TIP

By left-clicking on the runes inside the bag, you'll find that you can manipulate them and put them on the three-dimensional pattern in their center. A little experimentation shows you that you can hook the three particular symbols together.

When you start to move the pieces around, you discover some pieces have a natural attraction for others. The three that are copies of the symbols on the flyer stick together and start to form a three-dimensional puzzle.

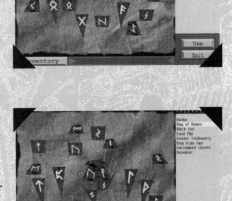

The downside, is that, with all 24 pieces, there appears to be an endless combination of how they can fit together. You're definitely going to need some more information.

The obvious place to get this would be from Helen Strauss. If she doesn't have a clue, it's a cinch—you don't know anyone else who does. At least, you don't know anyone else who would tell you.

For now, just keep the bag and the parchment sheets as your own little secret, one of the growing group you're hoping to acquire. It's hard to be a player in a game of high stakes when you don't have anything anyone else wants.

Ruling out the added mystery of the runes, which may or may not have anything to do with the messenger who was spreading the Brotherhood of Thule flyers out at Finster's munitions plant, you still have to find George Hansen.

It's later in the afternoon now. Maybe old George has decided to drop in at his favorite watering hole for a refueling. The only way to find out is to hoof on over there for a peek.

TIP   *Right-click on the mouse to pull up the supplemental list. Left-click on the World Map and then left-click on McGinty's Bar to go there.*

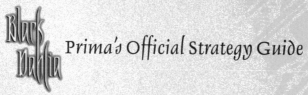

Only Sad Songs to Sing

The bar's atmosphere hasn't improved at all during your absence. The bartender still wipes glasses, and the toughs haven't gone anywhere. But Winslow apparently has given up his stakeout for the moment.

And there's a new face in McGinty's at the back of the saloon across from the pay phone. Doesn't take a trained investigator to see that this guy's nursing some deep problems along with that beer. Walk back to him and flash him your buzzer.

When you ask him about Hansen, the man owns up to being George Hansen. He also says that he didn't know the messenger from Adam more than a few weeks back. All Hansen remembers is that the man's name is Louie. No last name, just Louie.

Hansen met Louie in McGinty's. The man was complaining about being down on his luck. Feeling sorry for the guy, Hansen volunteered to take Louie in to see Finster—maybe get him a job. After getting Louie to the munitions plant, no one was more surprised than Hansen when Louie launched into his Nazi-sympathizing spiel. The next thing Hansen knew, he was fired. Since then, he's lost his house and his wife.

You thank Hansen for his time and turn around. Spotting the pay phone on the wall and seeing all the graffiti around it, make your way over to it. Your

experience has been that it's not unusual for someone to jot down a phone number and then to transfer it to a piece of paper or a matchbook later.

Sure enough, while you study the names and numbers on the wall, you find a listing for a LOU FIELDING. The number's hard to make out, but it looks like CMR-259.

TIP

Drag the cursor to the top of the screen to view the name and number after you get close to the phone. Be aware that there are two sections of the phone: the upper one and the lower one. The lower one gives you access to the dial.

So dial the number already. The voice at the other end of the connection sounds cagey and asks for a name. When you ask for Louie, you're told there's no one there by that name.

CMR-259

TIP

Type in any name you want at this point, but you won't get a positive response until you have uncovered the correct clues and followed the logic of the story.

Now that you have the Louie name, you've got another concrete fact on the messenger. Maybe another look through the mug book in Merylo's office would be in order. Get the dogs a-moving because, if you're going to swim, you've got to jump in.

TIP

Right-click on the mouse to bring up the supplemental list. Left-click on the World Map and then left-click on Merylo's Office to go there.

Louie, Louie

Detective Merylo isn't exactly overjoyed to see you step through his doorway again, but at least he isn't giving you the bum's rush. Open up the mug book again and see if you can match the description of the man Finster gave you to the name you got from Hansen.

Sometimes you get lucky, and sometimes you have to work hard for it. On page five, you find a bearded man named Louis—Louis Fischer. One of his known aliases is Louis Fielding. He's had convictions for theft, racketeering, forgery, and writing bad checks.

Okay, maybe the guy on the other end of the phone knows better than to take a call for Lou Fielding, but maybe he'll take one for Louis Fischer. Go back to the bar and call him again from there.

LOUIS FISCHER

TIP

Right-click on the mouse to bring up the supplemental list. Left-click on the World Map and then left-click again on McGinty's Bar.

The number (still) is CMR-259. But it's no dice because the answer you receive is still a big fat no.

During the time you have been gone, though, Hansen has been drinking steadily. Over the course of your short career, you have learned that some people have a tendency to remember things better after they've loosened up a bit—to remember some things that they couldn't remember even if they were sober.

Stop by Hansen and talk to him again. He says that he'll be talking to the boys later.

Give him some time. Go back to your office and take stock of all the leads you have so far.

TIP

Right-click on the mouse to bring up the supplemental list. Left-click on the World Map and left-click on your office.

Skimming through everything you have, you realize it isn't much. Unless you want to cough up the parchment sheets and the bag of ceramic tiles to Helen, you're holding nothing.

Not feeling exactly charitable at the moment, are you? And maybe Pensky trusted the professor and his daughter a little *too* much. That one will be tough to call until you're in over your head.

For the moment, take a run back to McGinty's. You let some more time pass. Let's see if Hansen has managed to talk to "the boys."

It's important to make all the stops along the way as they're described in this strategy guide. You must make them in order for the game logic to work properly.

Right-click on the mouse to bring up the supplemental list. Left-click on the World Map and then left-click on McGinty's Bar to go there.

Hansen is still at his table when you get there. And he's more talkative. When you ask him if he's checked around for Louie, he tells you that no one knows who this guy was.

As you turn to go, Hansen calls you back and says that there's one other thing that's bothering him, but it may not make any sense. One of the guys heard the argument between Louie and Finster. During that argument, Louie kept calling himself *Harold*. Hansen swears that he thought the man's name was Louie, not Harold.

Time to crank the handle on the phone again. Maybe Harold is Fischer's new alias that no one knows about yet. But when you dial the number and ask for Harold, you're told that no one is there by that name.

You're in a tough spot—and that's the truth. All the leads you have so far have petered out. You're down to one choice, and that's to trust pretty Helen Strauss and show her what you've got.

Get moving. The clock's ticking, and you're not getting any younger.

Right-click on the mouse to bring up the supplemental list. Left-click on the World Map and then left-click on the Museum of Natural History.

Written in the Runes

When you arrive at the museum, start slow. First show Helen the invitation with the 12 coats of arms on it.

To show Helen the invitation, right-click the mouse to bring up the supplemental list. Left-click on Inventory. Left-click on the Case File. Flip through the pages until you reach the Invitation. Left-click the Use button.

She's excited to see the invitation, but she's puzzled at the same time. As you listen, she tells you that these are family crests from the Thule Society in Germany—not the Brotherhood of Thule, she quickly goes on.

The Thule Society existed in Germany long before Hitler came to power. In fact, the group had considerable power in Germany before Hitler disbanded them. According to legend and stories Helen has heard, they supposedly were a cabal of black magicians. Their family crests belonged to a subgroup of Teutonic Knights that were excommunicated by Pope Gregory IX.

When she pulls a book off a nearby shelf and shows it to you, there's no doubt. Throughout the pages, you find the 12 crests on the invitation. Beside each of the stricken crests is a papal seal embossed in wax.

Henry Finster's family crest is on the seventh page in the lower right corner. The family used to be the Sergeant at Arms for the Knights of the Trinity.

That starts things clicking in your mind. If Louie or Harold was familiar with the family crests, he would have seen the one on the wall behind Finster's desk. He would have thought that he was speaking to a kindred spirit, not someone who would report him.

Helen goes on to tell you about the stained glass window her father is attempting to put back together. It's supposed to have all of the officers' coats of arms on it. Supposedly, the officers' names are hidden within the pattern as well.

Okay, you're not exactly sure where this is all leading, but you still haven't shown Helen everything you have. Show her the Finster stationery next.

TIP

To show Helen the Finster stationery, right-click on the mouse and left-click on Inventory. Left-click on Finster Stationery and then left-click on Use.

She examines it and tells you that the crest represents the involvement of the Finsterlau family in the outlawed knights. Ask her about the knights' crests, and you'll find out that there were four rankings of the officers. One of these positions was the Herald, also known as the Messenger.

Suddenly, it all clicks. Louie wasn't telling Finster that his name was Harold; he was telling the munitions plant owner that he was the *Herald*. Louie expected Finster to understand this.

After she's been this helpful, it's hard to resist showing Helen the parchment sheets and the ceramic tiles, too. Let her take a peek at the tiles.

TIP   *Right-click on the mouse and then left-click on Inventory. Left-click on the Bag of Runes then left-click on Use.*

After looking at the objects, Helen says that she's sure the tiles are runes, an ancient form of Germanic language. When she looks at the parchment sheets, she tells you that a partial transcription has already begun. She remembers the NINE GIFTS TO ODIN passage. The reference is to the sacrifices made to the god Odin. Usually, the sacrifice involved animals although there were occasional stories about a sacrifice of nine strong men. She says that it will take time to work out the rest of what is on the parchment sheets.

Well, you must be satisfied with that. But perhaps you can work on something of your own. Ask Helen if you can see the stained glass window her father is trying to piece together.

She doesn't hold back at all, taking you to the back of the room to the table where the stained glass fragments are laid out. She turns on the light, so that you can see it more clearly.

The possibility that all the officers' names of the Thule Society are on the window intrigues you, as do the jumble of pieces. You were always a fair hand at putting puzzles together, weren't you? Well, it looks as though you've got your work cut out on this one.

On the wall in front of you is a map with several notes and photographs thumbtacked to it. As you read and look at them, you realize that these pieces lying in front of you must have been Professor Strauss's journey to recover the stained glass window.

TIP

To view the entire wall, drag the cursor up and down and side to side.

By referencing the invitation and the book on family crests that Helen showed you, you start to get an idea of what the stained glass window is supposed to look like. Four officers' positions are represented by the window; the image has to be an amalgam of four of the crests.

TIP

You will find that you can left-click the mouse on the puzzle pieces to manipulate them. Left-clicking and holding the button down allows you to push the pieces more tightly together. This is a luxury that you cannot do without because the working space for the puzzle on the screen is very tight.

It may take you a long time to complete the puzzle, but you finally will be able to put the window together. Nowhere on the stained glass window can you find the names of the four families you're looking for. When you pull back from the window, you notice the light above the table to the left. Switch it on.

As soon as the infrared viewer is switched on, the four names are easily legible.

Landulph

Fischterwald   Muhlhaven

Finsterlau

You already know that the Finsterlau family was the Sergeant at Arms. Checking through the book you borrowed from Helen, you find that the other three families were assigned the following positions:

> Landulph—Chief Knight of the Trinity
>
> Fischterwald—Herald of the Order of the Trinity
>
> Muhlhaven—Scribe, Knights of the Trinity

Now that you have the names, a quick check against those on the Blacklist would seem to be in order. Sure enough—there's a Joseph Muhlhaven on the first page, but no Landulph or Fischterwald.

Still, chances are that Fischterwald is Louie's real surname. C'mon, it's worth the price of a phone call from McGinty's. Tell Helen you'll check back with her later and then leg it over to the Roaring Third.

TIP

Right-click on the mouse to bring up the supplemental list. Left-click on the World Map and then left-click on McGinty's Bar to return there.

The taps are still flowing at the saloon when you arrive. Make your way back to the pay phone. Dial 267-259 and ask for Louie Fischterwald.

TIP

When you're prompted to type, type LOUIE FISCHTERWALD in at the phone and press Enter.

This time the guy at the other end of the connection says sure, but Louie's not there. Have you tried the Raven Room, the swanky gentlemen's club up on Ninth?

Looks like you just ran Louie to the ground. Now get over to Ninth and put the arm on your pigeon.

TIP

Right-click on the mouse to bring up the supplemental list. Left-click on the World Map and then left-click on Raven Room to go there.

4

Death Takes a Hand

The Raven Room

No one seems to be working the foyer of the Raven Room when you arrive, but judging from the lavish surroundings, the club does a good business. It doesn't

look like the Depression ever touched this place.

At one end of the foyer over a small table, there's a large painting of a nude woman. A leather-bound book rests on the table beside a Tiffany lamp.

The door to the club itself is locked, with Officers Entrance clearly emblazoned on it. There's a buzzer to one side of the door. Press it—you never know; you may be able to talk your way inside.

A voice announces that they're closed, but you're thinking quickly now. You tell the guy that you're looking for Fischterwald. He hesitates a moment and then asks you for your name.

TIP

While talking to the guy over the intercom, you're given two options for a response. Neither of them gives you passage, but by lying to the guy and telling him Finster sent you, he mentions that Louie may be down at the Mission.

Well, I haven't seen many times that a Fed was welcome around a joint like this, so lie to him. Tell him that Finster sent you and that he wanted to reconsider Louie's offer.

The guy says that Louie isn't there right now. Did you try down at the Mission? You're so surprised by the answer that you lose your train of thought, asking yourself aloud what a convicted felon would be doing at a mission.

Immediately, the guy on the other end of the squawk box tells you to clear out; it then goes silent.

Okay, you've confirmed that Louie comes around the Raven Room, but what else can you find to work with? You have no idea when Louie will be back, or even if he'll be back.

Return to the table with the leather-bound book. It looks like some kind of guest or member register. Maybe it'll have something you can work with.

Look, you must be on the right track. Do you see the name at the bottom of the letter fronting the leather-bound book? It's got Joseph Muhlhaven's John Hancock there—bold as life and twice as brassy. He's listed as the Club Secretary—a fitting position for someone who's supposed to be a Scribe for the Brotherhood of Thule, don't you think?

Turn the page and scan the names. None of them rings a bell, right? Okay, those are the breaks sometimes. Catch a few going your way, and then there are a few more right behind them that don't cut you no slack.

Before you hurry and leave the table, take a look at the floor underneath it. Do you see the piece of paper under one of the legs?

Pick it up and look at it.

TIP

When you left-click on the piece of paper under the table, it automatically is added to your Inventory. To look at it, go into the Inventory and left-click on Holy Card to examine it.

Once you have it in the Inventory, left-click on it to flip it over and to look at the other side. This is important! Otherwise, St. Bartholomew's Mission won't be added to your World Map.

It's not a piece of paper. It looks like some kind of calling card.

Flip it over and see what's on the back of it.

St. Bartholomew's Mission, huh? And the card even gives the address—now that's service! Judging from the two names written here, it's an easy guess that Louie knows someone named Ernie down at the mission, and that they've got a game of gin going.

Well, what do you know? Maybe Louie really is down at the mission. So, get it in gear. You know from experience that Louie is a guy who gets around a lot. Your next stop is St. Bartholomew's Mission.

TIP

Right-click on the mouse to bring up the supplemental list. Left-click on the World Map and then left-click on St. Bartholomew's Mission to go there.

Knocking Doors Down at St. Bartholomew's

St. Bartholomew's Mission is definitely in a bad neighborhood. Looking around the lobby, it's easy to see that a lot of guys come here when they hit the skids.

Still, it appears clean and well run.

A big guy with a quick smile mans the desk. He watches you as you enter, but doesn't say anything.

It's up to you to break the ice. Flashing your buzzer impresses him. When he starts to speak, you get the idea that he's a little slow. Ask him what he does first to get him talking about himself, a subject he's probably comfortable with.

He says that he helps the fathers keep the place running, keeping it clean and keeping trouble away from the mission. When you press him, he says that he doesn't see much trouble. Usually, he just plays cards.

Now that you've got him talking, ask him if the mission has been busy.

He says that business is booming lately, partly because the hobos are afraid to sleep alone out in the open with the Torso Killer on the loose, and partly because Eliot Ness and his men have been burning down the hobo camps and running them off.

Chit-chat time's over. Get down to brass tacks and ask him about Louie.

The name brings a big smile to the guy's face. He tells you that Louie works at the Raven Room as a doorman. Then he looks worried and asks if Louie is in trouble. Catching himself, he says that he really shouldn't be saying anything about that.

Ask him how he knows Louie.

According to the guy, he and Louie go way back, to the time when they were kids. In fact, Louie helped him get the job at the mission. Louie also introduced him to Gloria DeMille, an aging pinup girl.

He shows you a picture of Louie and him with Gloria DeMille. There are some other characters in the photograph as well, but before you can take a good look, the guy puts the picture back under the counter.

From the way he handles the photograph, you know he won't give it up willingly. You can also tell that you really want another look at it. Maybe there'll be an opportunity to get it later.

Helen Strauss has had some time to work on the runes. Why don't you take a stroll over there to see what's up.

TIP

Although it's possible to trick the desk clerk and get behind the desk now, give the story logic time to work. Things will fit together better with this approach to gameplay than if you were to take the photograph now.

To get back to the Museum of Natural History, right-click on the mouse to bring up the supplemental list. Left-click on the World Map and then left-click on the Museum of Natural History.

Among the Runes

Helen seems happy enough to see you when you return. Ask her if she's figured out how to assemble the pieces of the runes.

Unfortunately, she says, she hasn't been able to do that. There are hundreds of ways they could fit together, and Helen has no idea where to begin until she has some kind of key.

Helen goes on to say that she's had more luck with the parchment sheets. From what she's discovered, the runes on the sheets were arranged to make a phonetic message that could be read in English once they were put together. The message on the sheets has to do with a two-part ritual. The first part supposedly summons the god Odin, while the second part supposedly gives the summoner Odin's power.

TIP *To access Helen's Notes, go to the Inventory and left-click on them.*

When she passes the decoded sheets over, take a look at them.

```
(1)  His Power Awakened
(2)  Nine gifts to Odin were there assembled
(3)  Seven messengers to the shepherds of stars
(4)  One each to bear the sacred silent cipher
(5)  To shatter heaven's sphere.
(6)  One singer to soothe the restless rolling earth
(7)  Who laments the children that she bore
(8)  That she may weep no more.
(9)  A herald to the misty haunted halls of ice
(10) Where the Aesir slumber beyond men's calls
(11) To lead the gray god home.
(12) Three vessels were there committed
(13) The skull of an aethling,
(14) a vizier and skald of great renown,
(15) who had drunk from Mimir's fountain.
(16) A cup of ash wood
```

(17) Fashioned by the Norns to hold all sorrows
(18) Cut from the root of the world tree.
(19) Thalia's dark prison
(20) Dusky, and fair as the seer's sad visage
(21) Surface scryed and bewitching.
(22) Each gift to him is now devoted
(23) Seven shimmering barriers thus are broken
(24) The warm earth is now soft and sated
(25) The frozen halls are lit and ringing
(26) Speak to the skald and share his quaff
(27) In the vessel that sprang from wisdom
(28) Shatter the prison and release the seer
(29) To summon the gray god to his throne

(1) Odin's Power Conveyed
(2) Nine gifts to the Norns are there assembled
(3) Seven messengers to the shepherds of stars
(4) One each to bear the sacred silent cipher
(5) To seal heaven's sphere.
(6) One skald to soothe the restless rolling earth
(7) Lest she balk beneath the new god's feet
(8) That reek with the blood of men.
(9) A willing bard to the misty halls of ice
(10) Where the Aesir stir in timeless slumber
(11) And must be consoled.
(12) Three vessels were there committed
(13) The skull of an aethling,
(14) a vizier and skald of great renown
(15) who had drunk from Mimir's fountain.
(16) A cup of ash wood
(17) Cut from the root of the world tree
(18) To hold the quaff of wisdom.
(19) The witness pure of heart
(20) Empty vessel to consummate the ritual
(21) and bear the brand of Hela.
(22) Three conveyances for the aspirant.
(23) The heart of the homeland

(24) Dark and dwarf delved from stony depths
(25) To conduct him to the oracle throne.
(26) Mimir's counterpart
(27) Innocent watcher that bears the brand
(28) To alleviate the master's pain.
(29) Thalia's dark prison
(30) Dusky, and fair as the seer's sad visage
(31) To link her master to his vessel.
(32) Suffer one night for each covenant
(33) And await the bearer of the brand
(34) Share Mimir's quaff with his skald
(35) Cast out the soft and sightless eye
(36) Now the black tomb begins to beckon
(37) Which will convey the sacred soul
(38) Watch the witness face his doom
(39) Thus is the gray god now usurped
(40) And Thule is become his tomb.

Disturbing stuff, right? I mean, all this mumbo jumbo about ritual and magic seems to take you right back in the direction of Pensky's last case—which, as you know, is not a good place to be. Still, you're a good detective; you can't ignore certain facts just because you don't want to deal with them.

There are three objects, Helen relates, that are supposed to be part of the ritual. A wise man's skull, a cup made of ash wood, and what she thinks is Phahlia's Dark Prison. Phahlia was a seer, a muse from old Norse legends, she says. She then mentions that there is a book about Norse mythology on the shelves.

Reading about old Norse make-believe isn't something you want on your plate right now, is it? Squeezing people is more your style, and Louie Fischterwald is your prime candidate for the moment, isn't he?

Hit the bricks back to the Raven Room and see if you can catch Louie there—then start squeezing.

TIP

Right-click on the mouse to bring up the supplemental list. Left-click on the World Map and then left-click on the Raven Room.

Leveraging Louie

Louie's waiting beside the door when you arrive. He gives you a once-over, but he doesn't seem concerned. Of course, he doesn't know you from Adam at the moment, but you're about to change all that, aren't you?

Exercise your ID case and give both his eyes the full badge. Then drop the agency's name on him and ask him about the invitation.

Despite the fact that you come down on him with both barrels, Louie remains confident that you can't do anything to him. He's got friends, he says. Guys who'll make sure you can't touch him.

For the moment, he's right. You don't have anything concrete on him. What you need is some leverage, and the only place you know you can get some is at the mission. Maybe the picture the mission clerk has will crack Louie open like an egg. Time to find out.

Get on back to the mission.

TIP *Right-click on the mouse to bring up the supplemental list. Left-click on the World Map and then left-click on St. Bartholomew's Mission.*

Take the Picture and Run

Arriving at the mission, you find the clerk still manning the desk. Thinking fast, trick him into leaving his station by telling him you're there to pick up a package the mission's fathers are supposedly holding for you. He's only too eager to try to help you look for it.

While he's gone, slip behind the desk and look for the picture.

TIP *Drag the cursor to the bottom of the screen to change the perspective and left-click on the spinning arrow to look beneath the counter.*

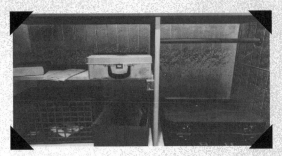

The photograph isn't in the metal cage on the left or in the wooden box with a pen, a comb, a knife and another photograph.

You hit the jackpot when you open the black suitcase on the right and go through it. The picture the clerk showed you earlier is at the bottom of the black suitcase under lots of papers and magazines.

TIP

The secret to getting the photograph from the black suitcase under the counter is to shift all the papers and magazines from the left side of the black suitcase to the right by clicking on them and dragging them with the cursor. Once all the papers and magazines are on the right, stack them neatly, this time on the left. When you reach the bottom of the black suitcase, you can add the picture to your Inventory by clicking on it.

Looking at the photograph, you realize that you don't know anyone in the picture, except Louie and the mission clerk. You do get the feeling, though, that these guys are probably known by the local law in Cleveland.

Time to see if you've worn out your welcome at Detective Merylo's office.

TIP

Right-click on the mouse to bring up the supplemental list. Left-click on the World Map and then left-click on Detective Merylo's Office to go there.

Louie's Ex-Friends

When you show Merylo the picture, he thinks you're onto something, too. The cast of characters includes Dutch Schultz, Lenny Coen, and Moose Malone. They're the head criminals in all of Cleveland.

Upon closer inspection, Merylo recognizes Fischterwald as Louie the Fish. He goes on to tell you the story of how Louie stole $10,000 from one of Schultz's booze operations and then went into hiding. Schultz is still looking for him, and Louie still must be hiding out.

You hit big. You were just looking for a little leverage, and now you have a crowbar to slam old Louie with. Return to the Raven Room. This is one trip you'll enjoy making.

 **TIP**   *Right-click on the mouse to bring up the supplemental list. Left-click on the World Map and then left-click on the Raven Room.*

Louie definitely is not delighted to see you again. He's even less delighted when you lean on him about the picture.

 **TIP**   *To use the photo of Louie, right-click on the mouse to bring up the supplemental list. Left-click on Inventory and then left-click on Ernie's Photo and Use it.*

With all the pressure you're putting on him, Louie caves. But he doesn't want to talk in the Raven Room. You can see the fear in him—smell it. Whoever it is that Louie's afraid of, he's got a bad case of the heebie-jeebies about it. He makes it sound as though this guy can see through walls or something.

Still, Louie seems adamant about not talking at the club. Seeing that you have no other choice about meeting places, you agree to meet him later.

With no evidence for an arrest warrant and no real intention of turning Louie over to Dutch Schultz, you simply have to hope that he's at least fearful enough of you to show up later that night.

Straight Shooter or Dead Man?

Louie gave you the address of an abandoned factory. You show up expecting the worst. With all the weirdness in this case—and all the money apparently connected to it—you decided not to trust anyone; you decided to come alone.

Now, looking across the factory loft, you begin to question that decision, don't you? Well, you're in a stew now.

Before you go much farther, a shadow jumps into motion. You yell at it to freeze, identifying yourself and pulling your badge and your gun. He takes a shot at you, sending you ducking and scrambling for cover.

The man shoots at you again as you follow him. He's close, but no cigar. Are you up to killing a man if you have to? Feel the way your gut tightens?

Inside the factory, you scan the open storage area ahead. The stairs look appealing, and you're certain that he's already taken the high ground. But there's a lot of open space to pass through before you reach cover again.

Take a look to the left and spot the narrow passageway through stacks of crates. It offers some good cover.

The way on the right, though, offers cover, too.

Go to the right. You've never been in a tighter pickle. Hunker down behind the crate here. Do you see the wine bottles lying on the crate? You can bet that a bottle would make a great diversion. Pick one up and toss it out on the floor.

Things happen quickly after that. The gunman comes boiling out of the shadows with blood in his eye and a blazing gat in his hand. It's kill or be killed—so shoot straight.

NOTE

No doubt about it—going straight up the middle on this play is going to get you as dead as last year's Christmas turkey. Either the fork to the left or the one to the right behind cover is a good move. You can't hesitate once you reach either spot, though. If you do, the gunman will break cover and burn you down before you can even get a shot off.

You also will find that you cannot retreat the same way you came. It's all or nothing once you get this far.

Blasting away with your pistol isn't going to do much good either. You've got to make a shot that counts.

If you take the right fork, as suggested here in the guide, simply left-click on one of the wine bottles to heave it onto the floor. Then target the gunman as he steps out of hiding. You have to shoot straight, true, and fast.

Taking the left fork requires a slightly different strategy. From your vantage point here, aim at the steam pipes the gunman is hiding behind rather than at the gunman himself. When your bullets strike the pipe, it ruptures and spews steam. The gunman then runs into the clear. Shoot him as soon as you have the opportunity.

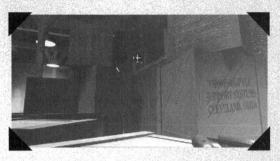

The gunman drops when the bullets strike him. Advance toward him cautiously. Even shot up, this bird is dangerous.

But the guy is dead when you reach him. After kicking his pistol away, kneel down and search his clothing. The only thing of interest that you turn up is a Hotel Cleveland matchbook. Inside the matchbook someone has written a name: Muhlhaven.

Now there's a moniker you've heard before. Another glance at the pistol you kicked away confirms what you thought you had already seen. The pistol is a Nazi-issue Mauser. You're dealing with the big boys now!

You walk out of the factory feeling beat. You've just killed a man for the first time in your life.

Before you get too far, a young boy approaches you with a box. He tells you a man said that you'd give him a nickel for delivering the box. Puzzled— wondering what the gag is—you pitch the kid a nickel and take the box. When you ask the kid what's in the box, he says he doesn't know.

Opening the box, you find Louie Fischterwald's severed head inside.

Lunch comes up in a New York minute, especially when you realize that the gunman you just drilled in the factory really wasn't the *first* man whose death is on your hands.

There's no doubt in your mind that Louie was killed because he was going to talk to you. Whoever murdered him has just sent you a message—they know *who* you are and *where* you are.

Welcome to the big adventure. Gonna be a hell of a ride, isn't it?

NOTE

Change to Disk #3.

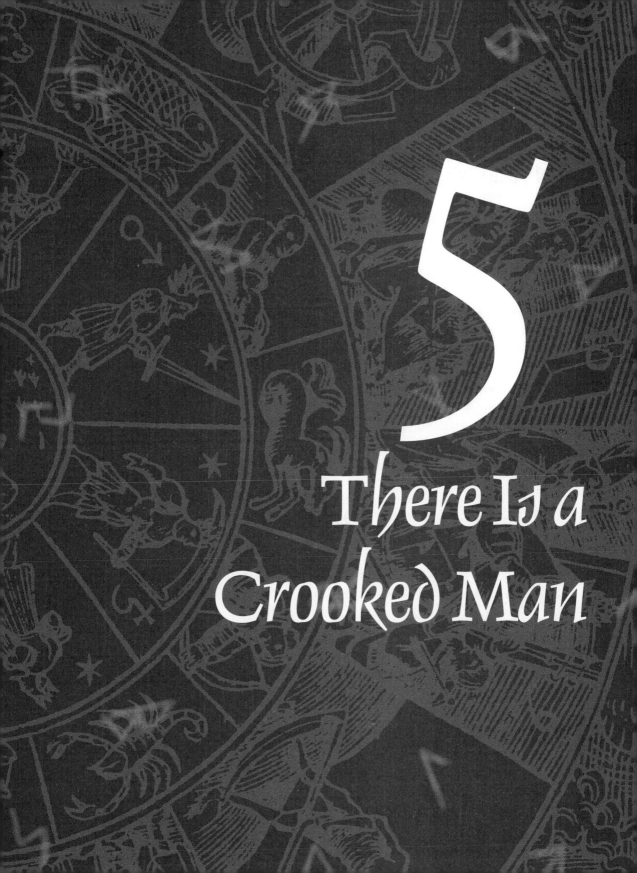

5

There Is a Crooked Man

Morpheus's Terrible Embrace
From the Casebook of COI Agent James R. Pearson

I knew I was dreaming. I don't always. But this time I did, and it was probably because everything was so weird about the experience. If I hadn't been involved in the case as I was, if it hadn't cropped so many references to magic and ritual and sacrifices, I wouldn't have included it in this log at all.

Dreams come from the unconscious, though, and I've been told that's where we do our deepest thinking. I know I do. Things or events I've been trying to make sense of kind of unknot themselves when I'm sleeping.

So I think some of it was my unconscious trying to make sense of everything that had happened yesterday.

And maybe the dream came to me because of all the death. The man I shot, and Louie Fischterwald. Killed both of them, I guess. Maybe most folks wouldn't see it that way, but I think I do even though I've tried to tell myself Louie didn't have anyone to blame but himself. He was an accident waiting to happen; always in the wrong place.

If he hadn't died because of me, somebody else would have seen to it his head ended up in that box. Or one like it.

Anyway, getting back to the dream since I seem to be avoiding it, I dreamed that I was in my office. That wasn't so strange, because I went to sleep there that morning. Couldn't keep my eyes open because I didn't sleep a wink during the night.

So I was in my office like normal, then I went out into the hallway. I heard a sucking sound behind me, then the hallway just seemed to melt away.

Next thing I knew, I saw a door in the distance. Just a door; no structure, no house, just a door. Then it opened and a man came flying out of it.

The man dressed in dark clothes, a frock hat and coat, I think, and looked thin, ruthless. He carried a cane. I could never forget that, I'm telling you. This guy flew over to me in an eye blink, and all I could do was stand there watching.

Before I could move, he pushed that cane to my forehead. For one split second, I saw some kind of glowing hot insignia at the end of it. He was so strong I couldn't get away as he held that burning insignia to my forehead. I heard the flesh sizzle, smelled my skin burning. Thunder exploded overhead.

Special Delivery?

A loud slam wakes you at your desk. The dream has left a chill on you, and for a minute, you think that maybe you're still sleeping and that things are going to get even worse.

Then you blink your bleary eyes and look up into the scowling face of Detective Merylo. He demands to know what's going on, wanting to know why the Torso Killer has started making personal deliveries to you.

You've developed quite a bit of respect for Merylo. After seeing Louie's head in the box last night, you know having a job like Merylo's, where he constantly looks at mangled bits of bodies isn't an easy one. And Merylo has been helpful.

Maintain your relationship with Merylo and tell him what you've learned so far. After all, you don't know anything about the Torso Killer, do you?

Merylo strongly believes that Louie was killed by the Torso Killer. He refutes the idea that the Brotherhood of Thule murdered Louie to keep him quiet. After all, when the rest of Louie's body was found, it had the word "Nazi" carved in his chest.

That throws you for a loop. You thought that you had this one all figured out, even with dreams about flying boogie men with burning canes. The Brotherhood wouldn't have carved "Nazi" in Louie's chest if they wanted to keep a low profile.

While you're mulling that over, Merylo asks you about the dead man in the warehouse.

Stay with the program of being truthful with the detective. You're in a new city fighting some powerful people. Merylo may not be inclined to cover your back if things get bad, but at the same time, you don't think he's the kind of guy to let you slide into the gutter without doing something about it.

Tell him what you know.

He tells you that the FBI has claimed jurisdiction over the murder. You'll have to negotiate with Special Agent Winslow for any information on the murder. Then Merylo takes his leave, telling you to get back to him if you come up with any more information on the case.

After he's gone, take a look at the morning paper he left behind.

 **T I P**

Left-click on the newspaper to bring it up. Once it's there, you can left-click again on either of the front page stories. You will want to read them both.

f Torso Victim's Remains Foun

The lead story is about Louie's death, describing how the rest of his body was found. As you study the picture, notice the man in the frock coat holding the cane in the background. Chill going through you? The bonus here is you get Louie's past address.

Then glam the second story. This one concerns the account of Henry Borasso's escape from a man he believes to be the Torso Killer. As you read the story, Borasso's description of the man—including the account of his strange accent, frock coat and tall hat—sounds a lot like the man in your dream, doesn't he? Even down to the cane.

The story also says that the man told Borasso that he ran a mission. The police are discounting the story, but maybe you shouldn't be so quick to write this one off.

Enough speculating. Get your dogs off the desk and hit the bricks. The only way you're going to get your man is to run him down. It's time to have a meeting with Sullivan and see what he has to say.

TIP *Right-click on the mouse to bring up the supplemental list. Left-click on the World Map and then left-click on Sullivan's Office.*

The FBI Has Sensitive Toes

When you reach Sullivan's office, though, you can hear that Sullivan already has company. The voices are loud and angry, and you have no trouble recognizing Sullivan's and Winslow's voices.

Special Agent Winslow makes no bones about not wanting you on the case. He says that you're too green, that you're too much like Pensky.

Sullivan defends you and Pensky.

It doesn't take you long to get a bellyful of it. It's like you to take the bull by the horns. So, you barge into the office unannounced.

Seeing you, Winslow immediately drops the conversation. He's polite to you on the way out the door, maybe thinking you're so much of a rookie that you won't be able to figure out when to get mad about something.

After he's gone, you apologize to Sullivan, who quickly brushes the apology away, saying he can handle anything Winslow wants to dish out.

Since you haven't talked to Sullivan about the case, update him now. His response is positive, and he seems to be more understanding than ever before.

Since he's feeling so magnanimous, you decide to ask him about Pensky. Winslow's comments have only made you more curious.

Sullivan gets really angry at this point. He obviously doesn't like Winslow at all. The COI chief goes on to say that Pensky stepped on some toes. The FBI

called in some favors, and before Pensky knew what was going on, he'd been packed up and shipped to a sanitarium.

That's all you're getting here. It's time to start burning shoe leather again and earning those big bucks. Remember the matchbook you took from the dead man last night? The one to Hotel Cleveland with Muhlhaven's name written in it? Well, take a look at it now to confirm the address. Go follow up on that lead.

TIP

You have to register the Hotel Cleveland on the World Map now. Looking at the matchbook in the Inventory gives you access to the hotel. Once you do that, you can go there.

Right-click on the mouse to bring up the supplemental list. Left-click on the World Map and then left-click on the Hotel Cleveland.

Doing the Hotel Cleveland Dodge

You can tell right away that the Hotel Cleveland is a swank place—the kind where dollars insulate you from the rest of the world, the kind where you can build your own world even, for a night or for as long as you can afford to stay.

The desk clerk is your best bet of finding out where Muhlhaven is staying. Approach him and see how pliable he is.

When you ask the desk clerk if anyone named Muhlhaven is staying there, he comes across as very officious. He says that a Muhlhaven—a very important client of the hotel—is indeed staying there. Before you can question the desk clerk any further, the phone rings.

The desk clerk takes the call, assuring the caller on the other end that a newspaper will be sent to the room immediately. He then calls a bellboy over to take the newspaper up and chastises him for not having the top button of his uniform buttoned.

When he turns back to you, ask him if Muhlhaven is in.

After assuring you that Muhlhaven is checked in, he goes on to tell you that he doesn't think Muhlhaven is presently in his room.

Pump him for more information about Muhlhaven. At least he's not cutting you off at the knees.

He doesn't seem to have a problem letting you know that Muhlhaven regularly keeps a suite of rooms at the hotel for business pursuits, but he doesn't go into what those pursuits are.

When you ask for the room number, he puts the brakes on in a polite but firm manner.

This leaves you with two choices: you can either attempt to bribe the guy or threaten him.

TIP *No matter how you approach the desk clerk, you're not going to get Muhlhaven's room number. You'll only acquire it through guile and subterfuge.*

The easiest route seems to be bribery in swank places like this. If anyone sees you flashing a fiver at the desk clerk, you can always claim you were just tipping the guy, not bribing him.

The desk clerk doesn't hesitate at all about turning down the money. Guys in this place must get paid real well.

You're going to have to be clever to get through this castle's defenses. Having watched the bit with the paper gives you an idea. Turn to your right and spot the phone on the wall.

Go to the phone and look at the Hotel Cleveland matchbook you have. See, the number to the hotel is written on the matchbook—GB5-637. Dial it up and then, when the desk clerk answers the line, act like a stuffy jerk with a lot of money. Tell him to get a newspaper up to Muhlhaven's room pronto.

TIP

When you access the Hotel Cleveland matchbook, you have to turn it over to get the number off the back. Put the cursor on the matchbook and wait until it turns into an arrow pointing to either side. Then left-click on the matchbook. The number is easy to read: GB5-637 or 425-637.

Jones, the desk clerk, assures you that the paper will be sent up. When you get off the phone, you watch as the bellboy grumbles that he's already delivered the paper. Jones sends him on his way anyhow.

See, all you have to do now is follow the bellboy straight to Muhlhaven's room, 23G.

When you arrive at Muhlhaven's room, you stand around a little while until the maid and the bellboy vanish from the hallway. Then take a look at the door—it's locked solid.

While the maid's gone, take a look at her cart. Maybe she left a spare set of keys to all the rooms there.

At any rate, there's a transom above the door.

Of course, getting up to that transom could be difficult. If you borrow the maid's cart, you'll be a lot closer, right? Sure you will. Move it over to the door.

TIP

To move the cart, left-click on it. You immediately pull it across the hallway.

Climb up on the cart—careful now!—and try to get through the transom. Stuck, huh? Figures it wouldn't be that easy. Maybe it isn't locked, though. Maybe you just need something to give yourself a little leverage to get inside.

Take a look at the maid's cart again.

There! Do you see the knife under the napkin? That's all the help you need.

TIP

Drag the cursor down to the bottom of the screen to focus on the maid's cart. Left-clicking on the knife under the napkin adds it to your Inventory.

This time, when you left-click on the transom, you automatically use the knife to force your way inside the hotel room.

Take the knife and climb back up to the transom. With a little prodding, you'll manage your first breaking and entering while in the employ of the COI. (When the agency was set up, you understood that some latitude was given to its agents to get their jobs done. But, you may have just blown that latitude all to bits.) Getting caught inside the room isn't a good idea.

And wow! Look at this room! Fit for a king!

At least, it seems to be fit for a Knight of the Brotherhood of Thule.

Enough gawking. Start tossing the room, and let's see what kind of secrets—if any—Muhlhaven's hiding here.

Go to the armoire on the left wall. It's locked. If you look close, you'll see that its keyhole has a really odd shape.

Nothing you can do will get you into the armoire at the moment. Go down to the bar—nothing there. Try the bedroom area.

When you check the vase on the night stand to the right of the bed, you see a spare room key and what looks like some kind of invitation in the vase. Take the key.

As soon as you're about to reach for the invitation in the bottom of the vase, the sound of keys jingling in the room reaches your ears. Moving quickly, you hide behind the drapes near the balcony.

The maid lets three men into the room. Judging from the way they move, one of them is in charge while the other two are there to watch over him. The maid gets nervous and starts giving the guys some lip.

One of the men starts for her, a dark rage on his face. The guy in charge barks at him, calling out his name, Hans, in a German accent. The man backs down, but the maid has gotten the message.

Evidently, knowing what he's after, the man goes to the vase where you were forced to leave the invitation. He takes the invitation out, but he puts something in the vase, too. A moment later, the maid and the three men leave.

Letting out a sigh of relief, step from behind the drapes and go see what the man left for Muhlhaven.

It's a photograph of a man and a woman. And, if that man is Muhlhaven, he's a man in a lot of trouble. Take the picture. Judging from the way the man handled the situation, the photograph is supposed to put pressure on Muhlhaven. It may be a good idea if you were in a position to put some pressure on Muhlhaven yourself. After all, the man who just left the room with his goon squad can probably get other pictures. This is the only one you've got.

When you turn the photo over, you find a message.

Here is a sample of my latest photographic essay. To receive the negative, meet me at the usual time and place.

No signature, which means that Muhlhaven—if he is the man in the photo—is used to dealing with these people.

You search the rest of the room, but there's nothing else here. You now have another piece of a puzzle. It may not be the same puzzle you were working on with Louie's case, but you're willing to bet it is.

For now, let's dust. You've got Louie's address. Let's go see what he had at his place.

TIP   *Right-click the mouse to bring up the supplemental list. Left-click on the World Map and then left-click on Louie's Loft.*

Looting Louie's Lair

Louie's place is in shambles when you get there. You go in with your gun drawn just in case there are any more nasty surprises.

Whoever went through the room was thorough. Despite knowing that the chances of finding something that was missed are slim, you do it anyway.

Louie used a cable drum as a table near the center of the room. A number of strange things rest on it.

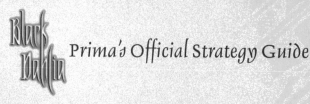

As you look around, you also notice that the walls are covered in weird markings, making you think of the runes.

A board squeaks underfoot as you cross to the other side of the room. The old coal stove draws your attention.

TIP

Left-click on the old coal stove to approach it and to get close enough to see the pile of ashes. Left-click on the small whisk broom nearby to use it to clean the ash away from the runes underneath.

But the pile of gray ashes at the bottom captures your attention even more. Doesn't it look as though something is under those ashes? Use the whisk broom to clear them away.

Yeah, you've stumbled on another clue. Look at the runes burned into the wood here. Get your notebook out and start copying them down.

The cold wind blows over you unexpectedly.

From the Casebook of COI Agent James R. Pearson

When that wind hit me, I was dreaming all over again. I mean, that's what it felt like. Only this time I was standing there with my eyes wide open.

I turned around, following the chopping sounds behind me. Then I saw him: that skinny old man with the queer language and the frock coat. Only he had the coat off at the moment because he was busy.

He was working at a table. Chopping something up with a big, heavy meat cleaver. Blood flew in all directions. Then he turned around and looked at me, shaking that meat cleaver at me while he spoke.

It was then that I saw the dismembered body on the table behind him. That's when I really started wondering if Detective Merylo was right, that maybe this queer old bird was in fact the Torso Killer.

He turned back around and smacked that body with another cut, and the thick sound of it let me know that he'd cut right through bone with that blow. Then all of the dream faded away, leaving me standing there in Louie's loft, staring down at the runes burned into the floor.

Okay, I don't know what's going on either, but pull yourself together. You ain't going to be doing anybody any good if you start losing your head. Oops, considering the scene you just witnessed in that dream, maybe that wasn't the best pep talk I could have given.

Turn your attention again to the runes in the floor. Don't they look like some of the ones in your bag?

Yeah, sure they do. Remember, Helen said something about needing to know what order the runes go in. The first three runes you fit together from the flyer that Louie was passing around at Finster's. Maybe these will fit together in this pattern, too.

TIP

To manipulate the runes, go to the Inventory and select the Bag of Runes. Left-click on them to put them together.

Yeah, that's the way. Connect the middle rune to the last rune in the sequence. See, the third rune is already on the three-dimensional puzzle frame. The middle rune goes directly beneath it; the one on the left goes to the left of it. Still, even with placing these runes, you have a lot of runes to go before you have the entire puzzle pieced together.

Move away from the stove and toward the dresser on the wall behind you.

Looking across the top of the dresser, you see an ashtray filled with cigarette butts, an empty whiskey bottle, a bottle of ink, and the strangely shaped fountain pen Louie must have been using to draw all over the walls.

The dresser's locked, so you can't access it. Head back to the door of the loft. You haven't come up completely empty, but you haven't found the answers you were looking for either.

Hey, do you hear the board creaking underfoot again? Why just the one board? I mean, this place looks as though a cyclone's been through it, but the floor's okay, right?

Take a look at the floor in the middle of the room.

TIP

The cursor changes into the spinning arrow when it's in the right place. Simply left-click on the floor to get a closer look.

Sure, Louie made himself a hiding spot here. But what did he hide? It looks like some kind of miniature house, or maybe a mill with that wheel on the side of it.

Take it out of the floor and get a better look.

Once you have the Lockbox in the Inventory after left-clicking on it, examine it. Also, you need to be there to manipulate the pieces of the Lockbox puzzle to get the key from it.

This little house is quite a contraption after you get the chance to study it. There are a lot of moving parts, but after considerable effort, you figure out its secret and find the proper sequence to open it.

1. Turn the lamp to the left of the large window clockwise.

2. Push the small window (the one on the left side) in.

3. Push the chimney down.

4. Slide the panel below the small window up.

5. Turn the mill wheel back away from you. This causes the panel below and to the left of the small window to sink forward into the side of the house.

6. Slide the panel below and to the left of the small window as far as it will go to the left.

7. Slide the panel that had been directly below the small window back down to its starting position.

8. Pull the chimney back up.

9. Turn the wheel toward you.

10. Turn the lamp to the left of the large window counterclockwise one half turn (until it stands straight up).

11. Slide the long panel below the large window to the left.

12. Pivot the door to the right of the large window all the way open.

13. Slide the open door to the left as far as it will go.

14. Slide the small square panel below the large window up.

Once you have done all this, watch how the house opens up and reveals a key and a ring.

TIP

To take the Lockbox Key and the Signet Ring out of the Lockbox, simply left-click on them. They immediately go into the Inventory. You can then look at them.
Left-click on the new items in the Inventory to inspect them.

Hang onto the key because it probably goes into the dresser. And the ring? Take a close look at the rune-shape plastered to it. Doesn't that look like the same shape as the one on the armoire lock in Muhlhaven's hotel room? Oh yeah, you're definitely onto something here.

We'll go to the Hotel Cleveland later. For now, let's give the dresser a shot. Cover up the hole in the floor. The more secrets in this little shindig that are yours, the better off you are.

Okay, the key fits, but it doesn't open the drawer. There must be a trick to it. Save the key for now. You have other fish to fry.

Yeah, yeah, that signet ring is burning a hole in your pocket, and you'd love to see what Muhlhaven is hiding at the hotel room. But let's get a proper view on things first. Jaunt up to Sullivan's office and see if you can get the skinny on Muhlhaven and the German who came calling while Muhlhaven was gone.

Information can save your butt.

TIP

Right-click on the mouse to bring up the supplemental list. Left-click on the World Map and then left-click on Sullivan's Office.

The German Spy

It's hard to restrain your excitement when you get to Sullivan's office, but give it a whirl. Sure, he's warmed up to you, but he was pretty warm toward Pensky, too, and Pensky's off in a nuthouse somewhere.

Ask him about Joseph Muhlhaven first.

Sullivan appears sincerely surprised that Muhlhaven is involved in the mess you're digging through. Muhlhaven is an industrialist with some political aspirations.

Tell him about the blackmailer.

From your description, Sullivan tells you the German you saw in Muhlhaven's room was probably Wilhelm Von Hess, a Nazi diplomat who's been suspected of spying for some time. Unfortunately, he's been able to use his political station to avoid deportation. If you can find something to tie him to, the Feds will only be too happy to run with the ball and kick Von Hess out of the country.

Getting a little more risky now, you decide to show Sullivan the picture of Muhlhaven.

Sullivan tells you that the picture was taken in a place called Flanagan's, a notorious illegal casino and brothel. Only men with Muhlhaven's power and money can afford a ticket there. Your boss is all ready to start the wheels turning to get Von Hess out of the country because something like Von Hess blackmailing Muhlhaven is all the Feds need to get to him.

You ask him to hold back on that for now, though, to give yourself a little room to work with first. You've got to gamble if you're going to bring in the high stakes.

With so much going your way and with Sullivan in your corner for the moment, ask him about Pensky's last case. Tell him that you'd like to see Pensky's case files.

That request puts Sullivan off. Even after you persuade him to see your side of things—and Pensky's for that matter—that the Brotherhood of Thule believes in the collection of mumbo jumbo, he tells you the FBI confiscated all of Pensky's files.

Blocked for the moment, you take your leave from Sullivan and hoof it over to Flanagan's. Since Muhlhaven wasn't in his room earlier, maybe you can catch up with him there. That's certainly less risky than going back to the Hotel Cleveland and possibly running into Von Hess or his goons.

TIP

Right-click on the mouse to bring up the supplemental list. Left-click on the World Map and then left-click on Flanagan's to go there.

Once you let yourself into the room at Flanagan's, you discover that Muhlhaven isn't there yet.

Okay, so maybe all the good breaks haven't caught up with you yet. Light a shuck here for the moment and try your luck with Winslow. After all, you received a personal invitation.

Winslow is your only access to Pensky's files, which seem more important by the second.

TIP

Right-click on the mouse to bring up the supplemental list. Left-click on the World Map and then left-click on FBI Office.

Shaken, Not Stirred

Arriving at Winslow's office, you find the agent somewhat overly involved with his secretary. It looks like more than just a professional relationship to your old peepers.

Winslow acts a little embarrassed to be caught with Candy, his secretary, and he shoos her along. When you tell him you're there for some information, he tells you he hopes you're not sore about this morning. He offers you a Turkish cigarette, the finest cigarettes he's ever tasted.

Ask him about the gunman in the warehouse.

Winslow says that they're still working on identifying the guy, but their opinion is that the guy was working for the Mob. Even when you point out that the gun was an SS Nazi issue, he maintains that it was a Mob hit. You also tell him about the connection to the Brotherhood of Thule, which he totally discredits and thinks nothing of. But he'll look into it for you.

Ask him about Joseph Muhlhaven.

Seeming somewhat hesitant, Winslow tells you that the FBI has had its eyes on Muhlhaven for some time. Muhlhaven is a guy who'll play both sides of the street if he gets the chance. He stands to make quite a bit of money if the United States jumps into the coming war. Winslow doesn't believe Muhlhaven even comes close to being a spy, however.

Ask him about the blackmailer, Von Hess.

Admitting to knowledge about Von Hess, Winslow doubts that the German diplomat is a spy. And if he were, what would he be doing in Cleveland?

You don't have an answer for that yet, so ask him about the Pensky files.

Winslow doesn't hesitate to tell you that he has Pensky's files in his safe. He's under orders, though, to keep them there—you can't even get a look at them. He goes on to say that everything in the files is utter nonsense, that Pensky went completely batty at the end.

Finished with Winslow, there's only one place you have left to go: Hotel Cleveland. So, get the lead out and get over there.

 **TIP**

Right-click on the mouse to bring up the supplemental list. Left-click on the World Map and then left-click on Hotel Cleveland.

Muhlhaven still isn't in his room when you arrive. Get out the Signet Ring you found at Louie's and try to open the armoire.

 **TIP**

To use the Signet Ring on the armoire, walk over to the armoire and then right-click on the mouse to bring up the Inventory. Left-click on the Signet Ring and then left-click on Use.

Just as you're about to open the armoire, you hear footsteps in the hall. You have just enough time to run and hide behind the drapes before the door opens.

Watching from behind the drapes, you see a man dressed in Nazi storm trooper black walk into the room. He turns to the table at the right and begins tearing pages from a book he's brought with him.

Angry at the Nazi's brass to parade around so publicly in his uniform, you move from your hiding place and confront him.

But I'm telling you now, there's no way to be prepared for what you're about to see.

6

Feather
and Fang

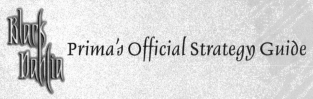
Death In SS Nazi Black
From the Casebook of COI Agent James R. Pearson

My God! In Muhlhaven's room in the Hotel Cleveland that night, I felt as though I looked into the eyes of Death himself!

And he was wearing my face!

Drawn to the figure of the Nazi storm trooper tearing pages from the book in Muhlhaven's room, I advanced on him. If Von Hess and his goons were involved in all the mess I was investigating, I figured this goosestepper had to be in it up to his pointy little ears.

So I reached out for him, intending to take him by surprise, and yanked on his shoulder. Only when he turned around, he was me!

Or at least he looked enough like me to be my twin. He shouted at me in German, offensive and cruel. But I didn't understand a word he said.

Then a white field settled over my vision. The next thing I knew, I was standing in front of the armoire with that signet ring in my hands, waiting to open the doors.

I was shaken down to the core of myself. Even the other 'visions' or 'walking nightmares' or whatever it was I'd been experiencing weren't as bad as this one.

Settle down. Some weird stuff is definitely going on around here, but stick to the basics and keep your head. Too many others are losing theirs—just ask Merylo.

Once you open the armoire, take a good look around inside.

Over on the left, under a stack of bills in a money clip, is a letter. Take it and read it.

Dear Mr. Muhlhaven,

We're all so looking forward to seeing you again next week. The girls just love the gifts that you brought with you last time and miss their Uncle Joe terribly. Kitty in particular sends her love and says that you are to bring her a bear named Theodore to go with her puppy. You know how children are, they can be so demanding, but she insists that you must have Theodore with you or she'll not let you in the house. I thought that story might amuse you. Please have a safe journey and give our best regards to your wonderful family. I only hope they realize how much your generosity means to us here at the orphanage.

With Deepest Regards,

Mrs. Flanagan

Well, it seems like old Muhlhaven is a hit with the girls at Flanagan's. And anyone not knowing what Flanagan's is wouldn't get a wrong idea about the setup at all.

But thinking about Kitty and her demand for a bear named Theodore makes you wonder. Suppose that's some kind of code? You don't know exactly what kind of business is going on down at Flanagan's for sure. At least, you don't know the parts that Sullivan didn't fill you in on.

Put the letter back and look at that stack of black booklets in front of it.

TIP *To get the Raven Room invitations near the money and letter, put the cursor on the black booklets. Left-click on the invitation again to open it.*

Hey, those are invitations to the Raven Room. When you open them up, you see that they're blank.

You are cordially invited to attend the gala premiere of the Raven Room.
This exclusive opportunity is extended to only the most prestigious members of local society.

*Contemporary entertainment provided by
Mel Fritz and His Fabulous Orchestra.
Cocktails and hors d'oeuvres
served until close*

– – – – – – – – – – – – – – – – – – – –

*Date: November 29, 1941
Time: 8:00 P.M.
Location: 1008 East 9th Street*

_____

Signature

November 29 is tonight. Better pocket one of these invitations, so that you can crash the party later. It'll be interesting to see who shows.

The right side of the armoire holds a camera, some letters, and girlie magazines on the shelf. There's even a Scrumpy's prophylactic.

The letter on the top is from the Hotel Cleveland, a detailed list of credit purchases Muhlhaven has made at the bar. Looking it over, it's easy to see that Muhlhaven is a man used to living high on the hog.

The letter under the girlie magazines is from Muhlhaven's wife, who's obviously living the good life and doing nothing but loving it.

On the lower shelf on the right, there's a USTC Telegram addressed to Muhlhaven.

```
PLEASED TO INFORM YOU THAT FIRST SHIPMENT LEFT ON
MORNING CONVOY STOP SECOND SHIPMENT DUE DAY AFTER
TOMORROW STOP AWAIT YOUR INSTRUCTIONS ON PROCEDURES FOR
STORAGE WHILE NEXT CONVOY FORMS STOP


   RUSSELL
```

Now that raises your eyebrows, doesn't it? What kind of convoy are we talking about here?

Okay, well at least you've got the invitation to use later. The raid here hasn't entirely proven to be a dry run. But what you really need is more information. The only place you can get that is from Pensky's files. Maybe it's time to go see if Winslow's chains can be rattled a bit more.

TIP

Right-click on the mouse to bring up the supplemental list. Left-click on the World Map and then left-click on FBI Office.

Safecracker!

You're in luck when you get back to Winslow's office. He doesn't appear to be around.

As you get further into the room, however, you realize that *that* isn't true at all. Winslow is there. From the girlish giggles and the crooning sound in Winslow's voice, you figure that his hands are full at the moment.

So come on, and take advantage of the situation. See about creeping into Winslow's office while he's otherwise engaged. (He's not exactly a straight-up Joe, is he?)

The first thing you notice is the pile of Turkish cigarette butts in the ashtray on Winslow's desk. The guy really puts them down, doesn't he?

Walk toward the grandfather clock to your right. A brief examination of the books in the bookcase shows Winslow's interests run from sports to murder novels.

Stepping back and turning around, go examine the short case against the opposite wall where the globe is.

The pictures on the wall near the globe draw your attention. They show Winslow in the company of a number of famous people, including FDR. He also has signed pictures from Tommy Dorsey and Mickey Rooney. Not exactly the top-shelf stuff you were looking for, is it?

But what about the picture of Winslow in the football get-up? Guy has an ego, doesn't he? And look, he even marked down the score of the Harvard/Yale game of 1933. Harvard 19, Yale 6.

There's a framed copy of the *New York Times* to the right, showing other college games, but none of them is Harvard or Yale.

Cross to the other side of the room to the door that leads to the adjoining room. The

sound of Winslow and the secretary are definitely coming from this room.

A world map above the filing cabinets on the left draws your attention for only an instant, but nothing's there. The picture of the boating classic to your right with all the notations holds your attention for a moment, too.

As you look at the picture of the pitcher and fruit to the right of the door, you notice that it doesn't sit on the wall right for some reason, but it still seems to sit flush against the wall.

To move the pitcher and fruit picture in order to reach the wall safe, left-click the arrow cursor on it and then left-click the arrow cursor on the left side of the frame *to open it.*

As you attempt to square it up, you feel the way it moves—like it's on well-oiled hinges. It turns out you're right. The picture pulls out and opens like a door, revealing the wall safe behind it.

And Winslow *did* mention that he had Pensky's files in his safe, didn't he?

Okay, dust off those magic fingers of yours and see if you can crack this safe. Winslow doesn't strike you as the type who'd trust himself to remember the number to the safe. He probably has it written down somewhere.

And since he likes to read those murder mysteries, maybe he'd even do an Edgar Allan Poe move with the safe combination, putting it out in plain sight so he can have his little laugh whenever anyone sees the picture. It would make him feel that much more superior to anyone around him.

There were lots of numbers on the pictures and newspaper from the armoire, weren't there? So which one would a joker like Winslow pick?

Well, if I were you, I'd put my money on the Harvard/Yale game. That seemed to be a moment of glory for Winslow, and it's a picture he'd probably show most people (while he laughed inside the whole time because they didn't get that he was showing them the combination to his safe).

So try the numbers 19, 6, and then 33—the score plus the year.

The safe dial works like most dial locks. Turn past the first number (19) to the right twice; stop on it the third time it comes around. Turn past the second number (6) to the left once; stop on it the second time. Turn back to the third number (33) and then try the handle to open the safe door.

To turn the dial to the right, put the arrow cursor to the right of the red indicator arrow on the lock. To turn the dial to the left, put the arrow cursor to the left of the red indicator arrow on the lock.

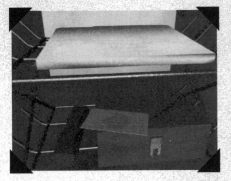

Attaboy! Got it on the first try. Look inside at that fat file sitting on the top shelf.

Opening them up, you see that these are the Pensky files. Even the quick glance you give them proves promising. More than anything, you want to take the file, but you know you can't. As soon as Winslow notices it's missing, he's going to come looking in your direction.

The Mystery of the Black Dahlia

Rare Artifacts Stolen

(Vienna) Officials from the Habsburg Museum of Natural History in Austria reported today the theft of several rare artifacts from the premises. Officials are perplexed as to how the burglar stole into the museum without tripping any alarms or alerting any of the guards. The work of a master thief would be expected, the curator notes, except for the fact that the stolen items were surrounded by several art treasures reportedly to be of far greater value. "The thief was clever, skilled, and bold," the curator said, "but if he'd put any time into researching the treasures on display, he could have come away with a far greater heist." Still, the curator noted, the artifacts were rare, one of a kind items that will be impossible to replace. "The museum suffered a great loss today." Officials from Nazi Germany issued a reward for any information regarding the theft. "Brazen theft of such icons of German culture will not be tolerated," was the official declaration.

Doctor Flees Austria

(London) Sources within the German government strongly denied reports from Vienna that renowned Austrian philosopher Doctor Heinrich Eisenstadt has defected from his homeland. Doctor Eisenstadt, once a prominent member of Austrian aristocracy and an early supporter of Adolf Hitler, was reported to have grown disenchanted with the Nazi party since its Austrian takeover. Doctor Eisenstadt's abrupt and unexpected departure from Austria reportedly caught the SS off-guard. Our own government officials refused comment on the missing doctor. "Any comment at this time would be baseless speculation," one spokesman stated. "We do not know for certain that Doctor Eisenstadt escaped his country's borders, or if he did in fact do so, how he managed to succeed." No further comments were elicited. Doctor Eisenstadt's current whereabouts and his destination remain unknown.

```
Date: August 15, 1941
To: Bill Sullivan
From: Walter Pensky
RE: Dahlia Investigation
```

Further investigations into the subject code-named "Dahlia" has turned up some interesting revelations. My sources confirm the reports from New York that several SS operatives have been dispatched to the area. I've made contact with an informant within an organization that I suspect could be a Nazi front. He was able to supply me with some new information on the case. Evidently, the "Dahlia" the Nazis are trying to recover is not a new technology at all, but rather a mystical artifact reputed to have some sort of supernatural power. Apparently, some members of Himmler's SS believe it could be the key to winning the war. I will continue my investigation into this matter.

LEVEL 3 SECURITY CLEARANCE

```
Date: August 1, 1941
To: Bill Sullivan
From: Walter Pensky
RE: Nazi Infiltration
```

Preliminary investigation supports conclusion of Nazi infiltration in the midwest area. I believe this infiltration to be pervasive. Although the large numbers of people in the area sympathetic to the German cause make it hard to separate the wheat from the chaff, I

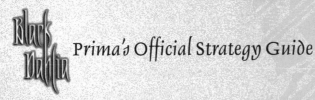

have strong suspicions regarding several key individuals
in both public and private sectors. I will continue to
devote efforts toward finding solid evidence of any
traitorous actions amongst these individuals. I will
make this my top priority.

I've stumbled upon another interesting piece of
information. When I last spoke to our New York offices,
an operative there spoke of an intercepted Nazi
transmission. The decoded message indicated their search
for an item code-named "Dahlia." An informant promised
to uncover more information on the "Dahlia" for me.
Given the large number of government contracts for
weapons manufacturers in the region, I have every reason
to believe that "Dahlia" is the name of some new,
possibly experimental technology that the Nazis plan to
steal in hopes that it will aid their war effort. I will
be investigating this further.

LEVEL 3 SECURITY CLEARANCE

Date: September 19, 1941
To: Walter Pensky
From: William Sullivan, Cleveland Bureau Chief
      Office of Coordinator of Information
Re: Dahlia Investigation

The COI has reviewed your reports and has determined
that the "Dahlia" investigation is no longer an issue of
departmental concern. As such, you are hereby ordered to
cease and desist immediately any inquiry into this case
or any related matter. I should not need to remind you
that your duty is to uncover evidence of Nazi
infiltration and traitorous actions in the area. Any
further insubordination shall result in immediate
dismissal.

Walt,

You're letting this mystical mumbo jumbo
get the better of you. Frankly, I
am concerned about your health. Let the
matter drop, for God's sake.

Yours,

Bill

LEVEL 3 SECURITY CLEARANCE

Date: October 31, 1941
RE: Review Board Findings for Walter Pensky

At the recommendation of the consulting psychiatrist,
Dr. Jorgensen, this board declares that Walter Pensky be
considered mentally incompetent, and, as such, be found
unfit to stand before this board. Herewith are the
board's findings: 1) Walter Pensky shall be relieved
immediately from all duties as an operative of the COI;
2) Forthwith, Walter Pensky shall be confined to a
board-appointed sanitarium; 3) The institution of his
commitment shall be the Sunnyvale Rest Home of Shaker
Height; 4) Walter Pensky shall be provided with board-
appointed supervision until such a time as he is
determined to be fit to return to society. In light of
Dr. Jorgensen's recommendation, this review board
declares that all motions shall be passed forth
immediately.

LEVEL 3 SECURITY CLEARANCE

Date: October 20, 1941
RE: Conduct Hearings for Walter Pensky

Walter Pensky is hereby given notice that conduct
hearings regarding his continuing status as federal
officer shall begin promptly on October 27, 1941, at
9:00 a.m. at the federal building. A federal review
board shall at that time determine whether or not Mr.
Pensky shall continue to serve the United States
government in active duty.

LEVEL 3 SECURITY CLEARANCE

Flipping through the pages, you get something even better than a copy of the file. You find out that Walter Pensky is at the Sunnyvale Rest Home. Not only will Pensky be able to tell you what's in the file, but you'll be able to ask him questions, too.

A leather ID case on the second shelf yields a security check pass in Winslow's name. Now that may come in handy, too. As you finish writing down the Sunnyvale name, you hear Winslow approaching the adjoining office door. Take the security pass and shove the file back into the safe. You're barely able to get the safe closed before Winslow comes into the room.

Agent Winslow is at once on the defensive, wanting to know how long you've been waiting in his office. He's grimly aware that you've probably figured out what was going on in the other room.

You lie and tell him that you just arrived there.

Winslow gives you the brush off, telling you there may be a better time to talk later. Having already gotten what you came for, you couldn't agree more.

Once you get back to your office, it only takes you two shakes of a dead lamb's tail to run down the address for the Sunnyvale Rest Home. Excitement fills you as you turn your tracks for Sunnyvale.

TIP *Right-click on the mouse to bring up the supplemental list. Left-click on the World Map and then left-click on Sunnyvale Rest Home to go there.*

7

The Pensky Interviews

Do You Believe in Magic?
From the Casebook of COI Agent James R. Pearson

Sunnyvale seemed harmless enough, but I knew some strings had been pulled to lock Mr. Pensky away. I thought it was best not to stir up any more trouble than was necessary, so I looked for a nice, quiet way in. The back door into the laundry room did the trick. It wasn't long before I'd found Mr. Pensky's room.

The problem was, Mr. Pensky wasn't alone. The nurse standing guard over him could have stopped a rampaging Viking with her tone.

"This room is restricted, sir," she told me with a harsh glare.

I checked my pockets and came up with the clearance I'd swiped from Winslow's safe. "I've got clearance." I flapped it at her.

She wasn't happy about it, but there was no denying it. "Oh, I'm sorry. I'll be out of your way in a minute." Then she turned her full attention to Mr. Pensky.

He was a broad man, going gray, but you could still see the lion in there. Mr. Pensky wasn't a man who could be easily railroaded from the look of him. Yet the FBI had found a way to get it done.

But now he looked pathetic. He sat in a geriatric chair, held in place by leather restraint bands around his legs and forearms. His eyes didn't seem capable of focusing on anything, and I started wondering if I'd come too late. Maybe he really had experienced some kind of breakdown.

The nurse shoved the pill she was holding at Mr. Pensky's face. He turned his head away from her. "Now, Mr. Pensky," she said in a harsh voice, "I don't have time to fight with you today."

Mr. Pensky kept his head turned from her.

The nurse's voice took on even more threatening tones. "Take it!"

Reluctantly, almost as petulant as a child, Mr. Pensky cranked his head over and let her put the pill in his mouth. Then he drank the water she gave him. Finally satisfied, the nurse left the room.

I moved closer to him, wondering how dazed his mind was going to be after all the drugs they were obviously keeping him on. "Mr. Pensky, I'm Jim Pearson. I'm with the COI."

All of a sudden, I saw the life come back into him. He swiveled a hard pair of eyes on me, taking my full measure at once. At least, that's the way it felt. He spat out the pill. "The COI, you say?" he asked indignantly. "Well, it's about time."

I didn't know how to respond to that, so I let it pass. "I've reason to believe that you were working on something that's all mixed up in my own investigations," I told him. "Can you tell me what it was you were working on?"

"Ha! That's what got me into this pickle in the first place." Mr. Pensky breathed out a sigh. "Do you believe in the supernatural, son? Spirits of darkness and forces beyond man's control?"

I answered honestly, knowing he could tell if I lied. "No sir, I don't. It all seems like a bunch of stuff out of pulp magazines and radio shows."

"I didn't believe in them much, either." Mr. Pensky smiled, showing me he wasn't too disappointed. "Everyone thinks I'm crazy. But I've seen things. Strange things. And if your case is at all tied up in this mess I was investigating, you better be prepared."

"Yes, sir."

Mr. Pensky shook his head sorrowfully. "You don't believe me. Some day you will."

"I found these in your office, sir," I told him, showing him the runes and the parchment sheets. "Professor Strauss's daughter helped to explain them a little bit. And I've also found some similar markings on some papers belonging to a group that goes by the name of the Brotherhood of Thule. But I can't make heads or tails out of it."

"You ever hear about a gem called the Black Dahlia?

"Just from your case files, sir."

"The Dahlia. That's what it's all about, my boy. That's what it's all about."

"What is this Dahlia?" I asked.

"It's pure evil. That's what it is. It feeds on blood sacrifice. Many men have tried to uncover its secrets and gain its power, and many men have been driven mad by it. Find the Dahlia; destroy it. That's the only thing that will make sense of this for you."

He was so vehement in his declaration that it sent chills up my spine. Still, I pressed on, not knowing how much time we had before someone saw through my flimsy subterfuge. It was hard not to think about the possibility that I could have been found out at any minute. "I'm not sure why, sir, but my instincts are telling me the Torso Killer is mixed up in all of this somehow."

"You follow your gut, son. The Torso Killer is at the center of all this madness."

"But how?"

"How many victims has he claimed?"

"Eight. At least, that's all we know of."

"Oh, you must find him quickly then. His bloody work requires the sacrifice of nine men and women if the prophecy—the ritual—is true."

"How can I find him? The police have been working on this case already for months, and they're still no closer to tracking him down. Do you know who he is?"

"Oh, I don't know who the killer is, but I was getting close, I tell you. That's why I was put in here. I was getting too close. Why, if they hadn't locked me away, I'd have had that man by now."

As I was listening to Mr. Pensky, I started getting that same familiar sensation of one of the walking nightmares, but I was in the middle of a conversation with a man. I couldn't just start dreaming in the middle of that, could I? Then his voice sounded hollow, as though he were a thousand miles away.

I looked around the room, noticing the mirror on the wall behind me. Something was wrong with it. The glass started getting all wavy, distorting the reflection. All of a sudden, though, I was no longer sure if it were a reflection at all. It looked like a totally different place on the other side of the glass.

I crossed the room and looked into the mirror. Without warning, the rune that's on the signet ring formed on my forehead with the sound of sizzling meat. It reminded me of my first dream, when the man with the German accent branded me with his cane.

I reached out to touch the image of the rune in the mirror, and the mirror sucked me through it!

A chill ran all over me, like a cold kiss in the middle of my back, when I realized I was standing in swirling mists on the other side of the mirror. It was as if I were on another planet with nothing familiar in sight.

I looked back through the mirror. On this side of the glass, the mirror seemed to hang in midair. But it gave me a view back into Mr. Pensky's room. He was still ranting, as if I'd never left the room.

"Lousy bureaucrats! The doctors and nurses here aren't any better. They feed me pills all day—when I could be out doing the job. But they don't give a rat's ass about a good day's work. All they want is government money. FDR's giving handouts to everybody who sticks their palm in the air."

Helplessly, I watched the doctor enter Mr. Pensky's room. The doctor put his black bag on the bed and opened it.

"Been wondering when you were going to stop by, Doc. It's been a while since I've been poked and prodded. You know, I feel like a slice of prime beef. You know that? What time is it? Seems like you were just here. So, what you got for me now, Doc, huh?"

The doctor pulled a meat cleaver out of the black bag; then he looked up at me. Only, when he looked at me, it wasn't the doctor who I saw. It was the man with the cane from my dreams.

He glanced up at me, knowing I was trapped on the other side of that mirror, and he grinned. Then he went for Mr. Pensky, my best lead in this whole mess.

I screamed a warning, but it was as if my voice didn't even enter the room.

"Maybe more pills," Mr. Pensky said sarcastically, not having a clue that anything was wrong, not having a chance to defend himself with the way he was tied down in that chair. "No. Maybe a shot in the ass?"

I slammed myself up against the mirror, but I couldn't break it, and I couldn't go back through.

"What's with you people?" Mr. Pensky demanded.

The dream man lifted the meat cleaver, and Mr. Pensky had no idea that it was even there. I tried to shout a warning again, but no one heard me. Without warning, the meat cleaver sliced down, straight for Mr. Pensky's head.

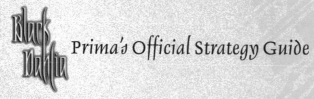

Before it touched, a flash of white filled my vision, and the next thing I knew, I was back in the room with Mr. Pensky. He was looking at me with concern.

"What's happened?" Mr. Pensky asked me.

"It's the strangest thing. I keep having these weird, uh..." I couldn't go on. I shook my head. "No. It's nothing."

"The man with the cane," Mr. Pensky said with sad confidence.

"How did you know?" I asked.

"I've seen him in my dreams as well."

I didn't feel all that much better when he told me. Maybe I was in as bad a shape as he was in. Or maybe there was no way to stop the man with the cane. Neither one of those options was something I wanted to live with. I took a deep breath to clear my head and then asked, "You've been troubled by dreams, too?"

"Yes. My dreams were violated by an evil man." Mr. Pensky grimaced as he spoke. "He wielded a cane. He drove me to the brink of insanity."

"How is this possible?"

"He who controls the Dahlia has the power to control dreams. But I found a way of stopping them."

"How?"

"There are three talismans. Sheltered by the wing of the Raven, protected by the fangs of the Wolf, and guided by the wisdom of the Dragon. The Raven feather shelters you from dreams. But if you had the other two items, you could fight back against your attacker."

The whole concept hit me like a ton of bricks. Even with the spiel I got to sign up for the COI, nobody ever talked about something this far from reality. "This is too much. It's like something out of The Shadow."

"It's your only hope," Mr. Pensky insisted.

"All right, all right. Where can I find these...things?"

"You'll find the Raven feather in my office inside my copy of The Crusades. But you'll need all three talismans if you wish to confront your tormentor. The others will be more difficult to attain. You'll need to get close to your attacker for those. Look for the totems of the Wolf and the Dragon. Return here with all three, and I'll show you how to fight back against your attacker."

"All right, I'll be back as soon as I can get my hands on the hoodoo trinkets." And maybe I would if I didn't find another solution to all these weird dreams. I shifted on to my next question. "In your investigation, sir, did your evidence ever direct you to a place called the Raven Room?"

"Nothing solid. More a suspicion than anything else."

"What did you suspect?"

"Well, that the night club was a front for something far more sinister. It wasn't long after I started putting my nose into their business that I was sent away here." Mr. Pensky swallowed hard and looked down for a moment before looking back at me. "There are some powerful people behind that club. If you're investigating it, better watch your step."

I agreed.

Although I continued to try to talk to Mr. Pensky, he refused to talk to me any more, telling me that I needed to find the three talismans before he could help me any further.

Having no other choice, I went back to my office, intending to check out Pensky's story about the Raven's wing.

TIP *Right-click on the mouse to bring up the supplemental list. Left-click on the World Map and then left-click on your office.*

Raven's Feather

Home, sweet office, huh? Well, don't get too comfy. You've got things to do. Get over to the bookshelves and look for the volume of *The Crusades* Pensky was talking about. Once you have it, open it up.

TIP *Get the book by left-clicking on the shelf just to the right of the locked cabinet where Pensky kept the note from Dr. Strauss. Left-click again on the black, bound book with the title* The Crusades: A Pictorial History. *Left-click on the black Raven's Feather inside the book to add it to your Inventory.*

There's the feather, just like Pensky said. Doesn't look so special, does it? Well, you got it. That's the first step.

Now there's just the Wolf's Fang and the Wisdom of a Dragon to find. And you'll only be protected if you figure on buying into all the hoopla a committed, strapped-down ex-COI agent tells you.

But he knew about the man with the cane, didn't he?

Your leads are slim and none—mostly none. There is, however, the key you found in Louie's Loft, and it did appear to fit the locked drawer. Hit the bricks and get back over there. You've got to skull out a way to get into that drawer.

TIP

Right-click on the mouse to bring up the supplemental list. Left-click on the World Map and then left-click on Louie's Loft.

Wolf's Fang

Nothing seems disturbed when you get back, and no one's lurking in the shadows. Let's take a look at that drawer again.

It takes you some time, but you're a bright boy. After a little experimentation you figure that what Louie's got here is a trick key and a trick lock. It seems that the key turns both ways real easy and that it pushes in and out. A little while later, you get the right combination of moves.

1. Push the key into the lock.

2. Turn the key left.

3. Pull the key out, but not all the way out of the lock.

4. Turn the key right twice.

5. Push the key in.

6. Turn the key back to its starting position.

7. Pull the key out.

TIP

Again, you've got to be precise in putting the cursor on the dresser's key lock. Drag the cursor to the bottom of the screen first and then left-click it on the lock.

Follow the combination of moves that opens the lock by making sure that the directional arrow on the key points in the direction you want it to go.

Clever boy that Louie. Look inside the lock mechanism—another hiding place.

And *that* looks like a wolf's fang attached to it. It's got to be the one Pensky was jawing about because it's covered in runes again.

Pocket the fang and count yourself lucky. Persistence does indeed pay off.

There's one other loose end you have to tie up: Muhlhaven. He could be the breeze that knocks down the entire house of cards you've been chasing. Get back over to Flanagan's and see if he's in now.

TIP

Right-click on the mouse to bring up the supplemental list. Left-click on the World Map and then left-click on Flanagan's to go there.

Making the Guest List

Muhlhaven acts pretty surprised when you barge in on him at Flanagan's. He's not happy about being caught with one of the little "orphan" girls, either. He makes loud noises, but when you show him the photograph, he folds like a bad poker hand buying into a pot that's a fiver into next month's rent.

After he sends the dame packing, ask him why Von Hess is blackmailing him.

Muhlhaven reluctantly admits that the German is blackmailing him to get into the party at the Raven Room. Von Hess is trying to find something stolen from Germany.

In the back of your mind, you start to remember those newspaper clippings you read in Pensky's file. Could that somehow tie into what you're working on, too? At any rate, the Raven Room is figuring into the scheme of things in a big way, so ask him about it.

Muhlhaven replies that it's simply a very popular social club. When you lean on him, Muhlhaven breaks like a soft-boiled egg. He says that there's an inner circle at the club, one that supposedly gathers to take pride in their heritage, to spite Hitler. But there's another reason, too. They want to restore an old order of knights. Muhlhaven believes that they're going too far, and Von Hess's blackmail is keeping him in the middle of things. He's clearly not happy about it.

Since the Raven Room appears to be the place, ask him how to get into the party.

Muhlhaven says that it's too late and that you need a copy of the invitation. Even if he could get you that, the party is so exclusive that you also need a copy of the original seal on the invitation to get in. Muhlhaven doesn't have access to the seal.

Surprise him by showing him the copy of the Raven Room invitation you lifted from his room. He hesitates only a moment, but signs it for you. He repeats, however, that it won't do you any good without the seal.

TIP

Go to the Inventory and select the Invitation. Use it on Muhlhaven.

Don't be disappointed that you won't be able to enter the Raven Room until you find the seal (and use it).

With the signed invitation in your pocket, things are looking up—or looking decidedly more dangerous, depending on your perspective. Are you feeling lucky?

Well, hoof it back to Pensky. You've got two of the three talismans and some information that he may be able to make some sense of for you.

TIP

Right-click on the mouse to bring up the supplemental list. Left-click on the World Map and then left-click on Sunny-vale Rest Home.

More Than One Way to Skin a Cat
From the Casebook of COI Agent James R. Pearson

Mr. Pensky was still strapped in his chair when I got back to the Sunnyvale Rest Home. He seemed more tired than he was earlier, but he looked at me with those alert eyes.

I got right to it because that's the kind of guy Mr. Pensky struck me as. "Do you have any idea why a Kraut named Von Hess would be so eager to get into the Raven Room? He's been putting the squeeze on a Thule member pretty bad to get into this party there."

Mr. Pensky didn't hesitate with his response. "You must go there."

Well, I'd been kind of figuring along those lines myself, so I wasn't too surprised. But I still wanted to know what his thinking was. "What for?"

His heavy sigh told me I'd disappointed him, making him explain things that I should have already known. "The Nazis have been in pursuit of the Dahlia for some time now. If Hitler were to get his hands on the gem, I mean, who knows what kind of suffering the world would see?"

Even though I still wasn't sure how much of his story I was buying into, I felt the weight of his words standing there in that small room. A lot of things were at stake—maybe more than I could imagine. "There's only one problem," I told him. "The party's by invitation only. And all the invitations have this seal from this old order of knights."

"The followers of Landulph," Mr. Pensky said.

"Yes, that's right. The invitation is no good without the seal."

"I've seen documents on display at the Museum of Natural History with that very same seal." A brief grin lighted his worn face. "I'll bet Miss Strauss would be willing to help you out."

I couldn't help but smile back at him, responding to the warmth in his expression. When he didn't feel like the whole world was against him, Mr.

Pensky was probably a Joe who knew how to enjoy life. "All right. If I can't wrangle an invitation out of someone, I'll make my own."

I said my good-byes and left him there, feeling an increasing excitement. But maybe it wasn't excitement at all. Looking back on it now, with the way things worked out, maybe I was just feeling an increased visceral fear. I couldn't tell you now.

When I headed back to the Museum of Natural History, I was feeling pretty good about things. I just didn't know how bad it was going to get. Or what it was going to cost.

But then, I guess none of us really do.

TIP

Right-click on the mouse to bring up the supplemental list. Left-click on the World Map and then left-click on the Museum of Natural History to go there. You will notice that it now pops up in your map.

Impressions

At the museum, Helen has no trouble knowing exactly which seal you're looking for. But standing there holding it in your hands in front of the glass display case, you're sure that this isn't the one you need. Helen says it probably just needs adjusting.

When you ask Helen if she knows how to adjust it, she says that she doesn't know. She tells you to hurry; the security guard will be along at any time, and she'll be in a lot of trouble—this leaves the problem in your hands.

Scan the paper in the center of the display case first. As soon as you reach for it, you feel another dream coming over you.

You're standing on the misty plain again, but there's a tree in front of you. Things hang from the tree branches. When you get closer, you see that the objects are bodies—all of them suspended by ropes.

One of them is Helen. She opens her eyes, looks at you, and then says your name.

Snap to—the lady's talking to you. See? Everything's jake. You're back in the museum, and nothing bad is going on. Now focus your attention on that lousy seal again, and figure out how to make it right. First thing you want to do is strip off the cover.

TIP

To strip off the Seal's cover, simply left-click on it. Notice that there are five color-coded rings on the Seal. For your convenience, start at the back of the seal and number that ring as 1, followed by 2, 3, 4, and 5, with 5 as the ring nearest the end of the Seal.

Be sure to watch which way you drag the arrow cursor on the Seal as well as which way you're supposed to be turning the rings.

If you move the incorrect ring—or move the right ring in the incorrect direction—simply click at the bottom of the screen to start over. Then left-click on the Seal in the display case again.

Yeah, it's a job all right. But after you've fooled around with it for a while, you've got it figured out okay. You have to move each one of the five rings in the right direction and in the proper order to change the seal face. Turn each ring until you hear a distinctive click.

What you're trying to achieve is to drop the darker colored seal to the bottom to replace the silver one.

❖ Turn Ring 4 to the right; the lower right quadrant of the seal sinks in.

- ❖ Turn Ring 1 to the right; the lower right quadrant of the seal is exchanged for the darker colored seal you want.

- ❖ Turn Ring 5 to the right; the lower left quadrant of the seal sinksin.

- ❖ Turn Ring 1 to the right; the lower left quadrant of the seal is exchanged for the dark colored seal you want.

- ❖ Turn Ring 2 to the right; the upper left quadrant of the seal sinksin.

- ❖ Turn Ring 1 to the right; the upper left quadrant of the seal is exchanged for the dark colored seal you want.

- ❖ Turn Ring 3 to the right; the upper right quadrant of the seal sinks in.

- ❖ Turn Ring 5 to the left; the lower left quadrant of the seal pops back out flush with the bottom of the seal.

- ❖ Turn Ring 1 to the right; the upper right quadrant of the seal shifts to the lower right quadrant of the seal, remaining silver.

- ❖ Turn Ring 2 to the left; the upper left quadrant of the seal pops back out flush with the bottom of the seal.

- ❖ Turn Ring 3 to the left; the upper right quadrant of the seal pops back out flush with the bottom of the seal.

- ❖ Turn Ring 1 to the left; the lower right quadrant of the seal is now exchanged for the dark colored seal you want.

- ❖ Turn Ring 4 to the left; the lower right quadrant of the seal pops back out flush with the bottom of the seal.

Once you have the right seal in place, Helen stamps your invitation in nothing flat. Signed, sealed, and delivered.

It's time to party and to see if you can shake up the Raven Room's roost.

NOTE *Change to Disk #4.*

8

Party Crashing
the Raven Room

Down Among the Filthy Rich

The party's already started by the time you get to the Raven Room. It looks as if nobody was holding their breath...until you got there.

Milling around in the crowd, you realize you're rubbing elbows with the city's elite and powerful. Makes you feel kind of small in your rented tux, doesn't it? Well, don't let it bother you. You're not here to soak up the atmosphere or impress anyone.

As you wander around, you spot Agent Winslow in the company of Eliot Ness and two good-looking women. But look over there. There's Muhlhaven and Von Hess.

So what do you do? If you go over and cause a stink, Von Hess will wonder where you got your information. His first conclusion will be Muhlhaven.

But maybe, if you lean on Von Hess and drop Muhlhaven's name, you just may take some of the pressure off of the industrialist. After all, Von Hess has already gotten into the party. It seems as though there's nothing to lose and everything to gain.

You address Von Hess, telling him you know the score. He already knows who you are because Muhlhaven has told him about your visit.

Good. This gets all the cards out on the table. After he dismisses Muhlhaven, you get in his face and talk tough with him. Still, Von Hess keeps his head. He tries to get along with you, telling you that he's just trying to get back some items that have been stolen. He says that the mix-up at the warehouse happened because they were after Louie's key.

He takes out a key that resembles a Maltese cross, saying that the key he's looking for looks a lot like this one. He scans your face, trying to read it to find out if you've seen the key.

Before anything further can be said, Agent Winslow comes over to the table and drags you away, telling you he wants you to meet Eliot Ness. At Winslow's table, he introduces you to Ness and the women they're with.

While you're occupied with Winslow, Von Hess makes his move and streaks to the club's back door. You saw that, didn't you?

Finished with the introductions, Winslow pulls out a chair and offers you a seat.

You don't have time to sit this one out. There's a burning feeling in the pit of your gut that Von Hess is going to cover something up that he's afraid that you'll see.

Give Winslow the slip and take off after Von Hess.

A doorman guards the private entrance to the backroom. Your conversation with him assures you that you're not getting in. It's a private party, and no one is in the room yet, the doorman says.

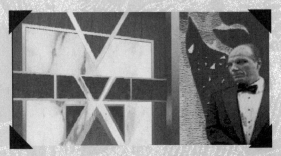

You try getting tough with him, but he's no weak sister. He doesn't back down at all.

Okay, so you know you need to get in the room—but how?

Peel your peepers to the left. It looks as though there's a screen over there behind the table.

Hey, it is a screen. And look at the lazy Susan built into the wall for the wait staff's convenience. From the way it's situated, you have to wonder if the lazy Susan connects to the back room, too. Reach out and give it a spin.

Oh yeah, the lazy Susan does open up into the private room. But what good is that going to do you?

TIP   *To give the lazy Susan a spin to see that it opens up into the back room, left-click on it.*

You want to put the nearby tray of glassware onto the lazy Susan and give it a spin, so that the glasses fall off and break in the private room. (You do have a mean streak in you—I like that in a guy.) So, get those glasses on there already.

TIP   *Left-click on the glassware to put it onto the lazy Susan and then left-click on the lazy Susan to spin it around.*

Good idea, but no dice. They're too well-balanced. Of course, if you had something to unbalance them, you'd be hitting on all cylinders.

Go back through the screen and see if you can borrow one of the soup bowls from the empty table you passed.

Yeah, this little dish should do the job just fine. Now, go back to the lazy Susan and put the dish on it. Stack the glassware on top of the dish and give the lazy Susan a whirl.

TIP   *Get the dish by left-clicking on it. The dish automatically goes into your Inventory. Use the dish on the lazy Susan from your Inventory and then left-click the glassware onto the lazy Susan.*

Now that's a lot of noise! And it looks like you're going to get all the audience you could have *ever* wanted.

The doorman and Winslow go through the door with a group of men. They catch Von Hess in the room and take him into custody. Winslow starts making jurisdictional noises, but everyone agrees to sort it out downtown.

You've already managed to snag a flashlight from one of the shelves in the wait station. When the action dies down, you clamber into the room going through the lazy Susan.

Here's Blood in Your Eye

The room is dark now, but the flashlight cuts through the darkness okay. Turn to your left and shine the flashlight around until you find the light pull cord hanging over the big table. Give it a yank and turn the lights on.

TIP *To turn on the lights in the room, left-click on the dangling pull cord with the arrow cursor.*

Now that's a big table. There's room for 12 people to sit around it comfortably. Notice the runes carved into the tabletop? That definitely proves you're in the right place.

Crouch down more closely to the table and look at the rune signs. I could be wrong, but they look like they open up to me.

Oh yeah, look at the bottom rune. That's the same symbol that's on the Signet Ring. And look, they open right up when you try them.

TIP *The easiest way to make your way around the table is to use the cursor. Follow the directional arrow to the left or to the right.*

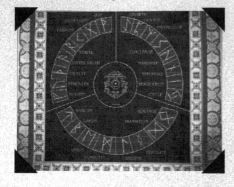

Well, at least you can open up 11 of them. Apparently, you can't open the one with the sideways hourglass rune on it.

Inside each panel is a small plate with some kind of motto. Starting at the black dragon panel that you can't open and moving clockwise around the table, you read the following mottoes:

- ❖ Transcend Joy

- ❖ All Men Together

- ❖ Compassion is not Apathy

- ❖ Stagnation Resists no Challenge

- ❖ Nurture by Valor

- ❖ True Heritage Merits Strife

- ❖ Constancy is its own Reward

- ❖ Hardship is my Birthright

- ❖ Of Intrepid Ancestry

- ❖ Excess Breeds Complacency

- ❖ Courage is my Mettle

Jeez, all you need now is a fortune cookie, and you've read the philosophy of all ages. Shelve that for a moment, and take a look at the brass disk in the center of the table. There's another motto engraved on it: EACH GIFT TO HIM IS NOW DEVOTED.

That has a familiar ring to it, doesn't it? Well, it should. Check out the parchment paper information that Helen Strauss translated for you.

Yeah, it's there all right. Look down at line 22 on the first page: Each Gift To Him Is Now Devoted.

Helen translated that from the runes on the parchment, which means the original parchment sheets should have that same line on it. Take a look.

There! Do you see it? Read off that line of runes. When you were looking at the panels, did you notice that it looked as though one rune was overlaying another? Well, they were.

And it seems as though these runes are paired up. Maybe a combination of these runes in this particular order means something. It's definitely worth a try.

Look at the table again, and let's reopen the panels. Use the black dragon that doesn't open as a starting point and number it as 1. Move clockwise around the table and open the panels in the following sequence:

❖ 6

❖ 8

❖ 11

❖ 12

❖ 9

❖ 4

❖ 5

❖ 7

❖ 2

❖ 3

❖ 10

❖ 1

After you have opened the other 11 panels, you'll find that the black dragon panel pops right out, and you'll find a book written in runes inside.

The book is bound in what looks like leather and must be what Von Hess was after. While you study it, you can't help but think about Pensky's comment about the last of the three talismans you're supposed to find: the wisdom of the Dragon. Could this be the third talisman?

As you stare at the book, blood drips down onto the pages. In horror, you realize that the blood is dripping from your eye. You try to staunch it, getting blood all over your hands.

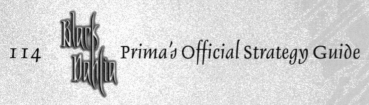

Then—in an instant—all the blood disappears. It was another dream. Apparently, the Raven's feather isn't doing its job.

Grab the book and run because you know that old man with the cane is gunning for you.

Outside, Winslow is arguing with Merylo over who has jurisdiction over Von Hess. You don't have time to get involved in that dispute now, and you certainly don't want to risk getting caught with the book you've just recovered.

With your heart hammering inside your chest, you hotfoot it to Sunnyvale Rest Home. If anyone can make sense of what you've just been through, it'll be Pensky.

Gone Missing!
From the Casebook of COI Agent James R. Pearson

My heart hadn't settled back close to anything normal by the time I reached the rest home. Luckily, nobody tried to stop me as I headed for Mr. Pensky's room.

But things had happened there anyway. I threw open the door and looked for him, but he was gone. As I stood there, not believing what I was seeing, the nurse who'd been attending Mr. Pensky earlier walked in behind me.

Then she looked at me like she'd never seen me before in her life.

"Where's Mr. Pensky?" I asked.

"I'm sorry, who is it that you're looking for?"

"Mr. Pensky."

"I'm sorry, there's no one named Pensky here."

"But he was just in here yesterday. You were there. I saw you."

The nurse shot me a doubtful look. "You must be mistaken, sir. This room has been unoccupied for some time. Are you sure you have the right place?"

"That's impossible! He was just here! I saw him!" I whirled around to point at the spot where Pensky had sat strapped into that chair. And for a moment, I saw him looking back up at me.

Without warning, he started melting, changing. And when I looked again, it wasn't Pensky sitting in that chair at all. It was the old man with the cane and the German accent. He laughed at me, like he'd just pulled one of the best jokes of all.

And maybe he had. My guts turned cold, like they were churning ice cubes.

"Sir!"

I finally realized the nurse was calling for me from behind.

"Sir. Are you all right, sir, you seem a little flushed? Perhaps I can find something to calm your nerves."

I had trouble finding my voice, but I finally did. "No," I told her. "No thanks. I'll be just fine." No way was I going to let anyone in that place put anything into me.

Somebody got to Mr. Pensky. That much was obvious. But who? Was it someone I bumped into and inadvertently led them here, to Mr. Pensky?

Or was it one of Mr. Pensky's old sins reaching out for him?

And that didn't really matter to me, because I was carting around a load of the same sins Mr. Pensky had taken on. Whoever got to him was going to be coming after me. Seeing that old man sitting in that chair laughing at me convinced me of that.

But I had some things going for me, too. I had the Raven's wing and the Wolf's fang, and the book I'd gotten from the black dragon at the Raven Room. They were the talismans Mr. Pensky had warned me to get.

I had something else going for me, too. I knew they were coming; I'd be ready, and I wasn't strapped in a chair and being force-fed drugs to keep me wiped out of my mind.

It was hard to say which was more scary, though. Thinking those people were actually out there waiting to try to take me, or thinking that maybe all of this was one big nightmare that I couldn't escape.

I've always considered my mind to be one of the strongest things about me. But the old man with the cane had shown me how it could be used against me.

While the nurse stood there watching me, lying through her teeth, I showed myself to the door and got the hell out of there.

9

Murder Written
in the Stars

Madame Cassandra

When you get back to the office the next morning, you know you look like hell. You passed the night sleeplessly, all twisted up thinking about what had happened to Pensky. Someone had gotten to him, but who?

You have more questions now than when you took over his caseload, but you've gotten further along than he did, right? At least Von Hess is out of the way, judging from the way things went last night. That should clear the board some.

As you take your seat behind the desk, you find a note that came in this morning's mail on the blotter. The name Cassandra rings a bell. It takes you a minute, but then you remember the name from the "Things To Do" list you found in Pensky's drawer.

Opening the letter, you discover a short, cryptic note inside.

Madame Cassandra
130 Memphis Avenue
Cleveland, Ohio

Dear Mr. Pearson,

Walter Pensky has asked me to contact you on a matter of utmost importance. He believes that you are in great danger and that I may be able to provide you with assistance in your hour of need. Please come to my home as quickly as possible. I await you.

Cassandra Rollins

Intriguing, huh? Well, don't wait for grass to grow—get moving.

A maid takes you through the old Victorian manor, and you find Madame Cassandra sitting on a couch wrapped up in a turban and shawl. Before you can address her, she begins to speak to you, telling you that your aura has been branded.

Once she breaks her monologue—and you can get a word in edgewise—introduce yourself.

She stops the swami act at once. After you ask her about the letter, she tells you she wrote it at Pensky's insistence.

Okay, sleuth, time to get back to the case. Ask her about Pensky.

She tells you that she wrote the letter in response to a letter she had just received from Pensky. He was concerned about you, and he also said that he would be out of touch for some time.

You can't help but wonder how far "out of touch." If Pensky simply had managed to escape the nursing home, the nurse wouldn't have been in on the cover-up there, would she?

Assuming that Pensky did in fact contact Madame Cassandra, tell her about your nightmares.

More concerned now, Cassandra tells you that the book, feather, and fang are only temporary devices against the nightmares. She says that she's the one who taught Pensky about these objects. She goes on to say that your aura is branded and that she has some psychic ability.

Her explanation becomes convoluted, but she tells you that you must find a way to track down the man who's been attacking you in your dreams. She offers to put you into a trance.

Even though you may not believe everything she's told you, allow her to put you into a trance. She pulls out a gold locket and begins to put you under.

Dreamworld Guardian

In a couple breaths, you're standing before the door you saw the Torso Killer attack you from earlier. Dark clouds and impossible sights surround you.

As you approach the door, a winged gargoyle above the door holds a skeletal finger to its mouth and silences you. But you open the door anyway. The surroundings change again, morphing into a room that traps you inside it.

Between two torches hung on the wall in front of you is a door. Go through it and you find yourself in what appears to be another world. As you turn around, you find that you are evidently at a nexus point joining four different places by some magical means. The torches mark the door that will get you back the way you came.

 **TIP**

Getting through the rooms inside this topsy-turvy world simply requires some effort. For those of you who get frustrated, the straight-forward solution is offered below. For those who have that stubborn streak, move around cautiously in the 360-degree environment and look for the hot points.

As you turn to the right from the Entry Point, you'll find the offices in this order:

Merylo's office. "The Crown and the Bird sit on his right and left," is the tag phrase that identifies it. Access Winslow's office by turning right and left-clicking on the desk area.

Once you're in Winslow's office, you'll hear, "The Keys are Creatures of the Sun." Turn to the right and left-click on the next hot point to get into your office.

Once you're in your office, you'll hear, "The Comet is seen after the Moon has risen." Turn to the right and left-click on the next hot spot to get to Sullivan's office.

Once in Sullivan's office, you'll hear, "The Star follows the Key."

To get back, start in Sullivan's office and left-click on the hot spot above the FDR picture behind the desk. You'll arrive in your office.

Turn right and left click on Winslow's office (the first hot point).

In Winslow's office, turn right and left-click on Merylo's office.

In Merylo's office, turn left and left-click on the Entry Point (you'll hear water sounds).

Voices sound around you.

Turn to the right, focusing on the voices. Keep moving around till you isolate each of the voices. A nightmare version of Detective Merylo's office comes first.

"The Sun loves the Bird, but only when she's alone."

"The Fish are creatures of the Moon, though she avoids their company."

"The Crown and the Bird sit on his right and left."

"When the Bird is away from the Sun, she's with the Moon."

The second place is a nightmare version of Winslow's office.

"The Serpent will chase the Comet's tail, if not chased itself by the Star."

"The Keys are Creatures of the Sun."

"The Serpent rises after the Sun, and sets after the Moon."

"The Bird and the Fish are the base of All."

These cryptic messages are found in the nightmare version of Sullivan's office:

"If West is the Right and East is the Left, You know on which side the Sun will rise and on which the Moon will set."

"A lonely Fish loves the Crown, though a lonely Crown prefers the Key."

"The Star follows the Key."

In the nightmare version of your office you find:

"The Comet is seen after the Moon has risen."

"The Key follows the Shield when the Moon is far away."

"No Twin can stand its Sibling."

"By day the Shield surrounds itself with the Sun and the Key; by night he prefers the Moon and the Fish."

Follow the offices back to the door that let you in. Approach the next door in front of you with all the symbols. The door is locked.

But, after listening to the clues you picked up from the whispered voices around you, it's only a matter of moments before you're able to piece together the order the stones go into the door slots. The left side of the door represents the day; the right side represents night. The stones go in the door slots in the following order (from top to bottom):

Day	Night
8. Crown	9. Bird
7. Key	10. Moon
6. Serpent	11. Shield
5. Star	12. Fish
4. Key	13. Serpent
3. Shield	14. Comet
2. Sun	15. Crown
1. Bird	16. Fish

As soon as you get the door open, bright lightning crackles in the entranceway. A monster wind sucks you through the doorway. And when you come to a stop, you know you're not on Earth anymore.

Two spinning crystal spheres hang before you in the starry blackness of space. Both spheres have symbols on them. The symbol on the glowing pale purple one on the lower right is, obviously, a crescent moon. You have no idea what the other one is, however.

With a little experimentation, you find that you can jump from sphere to sphere. As you jump, more spheres appear before you. In a short time, you discover that you can reach eight spheres; however, the ninth one—a huge silver sphere—remains beyond your reach.

Being unable to reach the ninth sphere frustrates you, and you get the feeling that this sphere is something important. Something this hidden must have an important meaning. You concentrate on Cassandra, trying to get back to her.

To get out of the sphere puzzle, simply hit your Esc *key once. Don't worry about this part of the mystery for now. We'll come back when we have all the necessary clues in hand.*

When you open your eyes, you're back in Madame Cassandra's home. Her hand is on your shoulder to steady you. Excited by your discovery, you ask her about the crystal spheres.

She seems as puzzled as you are, but she says that there must be a pattern to them. In astrology, connections are always made through patterns. Find the pattern, she assures you, and you'll find a way to get closer to the killer you're searching for. She offers you a book on astrology.

Looking through it, you find a quick summary on the subject and tables for the sun, for the moon, and for the planets in the solar system. You make notes of this information in your notebook, not knowing for sure what you're going to make of the numbers and symbols you found.

TIP

To copy the necessary information from the Astrology Book, turn the first page and then left-click on the page with the chart listings. You will need to have this in your notebook later.

As you make your list, stick to the eight spinning spheres you actually saw rather than recording information on all of the planets.

Color	Symbol	"Planet"	Number
Brown	⊕	Earth	4
Black	♄	Saturn	15
Blue	♃	Jupiter	34
Red	♂	Mars	65
Gold	☉	Sun	111
Green	♀	Venus	175
Purple	☿	Mercury	260
Silver	☽	Moon	369

TIP

The table that Pearson noted in his notebook is a definite clue and is exactly the kind of information you should look for. You may notice that not all of the planets listed in the astrology book come into play.

If you didn't notice this in your initial gameplay, you may want to put the book down for a while and see if you can't figure out the pattern and where to get it on your own. It's okay if you don't want to do this. The information is provided later in this chapter.

As helpful as Cassandra may be, you have to rake up some more questions and answers elsewhere. For the moment, you've followed this line of inquiry to its end.

Take a quick trip back to Sullivan's office. It's time that you brought the boss up to speed on these new developments.

TIP

Right-click on the mouse to bring up the supplemental list. Left-click on the World Map, and then left-click on Sullivan's Office.

Case File: Torso Killer

When you arrive at Sullivan's office, your first question should be what happened to Von Hess. Your instincts tell you that the man is eyeball-deep in whatever is going on.

Sullivan isn't too happy telling you that Winslow has Von Hess. The FBI is holding all the cards as far as the German is concerned. Sullivan feels that, at the very least, Von Hess is due to be deported.

You feel kind of nervous about mentioning the link between the Brotherhood of Thule and the Torso Killings, but you must. All your instincts and every clue you have turned up indicate that the two are part of a larger scheme. And, what if the Torso Killings are part of some sacrificial offering?

Despite Sullivan's misgivings, you make your case, tying the Brotherhood, the Torso Killings, the Nazis, and the Dahlia together. He gives you permission to exercise some latitude in the case and tells you to follow up your hunches with Merylo and Winslow to find more solid evidence.

NOTE

If you fail to tell Sullivan your thoughts about the Brotherhood of Thule and try to tie the case to the Torso Killings, he won't agree to let you talk to the police. Without his permission, Detective Merylo's Office won't appear on the World Map.

Sullivan also warns you that he wants things handled with more finesse than what was exhibited at the Raven Room, letting you know that he is fully aware of who got Von Hess caught with his hand in the cookie jar.

Chastised but excited, you decide to follow up with Merylo first. The tough cop will be more open with you than Winslow. The FBI is geared for grandstanding, not cooperative investigation.

TIP

Right-click on the mouse to bring up the supplemental list. Left-click on the World Map and then left-click on Detective Merylo's Office.

You're in luck because Merylo is working at his desk when you arrive. When you knock on the door, he looks up and tells you to come in. His voice sounds warmer now than before. There's even a smile on his face when you walk over to him.

Knowing that you stand a better chance of staying on his good side by

being up front with him, you ask to see the evidence on the Torso case.

He laughs at you good-naturedly, asking you why he should want to let another Fed into his case.

But you have a convincing argument, and Merylo's too sharp a cop to ignore the line of maybes you build up for him. In the end, he hands the file over. You examine it carefully, line by line.

NOTE

When handling the evidence file, you must go over it with care. There are 19 lines on the Evidence Tracking Log, and you need to look at each line.

Take special care with Line 1, the report on the first victim. When you click on it, be sure the cursor is placed along the right margin of the pages, so that you may look at all three pages. Angelo Santini's address is listed on the third page.

Once you have his address, left-click on it. If you fail to get the address, you can't go to the Santini home, an important place just a bit further in the game.

To check whether you have the address, exit from the Evidence Tracking Log and then bring up the World Map. If it does not appear there, get the case file again and look up Santini's address until the destination is available on the World Map.

The bloody newspapers pique your interest, don't they? But they're from different cities, and they have different dates. Yet, you can't help but feel there's something definite here—something that's right at your fingertips. That feeling grows even stronger when you see that the newspaper discovered under Louie's corpse has been impounded by the FBI.

TIP

Left-clicking on the first listed newspaper puts you into a conversation with Merylo. The big detective says that he feels certain that the Torso Killer has left clues behind deliberately to taunt police, but no one has discovered the pattern yet.

You briefly discuss the Santini murder with Merylo. The big detective points out that Santini and Louie the Fish were the only two victims identified. At first, given Santini's criminal history of street hustling and petty theft, his death was thought to be some act of revenge. When other Torso victims began to pile up, however, that idea was quickly discarded.

TIP

To discuss the Santini murder with Merylo, left-click once on the circled area of the third page of the victim report.

As you go down the evidence report list, the pictures of the crime sites catch your attention. Several bodies were found near sewer outlets. When you ask Merylo if any of the crime sites bear further investigation, he tells you about the canals along Kingsbury Run; a number of sewers connect to that area.

To prompt Merylo to talk about Kingsbury Run, simply left-click on Item 4.

As you go through the pictures, you discover that victim #'s 2, 4, 5, 6, and 7 were found around areas that could be accessed through the sewers along Kingsbury Run. This area bears further investigation, and after you speak with Merylo about it, you are able to go to Kingsbury Run.

You must, however, talk to Merylo about the area to have it placed on the World Map.

You also discuss the newspaper evidence that the FBI has impounded and the fact that the rest of Louie's body hasn't shown up—a standard practice of the Torso Killer.

Merylo is of the opinion that Winslow is sitting on the evidence to keep him from making the case. He is sure that there's a clue in it, but he has no idea what that clue may be.

To get Merylo to talk about the newspaper evidence, click on Line 19. Save before you do this in case you think that you may want to hear it again. Once Merylo speaks his mind, he doesn't repeat himself.

In this part of the game, you also find out that one of the puzzle solutions is located in the papers. Take a look at them again if you haven't already figured it out.

TIP

Numbers mean everything. A full explanation of the clue is given later in this chapter.

Handing the evidence file back to Merylo, you ask about Von Hess.

Merylo's grin lets you know that he's aware of your part in Von Hess's capture. He then hands you a folded invitation with a series of red, blue, and gold symbols on it. He says that the invitation fell from Von Hess's pocket when Winslow arrested him. He took it out of spite when Eliot Ness handed Von Hess over to Winslow.

The invitation intrigues you with all its strange symbols, but you don't know what to make of it yet. You pocket it and thank Merylo. You then ask about Von Hess's medallion, the one he had been showing you the night of the party.

Merylo says that, if Von Hess had the medallion at the party, the FBI probably has it in its custody, too.

Well, the big guy has been helpful, but you're pumping a dry well now (unless you can put some more pieces together). Winslow holds all the cards. It's time to see if you can get a hand yourself. Leg it on over to the FBI offices.

TIP
Right-click on the mouse to bring up the supplemental list. Left-click on the World Map and then left-click on the FBI Office.

Winslow and his secretary are acting cozy when you arrive. She grabs her notebook and leaves, and the FBI agent turns his attention to you as he sits back smugly behind his desk.

The first thing on your mind, of course, is what happened to Pensky.

The FBI agent immediately disavows any knowledge of Pensky's whereabouts, stating that, if anything has happened to Pensky, it must have been at his doctor's instruction.

Without proof, you hardly are in a position to shake his tree now. So, move to the next item on your agenda. Ask about Von Hess.

Winslow says that Von Hess is being questioned now. Von Hess insists that he had every right to be in that back room. He knows that he probably will be deported to Germany, but he still won't say what he was looking for in the back room.

Since you're discussing the subject of Von Hess, ask about the iron cross medallion.

Although he knows about the medallion, Winslow doesn't put much stock in it. Also, he is quick to point out that Von Hess is still a German citizen and that even the FBI isn't at liberty to pass around his personal possessions for you to inspect.

Growing more aggravated by his answers and his evasion, ask Winslow about the Torso case evidence that the FBI has impounded.

Winslow states that the Torso case is out of your jurisdiction. When you mention Louie the Fish, the FBI agent tells you that Louie worked in a lot of places with bad people and made a number of enemies. It's no surprise that the Torso Killer may have been one of those enemies.

The guy really gets under your skin, doesn't he? Sitting there at his big desk in his neat office, playing footsie with the secretary. So, ask him about the evidence that Merylo told you that the FBI impounded from the murder scene.

Winslow is defensive, saying the FBI is there to do a thorough job. He goes on to promise you that he will be the man to catch the Torso Killer. The only positive note in the conversation is that he says he will have his men return the evidence to Merylo—once they're finished with it.

Feel the need for some fresh air? Why don't you hit the bricks and get on over to Kingsbury Run.

TIP

Right-click on the mouse to bring up the supplemental list. Left-click on the World Map and then left-click on Kingsbury Run to go there.

Victims in Crime

Arriving at Kingsbury Run, you descend into the concrete run and follow it back to a locked iron gate that seals the sewer beyond, preventing entry. Even when you stand as close to the gate as you possibly can, you still can't see anything in the darkness, in the yawning maw of the sewer.

The lock on the gate looks rusty and cracked, but it holds up under your efforts to open it.

TIP

When the cursor lights up and shows you that the lock is interactive, you can left-click on it to get closer. A key is the logical choice to open it, but where will you find one?

Stumped and even more frustrated, you decide to take a look at Angelo Santini's home. The murders started with him. Thinking it over, you realize that maybe there's a reason he was the first victim. You already know why Louie the Fish was the last.

Crawl up from the sewer, and get over to the Santini House to see if there are any answers there—or only more questions!

TIP

Right-click on the mouse to bring up the supplemental list. Left-click on the World Map and then left-click on the Santini House to go there.

At the Santini home, Mrs. Santini leads you to her son's bedroom. She's obviously distraught, and having you in her home is unsettling to say the least.

You reassure her, telling her you'll be respectful. She stands there, waiting and watching. Knowing you won't be able to do your job well with her standing over your shoulder, you ask her about her son and if she knows of any motive a killer may have had for killing Angelo.

She insists that everyone loved Angelo and that a monster killed her son.

You agree with her (though you know Merylo's crime reports paint a different picture altogether).

TIP

To get Mrs. Santini to leave the room, left-click on her again.

More upset than ever, Mrs. Santini excuses herself, leaving the room in your hands.

Alone now, begin your search of Angelo's room. The desk holds a collection of books, papers, and baseball cards. Angelo apparently was a big Indians and Yankees fan.

The nightstand to the left of the bed holds a radio and a pack of cigarettes. When you open the drawer, you

find nothing helpful inside. A cheesecake picture is on the wall above the bookshelf. A game sits on top of the chest of drawers beside a baseball trophy and an alarm clock.

TIP

You can play the Peg Game, but it doesn't lead you to any clues. If you're stumped, though, it will give you something to do. The object is to get down to one peg.

Here's one solution.

Starting at the top of the triangle, number the holes 1–10. To take a peg out of the board, you must jump it with another peg, as you would in checkers. To get down to a single peg, follow the directions below.

Jump the peg from Hole #1 over the peg in Hole #3 to land in Hole #6. Remove the peg in Hole #3.

Jump the peg from Hole #4 over the peg in Hole #2 to land in Hole #1. Remove the peg in Hole #2.

Jump the peg from Hole #10 over the peg in Hole #6 to land in Hole #3. Remove the peg in Hole #6.

Jump the peg from Hole #8 over the peg in Hole #9 to land in Hole #10. Remove the peg in Hole #9.

Jump the peg from Hole #1 over the peg in Hole #3 to land in Hole #6. Remove the peg in Hole #3.

Jump the peg from Hole #10 over the peg in Hole #6 to land in Hole #3. Remove the peg in Hole #6.

Jump the peg from Hole #3 over the peg in Hole #5 to land in Hole #8. Remove the peg in Hole #5.

Jump the peg from Hole #7 over the peg in Hole #8 to land in Hole #9. Remove the peg in Hole #8.

That leaves you with one peg.

Okay, it looks as though Santini didn't have any secrets after all. Turn off the light and go make nice with the grieving mother.

Wait! What's that in the window to the right of the bed? It looks like something's up on the canvas screen. Cross the room and pull the window shade down.

TIP

Although you can get to the window while the light is on, gameplay prohibits you from pulling the shade down until the lights are off.

Left-click on the light switch to turn the light off and then cross over to the window. Left-click again on the window shade to draw it down. After you have pulled the shade down, the Santini Picture is added to your Inventory automatically.

Now here's an interesting wrinkle. This picture shows both Louie the Fish and Angelo Santini standing together, obviously sharing good times. They're both relaxed, kind of like old friends. With Santini's background, it's understandable that he crossed paths with Louie, but what brought them together?

But, more importantly, where would they go together to have this picture taken? Obviously, Santini must have thought a lot of it; otherwise, he would have gotten rid of it or never would have bothered to pose for the picture in the first place.

He also went to great lengths to hide it. So, was it a keepsake? Or, was it something dangerous?

Looking at the picture jars your memory. On the wall behind Angelo Santini and Louie the Fish is a tapestry you've seen before. It comes back to you in a rush—that tapestry was hanging on the wall in the Brotherhood of Thule's room in the Raven Room!

Now, here's a clue you were looking for! Get back to the Raven Room and see if you can find any more evidence linking Louie's and Angelo's murders to the Brotherhood of Thule and to the Torso Killer.

TIP

For a closer look at the photo, go to your Inventory and left-click on the Santini Picture. Note the tapestry in the background. When you return to the Raven Room, that's what you'll be looking for.

Now, right-click on the mouse to bring up the supplemental list again. If you're in the Inventory section, you must Exit first. Then left-click on the World Map and left-click on Raven Room to go there.

Von Hess's Special Invitation

No one's working at the Raven Room when you arrive. Using your lock pick set, you're inside the club in a matter of seconds.

Thinking that you may be able to enter the back room through the lazy Susan again, you make your way back to the wait station. Only when you get there, you discover the lazy Susan is locked up tight.

From your earlier trip inside the room, you know that this only leaves one way in—the door. Get back to the door.

Okay, the door is locked, and you don't have a key. Your lock picks don't work here either. Thinking back on it, Von Hess didn't use a key to get in. He pressed sections of the door.

Maybe there's some kind of secret combination on the door. Inspecting it, you notice that the door's geometrical shapes do indeed move when you press them. The problem is to come up with the right combination.

Remember what Merylo said about Von Hess becoming really concerned about losing the invitation? Maybe you should take a look at it.

Yeah, look at the fold lines across it. It looks as though it had been folded into some kind of shape—maybe a geometrical shape? Better start folding.

NOTE

Left-clicking on the geometrical shapes on the door moves them. You still need the right combination, however.

The secret to folding the invitation and getting the geometrical designs to appear is to fold the invitation so that all the gold shapes are on one side of the page. To do that, follow the drawings below.

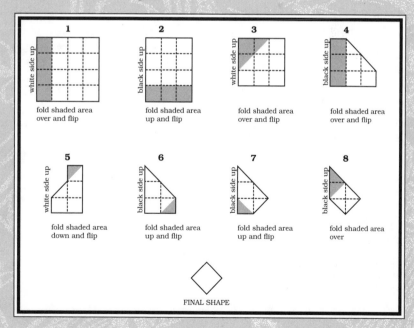

Solution:

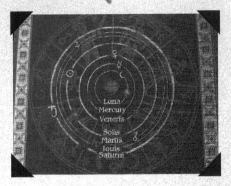

As soon as you trigger the right sequence of patterns, the door opens. Enter the darkened room beyond.

Once you're inside the room, turn to the right and look at the wall to find the tapestry that is behind Angelo Santini and Louie the Fish in the picture. As you study the tapestry, you notice that the planets resemble the spheres in your dream. They all have zodiac signs, too. A quick comparison against the list in your notes (from the book at Madame Cassandra's) shows you that the names and symbols do match.

The tapestry must be important to the Brotherhood of Thule and to the Torso Killer. There must be something in the design.

Got an idea now? The tapestry reflects a pattern, and Madame Cassandra told you that you need to know a pattern to get inside the Torso Killer's mindset. What if each of the Torso Killer's victims was, in fact, a sacrifice to one of the planets on the tapestry?

If you check back through the notes Helen gave you, you find that both pages refer to the seven messengers of the shepherds of stars. Together, they were supposed to seal heaven's sphere.

Given that there is a pattern to the killings, you know that you have to figure out what that pattern is. Go back to Merylo's office and reexamine the evidence. It's time to see if Winslow made good on his promise to return the things he took.

TIP

Right-click on the mouse to bring up the supplemental list. Left-click on the World Map and then left-click on Detective Merylo's Office.

Murder by the Numbers

Back in Merylo's office, ask if Winslow returned the evidence he appropriated.

Merylo says yes and then takes out the file for you again. He tells you that the newspaper has been returned.

Your gut instinct tells you that the victims were deliberately chosen and that the Torso Killer has left a clue behind. As you scan the bloody newspapers in succession, you notice that certain numbers were left uncovered. Was this deliberate?

Following the insight from the tapestry, jot down the uncovered numbers as they appear.

First newspaper—15

Second newspaper—65

Third newspaper—260

Fourth newspaper—175

Fifth newspaper—111

Sixth newspaper—369

Seventh newspaper—34

Eighth newspaper—4

Eight victims. Eight numbers. Eight planets. Eight spheres. That's too coincidental. And the numbers look familiar too, don't they? Sure they do. They're in your notebook. You copied them down from the astrology book at Madame Cassandra's. Match the numbers to the planets from your list.

Numbers	Planets
15	Saturn
65	Mars
260	Mercury
175	Venus
111	Sun
369	Moon
34	Jupiter
4	Earth

If you're right about this—and if Madame Cassandra were right about the pattern you needed to get through the spheres—there's only one place for you to go. You give the evidence file back to Merylo and then beat feet back to Madame Cassandra's house.

TIP

Right-click on the mouse to bring up the supplemental list. Left-click on the World Map and then left-click on Psychic Parlor.

The Iconic Stones

The maid lets you back in at Madame Cassandra's house and then leads you back to see her. Cassandra doesn't appear too surprised to see you. After sitting down, you ask her to put you into a trance again.

After a brief moment staring at the locket, you find yourself back in space looking at the spheres again. Matching the symbols carved on the planets with your notes, you jump through them, wondering where you'll end up if you're right.

Planet	Color
Saturn	black sphere (on the left)
Mars	red sphere (on the right)
Mercury	purple sphere (on the right)
Venus	green sphere (on the right)
Sun	gold sphere (on the right)
Moon	silver sphere (on the right)
Jupiter	blue sphere (on the left)
Earth	brown sphere (on the left)

As soon as you complete your passage through the silver sphere, a force grabs hold of you and drags you down into the silver sphere. Before you know it, you arrive at a strange clearing evidently on the silver planet's surface.

A fire burns ahead to the right be- side an ornate pool. You approach the pool cautiously, feeling very much out of place here.

At the pool's edge, glance down to see the pool ahead of you. Seated on their haunches and looking away from you, bizarre carved stone creatures

are, evidently, holding sentry duty around the pool.

Upon closer inspection, you no- tice the smooth rocks at the water's edge. Each of the seven rocks has a symbol on it. But why would they be so close to the pool?

The symbols on the rocks are a shamrock, a fish, hands, a locket, a glass, a knife, and glasses.

Since it was a locket that brought you here, examine the stone with the Locket painted on it. When you pick it up, though, it tugs at you with noticeable force to make you drop it into the pool. As you stare into the water, a vision comes over you. In the vision you see yourself sitting beside Cassandra in the Psychic Parlor.

Shaken, but definitely interested, you move down the line of stones. Your next vi- sion comes from the Hands stone. In it, you watch Angelo Santini walk into his bedroom, then hide an envelope in a space behind the baseboard next to his desk.

The Shamrock stone gives you a vision of Louie and Ernie playing cards.
The Fish stone gives you a vision of Louie going into his loft.
The Glass stone gives you a vision of a man getting a drink at McGinty's.
The Glasses stone gives you a vision of Mr. Pensky at his desk.

Only one more stone, the one with the knife, yields a vision. The vision you see this time involves the old man you know to be the Torso Killer. As you watch, the man walks to the sewer grate located at Kingsbury Run and enters. But he isn't alone. Two other men are with him. One of them you recognize immediately as Louie the Fish, very much alive. But the other man's identity remains hidden from you. This surprises you. You had assumed that the Torso Killer was working alone. Yet, with the Brotherhood of Thule involved, as you believe it to be, the old man wouldn't have to work alone, would he?

Okay, time to get away from all this mumbo jumbo and get back to serious detective work. These visions wouldn't stand up in a court of law even if you could get a judge and jury here to see them. In fact, they could even be figments of your own imagination—even though your gut tells you that they aren't. The only way you'll ever know is by taking a look at things yourself.

Wake up from your trance.

TIP

To get out of the trance at this point, back away from the Pool and then hit Esc. *This puts you back in the Psychic Parlor with Cassandra.*

Cassandra helps steady you as you come back to your senses. You're filled with excitement about your discovery. Tell her about the stones and the pool you saw in your vision.

She tells you that they were iconic stones. These stones allow you to see who you want to see in your visions. She also tells you that the stones are easy to create. All you need is a personal item of the person you want to see.

If that's true, though, how did you see yourself in the pool? Tell her that you saw yourself in the pool.

Cassandra tells you that your attacker must have one of your personal items, something you cared about very much.

You tell her about your St. Christopher's medal, which has been missing since the night Louie's head showed up in the box by special delivery.

Agreeing that the St. Christopher's medal would be something the killer could use, Cassandra also tells you that you can turn the tables on your attacker by finding something personal of his. Finding the right item won't be easy, though.

Thank her for her time—the game's afoot. It's time to follow up on the Santini and Kingsbury Run leads. Go to Santini's first to see if the hidden envelope is still in the boy's room.

TIP

Right-click on the mouse to pull up the supplemental list. Left-click on the World Map and then left-click on the Santini House.

Angelo Santini's Secrets
From the Casebook of COI Agent James R. Pearson

Mrs. Santini had no problem with me returning to search her son's room again. I have to admit, I don't know if I would have remained civilized enough to simply go away if she'd turned down my request. There were too many things I needed to know. I believed in the visions Cassandra had helped me see.

The woman seemed to be in better spirits as well. When we got to Angelo's room, she crossed herself, then turned to me and said, "When you're finished, you come into the kitchen. I make you a good meal."

"There's no need for that, ma'am," I told her. I felt like a heel standing there talking to her. I knew stuff about Angelo that would hurt her a lot if she found out. And if I needed to use that information to shut down the Torso Killer, I knew I was going to use it.

She waved away my answer. "Look at you. You're all skin and bones. You come in the kitchen before you go and you eat."

I looked at her, feeling like I was listening to my own mother all over again. There are some women that just make you feel like a little boy all over again. Mrs. Santini was one of them. I laughed at her insistence, but maybe it was at myself because I found that I couldn't do anything but accept the offer. "All right. A home-cooked meal does sound good right about now."

She smiled at me, a smile that would have normally made me feel like a good Joe. Only I knew what I was there for and she didn't.

After she left, I turned my attention to the baseboard beside the desk. I knelt down beside the desk and, with little difficulty, removed the baseboard. Then I peered inside.

TIP

When you were first in this room, gameplay would not let you access the baseboard. Now that you know the envelope is hidden behind the baseboard, you can get to it easily by left-clicking on the hiding place.

Left-click on the items inside to put them in your Inventory.

Evidently Angelo Santini was something of a pack rat. Inside the hiding place were cigarettes, a knife, firecrackers, and papers. And money, what looked like a lot of it. The papers immediately captured my interest.

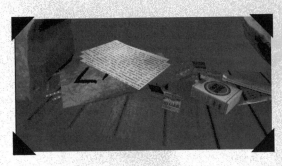

I took the papers out and flipped through them. A few of the papers looked like they'd been ripped from some kind of scholarly journal. There was also a note from Mr. Pensky and another paper that had more of the Norse runes written on it.

I copied the runes into my notebook, then took a look at Pensky's note.

Mr. Santini,

I am indeed interested in the items that you described to me at our last meeting. I have made arrangements to

supply you with payment in the amount that you
requested. Meet me on Thursday at the usual time and
place where the exchange can occur. I promise you that I
will not be late this time and that your security will
not be compromised.

W. Pensky

The note definitely made the connection between Mr. Pensky and
Angelo, tying in the Brotherhood of Thule and the Torso Killer as well. I
had no idea what Mr. Pensky had bought from Angelo Santini. Maybe it was
the bag of runes I'd found hidden in the office. But it was obvious from
the stack of money that Angelo had been paid well.

I also had an idea where Angelo had gotten the items he'd sold to Mr.
Pensky. Louie the fish already had a history of double-crossing the people
he worked for. Either Louie or Angelo had found out about Mr. Pensky's
interest in the case, then swiped things from the Raven Room to sell to
Mr. Pensky.

I had a gut feeling that Louie helped Angelo, or set the boy up.
Angelo had been killed on the night of August 17 or early morning on
August 18. Maybe even as far back as August 15. Louie hadn't been killed
until November 23. It was possible that Louie had ratted the kid out to
save his own miserable hide and had escaped detection by the Brotherhood
of Thule until I leaned on him and made him talk to me.

No wonder Louie had said they'd kill him if he talked. He'd already
had first-hand experience that they would.

I knew then, even if I'd been doubting it before, that a lot of Louie's
death was my responsibility. Maybe it should have made me feel kind of
lousy, but it didn't. Louie had put his head on the chopping block a long
time before I'd met him. And he'd probably given up Santini to buy himself
some more time.

I glanced through the journal papers and found them to be just that.

interesting variation on the "Paganism Resurgent" theme
that was prevalent at the height of the Middle Ages is

the legend of the "Trinity Knights." These warriors were
an actual set of the Teutonic order that played a small,
if not bloody, role in the ongoing saga of the Baltic
Crusades. Accused of paganistic ties in 1234, their
faction was disbanded and its members excommunicated by
a surprisingly vehement Pope Gregory IX.

Pope Gregory was a name I remembered from the notes Helen had
given me. He was also the guy listed in the book on family crests who'd
thrown out the members of the Brotherhood of Thule.

There are few scholars who devote much energy to the
study of the obscure, semiautonomous groups of the
Teutonic Knights, which evolved in isolated castles on
the Prussian frontier. Among these scholars, there is
considerable debate as to whether the Pope's actions
against the Trinity Knights were motivated by legitimate
evidence or a cynical grab for wealth, much like the
destruction of the Knights Templars in 1314.

Though facts of this case are well documented elsewhere
(see the elder Strauss's "Holy War by the Baltic Sea"),
I have discovered a little known legend about events
that occurred after the order had been disbanded that
may be of interest. According to one Ogland of Karpina,
a fourteenth-century Dominican Monk known more for his
bawdy tales than his prowess in historiography, the
exiled military leaders of the Trinity sect did not go
quietly into obscurity after their excommunication. He
contends that they made their way in secret to the then
Franciscan monastery at Alberg, which had been their
chief source of financial support during their
campaigns.

That passage reminded me of the map Dr. Strauss had on the wall above the stained glass window I had reassembled at the museum. And I was certain the "elder Strauss" mentioned in this document was Helen's father.

The monk tells us that, beneath the seemingly Christian surface of this institution, there existed a still functioning pagan shrine dedicated to the Germanic god Wodan or Odin. It was here that these unholy knights went to conduct a sacred blood ritual for the purpose of granting supreme Aesirian powers to the Master of the Order (a direct descendent of the notorious Landulph of Capua, no less).

According to Ogland, the ceremony that they gathered to pursue had originally been recorded in an ancient runic text called "the Thule prophecy." Independent inquiries into the validity of this document indicate that it does indeed exist. It is an odd mix of pagan and early Christian sophistic folklore which originated among the rebellious proclamations of East Frisian tribal leaders who, in 800 A.D. and under the influence of their Viking cousins to the north, conspired to throw off the Holy Roman yoke and return to the free and easy lifestyle of their pagan ancestors. The rebellion was of course crushed by Charlemagne who subsequently ordered the codification of Germanic tribal law in order to protect such disgruntled citizens from future predation by unscrupulous church officials. (See Treitschkes, Cologne Lectures, Circa 1891.)

Ogland tells us that the text of the original prophecy ritual was actually intended to awaken Odin and his court of Norse gods from slumber in the mythical land of Thule. From there they would return to Midgard (Earth) to rule in the place of Christ and his saints. This ceremony was then later perverted by the hero Eodulph (banished by Charlemagne as a result of the Frisian uprising) in his quest for supreme power. According to

this saga, this errant thane had discovered a way to
transpose most of the Awakening Ritual and then twist
parts of it to his own ends in order to kill Odin and
assume his power. Be that as it may, a certain Estefan
of Tauren, the Arch Abbot of the Arlberg monastery,
objected to these proceedings (as one might expect of a
church official in his position). Where the tale becomes
truly interesting is in Ogland's contention that the
Arch Abbot actually protested on the grounds that the
Order's true purpose was to carry on the work for which
its members had already been excommunicated, i.e., bring
about the Gray God's (Odin's) return and not his
destruction.

From here the story begins to grow even more fanciful
and fascinating. It seems that the warriors of the Order
were in no mood for compromise at this point. Having
lost all their Baltic holdings by Papal Bull, they
claimed to have been abandoned (as did Eodulph,
incidentally) by their god and declared it high time
that they took over for him. The Arch Abbot, seeing that
he was outnumbered by the returning knights, contrived
to thwart their efforts through trickery. It turns out
Brother Estefan, more than your average mild-mannered
monk, was actually a pagan high priest in friar's
clothing. His own mystical powers must have been
considerable, for he used them to instigate a scheme to
protect his deity and administer divine justice to those
who intended to betray it.

There were three ritual items central to either of the
ceremonies. These objects, which are supposed to be the
basis for the Order and the source of its name, are the
"Skull of Landulph," a holy grail known as the "Cup of
the World Tree," and a large piece of black amber called
Thalia's Prison (later referred to as "The Black
Dahlia").

That revelation sent my mind spinning. The Black Dahlia was a chunk of black amber, and the rune tiles I'd been assembling were starting to take on a definite shape. I didn't think the runes were the Black Dahlia because they weren't one piece and, according to this, the Dahlia was one piece. But I knew then that I was holding onto an important piece of the puzzle I sought to unravel.

The clever Estefan took this last item from its rune inscribed case and replaced it with a piece of coal that had been intricately carved and mystically camouflaged.

So the tiles I now held were indeed the case that had once housed the Dahlia! But where was the Dahlia now?

The introduction of this new item into the proceedings would prove to be cataclysmic for Estefan as well as the Trinity Knights.

Now the purpose of the Dahlia in the divinity ritual was to act as a medium that would convey the soul of the performer into its "new vessel," which was the living body of the last of nine human sacrifices. (The details in which the sacrifices were to be consigned to astrological guardians and then ritualistically butchered make for fascinating, if not grizzly, investigation. Again Treitschkes's lectures are the most coherent source for such inquiries.) Before the performer could culminate the proceedings, however, he must first take his own life, which the grand master dutifully did. It just so happened that our Abbot, Estefan, whose disloyalty was suspected by the knights, had been selected to be the ninth sacrifice and, thus, the recipient of the aspirant's soul. As a necromancer, old Estefan knew well that the fruits of his deception

would cause quite a severe supernatural reaction, but it
seems even he had underestimated the metaphysical
prowess of the Order Master. According to the legend,
when the Master's soul went forth from his dying body,
it became trapped within the empty Dahlia casing, just
as Estefan had hoped. In desperation, the warrior
realized that Estefan had duped him, and he reacted
violently. Using all his supernatural might, the Master
lashed out at his tormentor and drew forth Abbot
Estefan's own essence for one last bout of mystic combat
within the Dahlia's empty shell.

The spiritual duel that followed was so violent that the
vessel was shattered by its impact. In the end, the
descendent of Landulph was destroyed in the cataclysm,
and his soul sent off to eternal torment; but the crafty
Estefan was, at the last instant, able to install his
spirit into the shards of the fractured case. The legend
goes on to speculate that, when the shards are
reassembled and returned to Estefan's tomb, this action
will free him to meet his eternal rest.

The thought that I might be carrying around the spirit of a monk
trapped in those runed tiles was unsettling to say the least. I just couldn't
believe it.

Yet, until a few days ago, I wouldn't have believed in the visions I'd
had. Nor would I have believed the things I'd seen while in a trance under
Madame Cassandra's care.

Thinking about the lives the Torso Killer had claimed so far grounded me,
though. It didn't matter if I believed or not. That insane butcher did. And to
catch him, I'd have to know as much about what he believed in as he did.

As with all good fairy tales, the kind and handsome
prince (this time in the form of the Emperor Frederick
II) makes his appearance in the nick of time and

slaughters the evil Trinity Knights while they stand
dumbfounded by their botched ritual. The heathen shrine
was razed, and the closet pagans among the monastery
brethren were rooted out and packed off to the
Inquisition. Much to Ogland's dismay, however, the Arch
Abbot Estefan emerged a hero in this story. His pagan
ties were hushed up, and claims were made that, in the
end, he had received the enlightenment of Christ, which
gave him the power to overcome his infidel opponent. At
any rate, Estefan was actually credited with denying the
heinous Odin heathen ritual. His battered body was
buried, in state, on the site of the Old Aesirian altar
in the crypt of the monastery chapel, where it remains
to this day.

The monastery complex itself lived on for centuries and
still stood, though now abandoned (since the Great War),
when I last visited the area in 1933. My inquiries with
the local villagers indicate that the place still
carries the stigma of rumored pagan sympathies and folk
tales about secret passages filled with heathen ghosts
and treasures. Having seen the site of Estefan's
sarcophagus with my own eyes, I can corroborate that
there is in fact a distinctly exotic and unchristian
feel to the place. Indeed, there is a basin in the
surface of the stone coffin where a pagan sacrificial
offering may have once been placed. Beneath this is a
Latin inscription that translates as follows:

Within the heathen letters hid

The secrets to their god's destruction

Upon lamb's blood he has fed

To make a mocking resurrection

Obviously someone in our mediaeval past has taken the Legend of the Trinity Knights more seriously than modern scholars.

Recent reports from within the Nazi Reich indicate that some of the monastery buildings are in the process of being refurbished as a monument to "Aryan Culture" as are many locations that played an important role in the rather bloody legacy of the Teutonic Crusades. If this is true (which I suspect is indeed the case as I myself have received communications from the Reich Ministry of Culture inquiring about the possible purchase of certain items from my own collection), then students of the Baltic Crusades will be well advised to visit it for themselves. If for no other reason, it will at least provide them with a more whimsical sojourn into one of the many obscure legends that, over the centuries, have attached themselves to the Christianization of Western Europe.

In this same vein of study, there is also an interesting folk story that I discovered in Southern Bohemia. It relates to the saga of a group of "child knights" credited with a significant role in the death of Ughetiai, the leader of the invading Mongol hordes in 1241. It would

The pages ended there, but the questions that entered my mind went on and on. Staggered by what I had learned, what I now guessed, and the little voice in the back of my head that insisted it might all be true, I shoved the papers into my jacket pocket.

Then I reached for that pile of money. I raised my voice. "Mrs. Santini. Mrs. Santini."

She came at once, drying her hands on her apron. "What is it?"

I presented her with the money. "I'm sorry to have disturbed this room, but I found something." I indicated the baseboard hiding place. "I know this can't compensate for your loss, ma'am...but I know that Angelo would have wanted you to have this."

Tears filled her eyes as she took the money and hugged me. "Bless you, Mr. Pearson. You are a good boy."

And somehow, her words warmed me up in spite of the chill that had filled me after reading those pages. I took her up on her offer of a meal, trying not to show how anxious I was to get out of there.

When I got the opportunity to go without offending her, I left. My destination was clear-cut in my mind. I didn't know what I'd find at the sewer grate in Kingsbury Run, but now that I'd seen it in that vision, I wanted to take another look at it.

TIP   *Right-click on the mouse to bring up the supplemental list. Left-click on the World Map and then left-click on Kingsbury Run.*

NOTE   *Change to Disk #5.*

Only Flesh and Blood

The moon beams down in a big way when you get back to the sewer. Your mind is so overwhelmed with what you've learned that it takes you a minute to realize that someone is moving toward the locked grate.

You peer through the darkness and recognize the old man from your visions. You shout out at him, startling him as he opens the grate.

He turns, holding onto his hand painfully. You can see the blood streaking his palm. Then he turns and dashes into the sewer, leaving the grate open behind him.

Draw your gun and follow him. You're not afraid, are you? The guy's only flesh and blood, right?

But it's still pretty nerve-wracking stepping into the darkness.

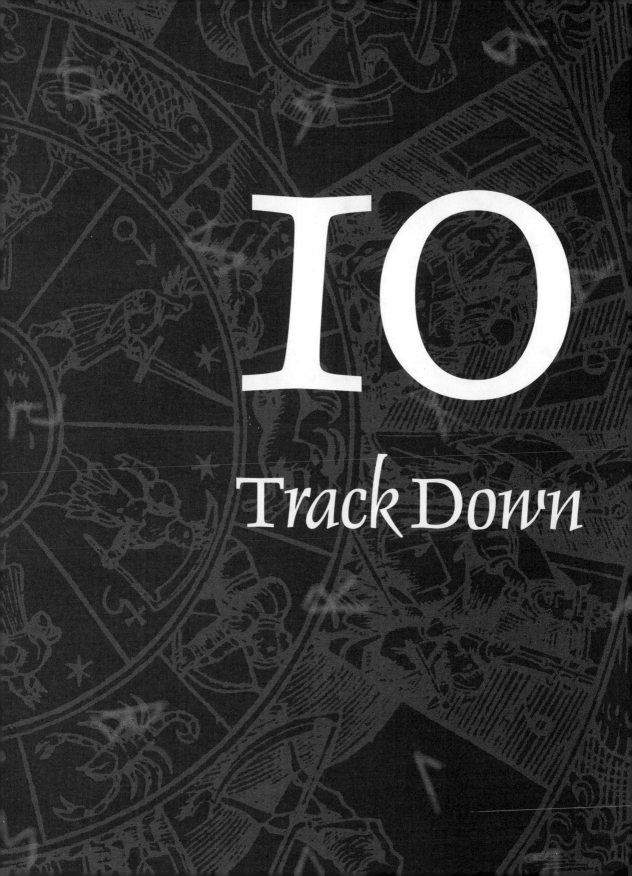

10

Track Down

Sewer'd He Go?

The sewer stretches in front of you; murky water runs through it. You listen, but you can't hear any footsteps ahead of you. Still, there's no ready way out. Keep going forward.

TIP

To get through the tunnels in this section, refer to the map entitled CLEVELAND SEWERS in this chapter. All the twists and turns may confuse you, so pay attention to the number of left-clicks you make and to your direction.

Also, there's no need to follow all the various routes unless you simply want to do so. Once you have found the Valve Room, you automatically end up there every time you return to Kingsbury Run.

After many twists and turns down the long, dank tunnels, you end up in a room with a number of pressure release valve wheels on the wall.

TIP

In the Valve Room—if you follow the map—it will appear that you have arrived at yet another dead-end. If you turn immediately to your right, however, you will see the adjustment valves. Approach them by left-clicking on them. You will find the bloody handprint that allows you to work with the valves.

Look at the wall to the right of the valves. The bloody handprint is a dead giveaway that the Torso Killer was here.

A quick observational check also lets you know that there are five valve gauges, but only four adjustment wheels. It doesn't take a rocket scientist to figure out that there's a hidden door somewhere around here. The Torso Killer didn't just disappear into thin air. Despite all the stories

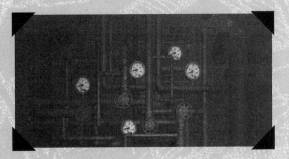

Cleveland Sewers

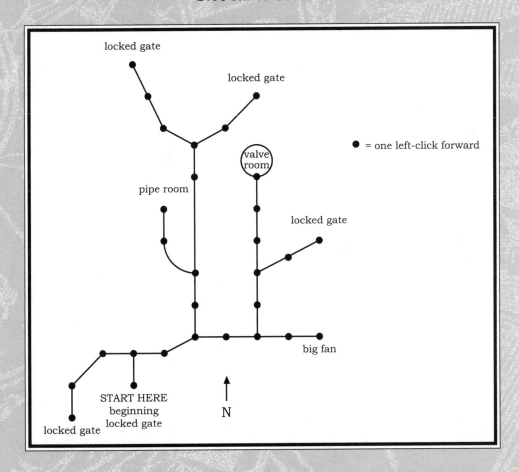

and legends you have heard, you still believe that the old man is as human as you.

To find the door, you must figure out the secret to the pressure release valves.

NOTE

Resist the temptation to start twisting the valve wheels for the moment. Save the game here. Below is a key to opening the hidden door. If you accidentally twist a wheel too far or get lost in the directions below, simply Restore to start over.

Number the gauges 1–5 from left to right. Number the wheels 1–4 from left to right.

You will find from experimentation—if you choose to move on without this guide for the moment—that you can affect the reading on every gauge except Gauge #2. To change the reading on the gauges, left-click on the wheels and drag the cursor clockwise or counterclockwise. The rest of the gauges and the wheels go together as follows:

Wheel #1 operates Gauge #4.

Wheel #2 operates Gauge #1 and Gauge #5, although it sends them in different directions.

Wheel #3 operates Gauge #1 and Gauge #3, although it sends them in different directions.

Wheel #4 operates Gauges #1, #4, and #5, although it sends them in different directions.

It gets complicated really fast. To solve the puzzle, your objective is to get all the gauges to have the same reading. Since you cannot move Gauge #2, you must line up the other gauges, so that they have the same position as the needle on Gauge #2.

1. *Rotate Wheel #3 clockwise until Gauge #3 reads 30.*

2. *Rotate Wheel #2 clockwise until Gauge #1 reads 40.*

3. *Rotate Wheel #2 counterclockwise until Gauge #1 reads 25.*

4. *Rotate Wheel #2 clockwise until Gauges #1 and #5 read 30.*

5. *Rotate Wheel #1 clockwise until Gauge #4 reads 30.*

Once you have all the gauges properly set, the hidden door slides open.

When you get the pressure gauges set correctly, a door in the wall to your left opens. On the other side of the door is another door. Upon closer inspection, you see a strange-looking keyhole.

TIP

Be sure to left-click on the door to get a close look at it. This also lets you copy the runes from the door into your notebook. You need all the runes to solve the case.

Be sure you click on the keyhole itself; otherwise, you won't have anything to discuss with Winslow when you return to see him.

The keyhole looks exactly like the shape of the iron cross medallion Von Hess showed you last night in the Raven Room, doesn't it? And guess who has the medallion?

No matter how hard you push, the door won't budge. Leg it back to the FBI Office. You have no choice but to try to cut a deal with Winslow. If he won't give you the medallion, maybe he'll at least let you borrow it.

TIP

Right-click on the mouse to bring up the supplemental list. Left-click on the World Map and then left-click on the FBI Office.

Don't worry about having to find your way through the tunnels again. Once you have found the pressure gauges, you're allowed to return to them.

Viking Blood

Winslow must have one of the most devoted secretaries you have ever seen. It's hard to figure out how she gets any work done at all, perching on Winslow's desk like that all day.

Seeing you, Winslow sends her packing and then asks you what you want. Ask him for Von Hess's medallion.

The FBI agent waffles at first, not wanting to help you out. Having no other choice, you open up to him. You tell him how you followed the man whom you believe to be the Torso Killer into the sewers. You also tell him about the door with the strange-shaped lock.

Winslow wants to know the door's location, but you play your cards hard and close to your vest. Having no other choice of his own, Winslow makes a deal with you. He gets the credit for catching the Torso Killer, while you receive the credit for breaking up the Brotherhood of Thule.

Back at the sewers, Winslow does nothing but whine that he's too good for the sewers, apparently.

TIP

Once you get back to the locked door with Winslow, all you have to do is left-click on the keyhole to open the door.

When Winslow gives you the iron cross medallion, first draw your pistol. Then insert the iron cross into the keyhole. Lead the way with Winslow following along at a distance.

Inside the next room, Winslow decides to hang back. A pool of water to your right has carved stone faces that resemble Vikings. There are three other

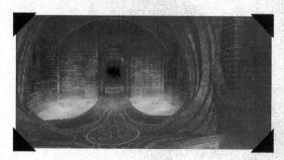

pools in the room, too. A large rune is painted across the floor, leaving you no other option but to step on it as you cross.

Without warning, the water starts glowing red. In heartbeats, it takes on the appearance of blood spilling from the mouths of the carved stone faces. Winslow's nerve snaps, and he tells you that he's going to let you have this one all on your own. He turns and leaves you there.

Almost as soon as his footsteps fade into the darkness, the water resembles water again, not blood. You call after Winslow, but he's long gone.

With the gun still tight in your fist,

you cross the narrow walk between the four pools. Your way is blocked by another door.

Instead of a key, this door has a locking mechanism that consists of levers and bars, which undoubtedly make up the combination.

NOTE

As you study the locking mechanism, you notice that there are six bars and eight moveable toggles. Number the bars from the top 1–6, and number the toggles from the top 1–8.

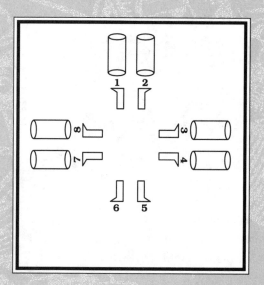

Experimentation shows you the following:

Moving Toggle #1 up pulls Bar #2 down.

Moving Toggle #2 up pulls bars #4, #5, and #6down.

Moving Toggle #3 over pushes Bar #5 back into a locked position.

Moving Toggle #4 over pushes Bar #2 back into a locked position and pulls Bars #3 and #5 down.

Moving Toggle #5 down pulls Bar #1 down and pushes Bar #6 back into a locked position.

Moving Toggle #6 down pulls Bar #5 down and pushes Bar #6 back into a locked position.

Moving Toggle #7 over does nothing.

Moving Toggle #8 over pushes Bar #1 back into a locked position.

You need to get all of the Bars down at one time to open this door. Move the Toggles in the following order: #5, #4, #2, #3, #7, #5, and #2. The door opens automatically.

On the other side of the door, you follow the stairs down to another door covered with glyphs, runes, and carvings.

This door has no obvious lock or locking mechanism, though. Turn to

your left and look up. High above is a ledge with iron bars.

That's within jumping range. At least you can take a peek through the iron bars.

TIP *Locating the ledge can be difficult if you're in a hurry. Turn 90 degrees (about halfway around) to the left and look up at the top of the screen. The ledge is there. Touch it with the cursor, and you will find that it's interactive. Simply left-click on the ledge to climb up.*

Peering through the bars, you discover that you are looking into the back room of the Raven Room. Several men are inside the room, but you're positioned in such a way that you cannot see who they are. Finally, one of them steps over to a wardrobe against the wall.

You recognize the old man with the cane at once. Quietly, you hang onto the bars and watch as he picks up a candleholder, puts a robe in the wardrobe, and leaves. Your attention is grabbed by the pendant on the necklace with the robe. It kind of reminds you of the icons you saw in the Dream Pool.

When he's gone, lower yourself to the ground again. Now here's your chance. With everyone out of the room, you can sneak into it and try to grab the pendant. Madame Cassandra told you that, if you had an item of some personal nature or value, you would be able to spy on the Torso Killer. Time to find out if it's true.

TIP *Right-click on the mouse to bring up the supplemental list. Left-click on the World Map and then left-click on the Raven Room.*

Dreaming of Death

Getting into the Raven Room is easy. (In fact, they should give you your own key. Of course, considering the invitation you have from Von Hess, perhaps it's as good as done.) When you're in the back room, go over to the wardrobe.

The door is locked, preventing you from simply reaching in and taking the pendant. It hangs there against the robe on the other side of the glass.

Breaking the glass *would* be an easy solution, but it also may alert the Torso Killer that you were onto him. If he knows the pendant is missing, he may have a way of blocking you from spying on him at the Dream Pool. Stealth is the way to go.

Picking the lock would be a good start, but this one is like nothing you've ever seen before. Then you remember the Torso Killer picked up a candleholder before he opened the wardrobe.

On the table to the right of the wardrobe are two candleholders.

After inspecting the candleholder on the right, you notice that the bottom

of the left one has been sectioned off in shapes that resemble the wardrobe's keyhole. The candleholder has five sections that turn, too. When you twist them, the shapes on the bottom begin to protrude. It's obvious that you must twist the candleholder in the right manner to make it fit the wardrobe's keyhole.

NOTE

The solution to the candleholder puzzle is a little tricky. The five sections twist to the right and to the left. Number them from 1 to 5, starting at the top of the candleholder and working your way to its base.

In order to make the key, you must make the following twists:

Twist Section #4 to the right twice.

Twist Section #5 to the left twice.

Twist Section #3 to the right twice.

Once you have the candleholder in the right shape, you automatically open the wardrobe door.

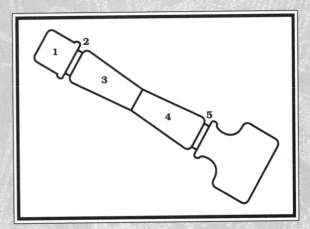

Pretty good. Now put the candleholder back on the table and swipe that pendant from the robe.

TIP *Left-click on the pendant to take it. The pendant is added to your Inventory as Talisman.*

Feeling pretty good about yourself now, aren't you? Well, you haven't caught the Torso Killer yet. Hit the bricks and head back to Madame Cassandra's to see if she can work that voodoo that she does so well to help you crack this case.

TIP *Right-click on the mouse to bring up the supplemental list. Left-click on the World Map and then left-click on Psychic Parlor.*

Back at the Psychic Parlor, ask Cassandra to put you in a trance again. Once she does, walk over to the Dream Pool and locate the icon stone that has the Talisman's shape on it. Pick it up and toss it into the pool.

The vision pulls you into it at once. You can immediately tell that you're back in the Raven Room. The Torso Killer sits at the table and reads a book. As you watch, he crosses the room to a set of bookshelves and pulls one of the books out, releasing a hidden door somewhere in the room behind him.

He crosses the room and walks down the stairs into a room that looks like some kind of dark, unholy chapel. The bloodstained altar only sets the tone for the demonic shapes around it.

As the vision fades, you realize that you may have the key you need to trap the Torso Killer. But what else has happened? Force yourself out of the trance.

TIP *To get out of the trance, back away from the Dream Pool and hit* Esc.

Cassandra sits beside you when you return to your senses. She steadies you, but you push yourself to your feet and rush off. If you're going to catch the Torso Killer, you get the feeling that you're going to have to hurry.

TIP   *At this point, gameplay automatically runs as you get Merylo and head for the Raven Room.*

Scene of the Crime
From the Casebook of COI Agent James R. Pearson

When I reached Merylo's office, I was excited, ranting almost. I also wasn't going to take no for an answer. I leaned over his desk, trying not to shout. It wasn't working. "I'm telling you I saw his secret lab. I saw the way in!"

"Are you crazy? I can't get a warrant out of your trip to a crystal gazer!" Merylo was almost apoplectic.

But I knew I had him. I could see it in the fire in his eyes. He'd hunted this man far longer than I had, and he was buying into my story no matter how crazy it sounded. I pushed him, getting louder. "There's no time for a warrant. I thought you'd want to know if I came across the killer. I guess I was wrong. But something weird happened down there, and I'm going to find out what it was. With or without you!"

"Wait!" Merylo exploded, pushing himself up from his desk. "Kid, I want in on this cockamamie scheme of yours!" He grabbed his coat and followed me out the door, both of us running now.

At the Raven Room, everything was quiet. Like a dead man's tomb. I kept remembering that terrible scream I'd heard at the end of the vision. I guess it rattled my nerves some. I turned to Merylo, who wasn't looking exactly brick solid himself. "Got a smoke?" I asked.

The big detective looked up at me in surprise. "I didn't know you smoked, kid."

"I do now." I needed something to calm my nerves, something to do with my hands. I didn't know what we were going to find in that room. I lit the cigarette he gave me with his lighter.

Inside the room, I turned to the right and crossed over to the book shelves. Then I pulled out the book I'd seen the Torso Killer move.

TIP

To move the book, left-click on it. The door opens automatically.

The sound of rolling casters echoed across the floor as the wardrobe behind us opened. I glanced at the open throat of the secret passageway, then at Merylo. He grinned.

I took the lead. "Are you ready, detective? His hideout's right down those steps." We both drew our weapons.

"I called some of my men," he said. "They should be here soon to back us up."

I knew we weren't going to wait. We couldn't. I took the lead down the stairs.

I didn't know what to expect as I went down them into that strange room, but finding the Torso Killer butchered and laying across his own altar was definitely the last thing.

"What the hell?" Merylo asked from beside me. "Looks like we're a little late to help victim number nine."

It took me a minute to understand what he just said. Then I tried to correct him, to let him know THIS is the Torso Killer. "But...but that can't be. It's him!"

"You know the stiff?"

"This is the killer!" I told him. "I'm sure of it."

He looked at me and shook his head. "You were wrong, Jim. That poor sap couldn't be the killer. But at least we've found his hideout, even if he isn't in it. You did good work. We'll get clues we can use out of this."

"And they'll all point to that man on the altar there, detective," I assured him. "He's the killer. I'm sure of it. There's his cane." I knelt down to get a better look at it, searching for the black stone I knew to be set in the top of it. "Someone took it."

"Took what, kid?"

I didn't even realize I'd spoken out loud. "The Dahlia. It's missing."

"Nobody had better have taken anything," a cold, steely voice announced behind us.

Merylo and I both turned around and looked up the stairs. Eliot Ness and Dick Winslow stood there at the head of a pack of uniformed policemen. Neither of the FBI agents looked happy to see us.

"Eliot," Winslow said, "I want these amateurs removed immediately. They've botched everything. Why, if we hadn't been tipped off that they were down here...."

I cut him off, my anger getting the best of me then. I'd always been a man of convictions, and they never ran any higher than at that time. "Amateurs? We just busted this case wide open. We weren't too chicken to...."

"I had enough sense to get a search warrant," Winslow replied suavely. "Now we won't be able to use one shred of evidence from here."

Merylo lit into him, sounding good and mad himself. "You're just sore 'cause we found the killer's hideout first. You're afraid our mugs'll get in the papers insteada yours."

"There'll be no contact with the press about this," Ness stated.

"Mr. Ness?" Merylo looked like he couldn't believe it.

Ness went on in a flat voice. "You busted illegally into a club owned by some very important people. People with connections to Washington—all the way to the top. They're not going to like what we found here."

"You can't just cover this up," I argued.

"Mr. Pearson," Ness said, fixing me with that hard gaze, "you are way out of your jurisdiction here. You're in no position to be arguing with anyone."

"But how can you just...."

Ness interrupted me in a harsh tone. "We're going to do what's in the best interests of this country."

Before I could say anything else, one of the uniformed men spoke briefly to Ness.

When the FBI man turned around to face us, his eyes held a gray winter chill. "President Roosevelt was just on the radio. The Japs bombed Pearl Harbor."

I felt overwhelmed at that moment. I'd been chasing after a sick, sadistic killer—now the whole world was at war.

II

Recovery of the Black Dahlia

1945

From the Journal of Captain James R. Pearson, Office of Strategic Services

I've served my country well over these past four years. In 1941, after Pearl Harbor, the COI got a makeover into the OSS. I fought with them across Europe, making my present rank of captain. I saw a lot of things a man shouldn't have had to see—things I knew I couldn't forget if I lived a hundred lifetimes.

Yet, with all that pain and agony I was witness to, I've never been able to forget those killings in Cleveland. All that business seemed only half-finished. The truth was there somewhere. I stayed in touch with Merylo over the years, but he never got any closer to the answers we were looking for either.

Imagine my surprise when this current assignment brought me full circle back to the mystery that had so haunted me. I had recently arrived in Nuremberg to help log and identify art treasures the Nazis gathered during the war. My special interest in SS occult artifacts has become legendary, much to my chagrin. But I am in the military, and I go where I am sent.

At the vault site, I was met by a wiry private with the habit of talking incessantly. He led me down into the vault and to the scene where I was to take up arms against the legacy of the Brotherhood of Thule once more.

Lines of electric lights ran down the lengths of the tunnels. Still, the shadows continued to gather in every irregular surface.

"We've been pulling junk out of that joint for hours now," the private who escorted me said. "I swear those Krauts hoisted everything but the kitchen sink. I think they even got one of my paintings in there. And I ain't painted nothing since Mrs. Kaufman's art class in the fifth grade. Say, that reminds me...."

"You ever come up for air, kid?" I asked.

"What's that, sir? Oh, yeah. The mouth." He nodded, letting me know there were no hard feelings. "Yeah, the boys all say I put the patter in Patterson. Patterson, New Jersey, that is. That's where I'm from."

We walked past another enlisted man coming out of the tunnel leading to the vault.

"What's your name, private?" I asked as two men carrying a crate navigated down another of the tunnels.

"Private Benjamin J. Schwartz, sir. Most folks just call me Benny."

"You're okay, Benny. How about filling me in on this room you found?" I followed the private into another tunnel, already starting to feel lost.

"Oh, yes sir. It's a real creep show back in there. Make Boris Karloff crap in his drawers. You know what I mean? Yeah, some of the boys tried to go back there, but they got that place all rigged up. Petey was nearly crushed to death when that big door shut on him. Whatever it is they got hidden back there, they sure didn't want just anyone waltzing in and hauling it off."

I felt the weight of the rock above us start to settle in. You get this deep in, with remnants of the war all around you, you can't help thinking about graves. It wasn't a good thought.

"This is it, Captain," the private said as we turned a final corner. He patted me on the shoulder. "Good luck."

"Thanks, Benny." Then I turned my attention to the huge door in front of me.

Take a good look at the door in front of you. It's easy to figure out that this is a representation of the solar system, but when you touch one of the planets, you find that the representation is mobile.

NOTE

Left-click on the door to get close to it. To move the planets, left-click and hold down; then drag the planet in whichever direction you choose.

Instead of calling each planet by its name—if you're curious, you can match the symbols on the circles with the information in your notebook. Starting with the planet closest to the sun and counting back to the outer orbits, number them 1–7.

At this point, you may think you have to move the planets, so that they all face the sun. That would be wrong. The objective here is to line all seven planets up facing the mural of Odin above. Once you have them lined up, left-click on the sun to go through the door. When you finish, the planets should be lined up as follows:

To do this, make the following moves:

Move Planet #7 three complete revolutions clockwise, slowing down and stopping as Planet #5 locks into position.

Move Planet #1 counterclockwise slowly to put Planet #6 in place. **Important:** Keep Planet #6 moving until it almost turns out of position. If it does, simply use Planet #1 to drag it back into place.

Move Planet #3 counterclockwise until it just goes into place. Try not to go much further.

Move Planet #6 counterclockwise to put Planet #2 into place.

Move Planet #4 clockwise to put Planet #1 in place.

Left-click on the sun to open the vault.

Above the door is a mural. Going back over all the history and mythology you have learned these past few years, it's easy for you to recognize the central figure in the painting as Odin, ruler of the Norse Gods. He was also the one mentioned in the papers Helen helped you decipher four years ago.

Once you have lined the planets up so that they face the mural of Odin, press the sun in the center. The sound of gears engaging behind the door echoes through the dimly lit cavern.

Benny shows up again; he's really excited for you. Then he goes off to file a report.

Walking into the room behind the door, you discover three vaults lining the walls. All of them are locked. Start with the vault on the left. The locking mechanism on this vault looks something like a manual transmission gearshift.

TIP

The three vaults in this room can be opened in any order. They are in a certain order in this guide for convenience.

The first two vaults you open—it doesn't matter which one it is—contain only empty holders for the Skull and the Cup. The third, however, will have the Black Dahlia. In order to get the Dahlia, you must be able to get through all three puzzle locks. No one ever said that it was going to be easy.

NOTE

In the puzzle on Vault #1 (the one on your left), you must maneuver the lever like a gearshift until you get all the retracting bars to unlock and open the vault. To do this, move the lever in the following fashion:

Push the lever left one move.

Push the lever up one move.

Push the lever right one move.

Push the lever down one move.

Push the lever right one move.

Push the lever up one move.

Push the lever left two moves.

Push the lever down one move.

Push the lever right two moves.

Push the lever down one move.

Push the lever left one move.

Push the lever up one move.

Push the lever down one move.

Push the lever right one move.

Push the lever up one move.

Push the lever left two moves.

Push the lever down one move.

Push the lever right one move.

Push the lever up two moves.

Push the lever down one move.

Once you have completed all the moves, the vault unlocks automatically.

When you have the first vault open, you find an empty case inside. It must have fit the Cup of the World Tree you found out about in the papers in Angelo Santini's bedroom. The Cup itself is gone, however.

Turn your attention to the second vault now. This door has a series of eight keys and eight locks. Experimentation quickly shows you that many of the keys fit into more than one lock and that some of the keys can be turned in more than one direction.

NOTE

To solve this puzzle, first get organized. Number the keys 1–8 from left to right. Then number the keyholes 1–8 working from left to right and top to bottom.

Be very careful about working with one key at a time. The keys go back on other hooks than the ones they originally came off of.

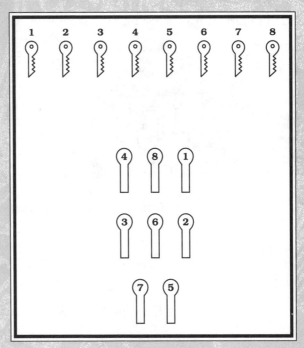

NOTE

The proper order of keys and locks follows along with the directions you should turn them:

Key #4 goes in Keyhole #1; turn it to the right.

Key #8 goes in Keyhole #2; turn it to the right.

Key #1 goes in Keyhole #3; turn it to the right.

Key #3 goes in Keyhole #4; turn it to the right.

Key #6 goes in Keyhole #5; turn it to the right.

Key #2 goes in Keyhole #6; turn it to the right.

Key #7 goes in Keyhole #7; turn it to the right.

Key #5 goes in Keyhole #8; turn it to the right.

When all the right keys are in the right holes—and when they have been turned—the vault door opens automatically.

Inside the second vault you find an empty case that probably would have fit the Skull of Landulph, but you're too late here, too—it's long gone. Move on

to the third and final vault, and hope you get lucky—you're definitely due.

The locking mechanism on this one has seven levers, a button, and gears. After working with it for a few minutes, it starts to make sense to you; you manage to get it open.

NOTE

The solution to the third vault door puzzle is as follows:

Number the levers 1–7 from left to right.

Flip Levers #1, #4, #6, and #7 down by left-clicking on them.

Press the red button eight times.

Keep on pressing it until the gear flips over and allows the vault door to open.

Opening the third vault door reveals that the last item has not been taken. The Black Dahlia itself sits on a perch, its runed sides gleaming at you.

Don't hesitate. Reach in and take it. This is the prize that's haunted your dreams for four long years.

From the Journal of Captain James R. Pearson, Office of Strategic Services

I closed my hand on the Black Dahlia, somehow fearing that it might burn me and scar me forever. Physically, I mean. Mentally, I didn't think there was anything worse it could do to me.

Instead, the gem felt cool to the touch. I felt the runes beneath my fingertips. I knew them all from memory, and now I could see some of them in the order I had assembled them in.

Footsteps sounded behind me. I turned and watched a pair of Military Policemen approach me, a third man trailing them.

"Good work, Captain," one of them said, holding onto a clipboard. "We'll take over from here."

"Take over what from here?" I demanded, but I had a sneaking suspicion what was going on. The military could be very covetous of the secrets they discovered.

"That gemstone there," the MP said, pointing at the Black Dahlia in my hand. "I'm going to have to ask you to hand it over. We're cataloging every item we take out of the place."

"I'll do no such thing. I've searched high and low for this gem, and I'll be damned if I turn it over to anybody but my superiors." I made my words harsh, making sure he remembered who was the ranking officer here.

"Sorry, Captain," he said with a sarcastic grin to let me know I didn't scare him a bit. "We're just following orders from General Bradley. If you like, you can take it up with him. In the meantime, I'm going to have to insist you hand over the gemstone."

I punched him in the chest with my finger, driving home the anger I felt. "All right, sergeant, I'll play it your way. But you can be sure as hell I'm taking this up with your superiors."

"If you like, you can file a requisition order with the quartermaster. I doubt you'll have much luck, but you never know."

And with that, they were gone, taking the Black Dahlia with them. I followed them for a while through the tunnels, drawn by the mystery that clung to that black gemstone. In a short time, they disappeared, leaving me there with my anger and frustration.

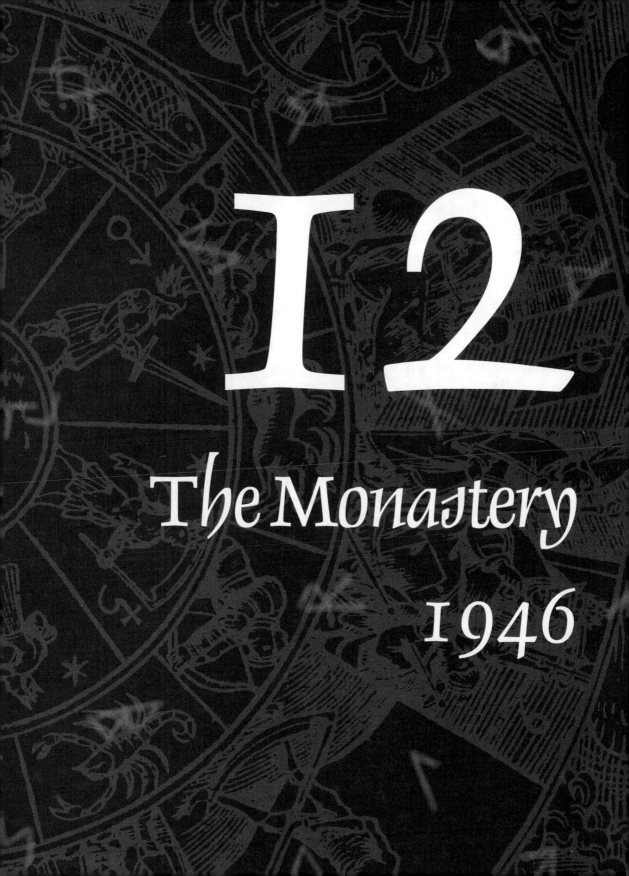

12

The Monastery

1946

The Wine Cellar
From the Journal of James R. Pearson

After the war, I stayed with the OSS for a time, but they were soon disbanded. No matter how many requisitions I filled out, I never got to see the Black Dahlia. I think by the time I turned in my resignation, I'd about worn out my welcome with all the paperwork I kept pushing at people.

I also kept up with all the supply sergeants and other personnel I thought might be instrumental in helping me find the Black Dahlia. That included helping out with the take-home pay of several of them.

But I never caught a whisper of the Dahlia. I'm sure the military moved it out of Nuremberg, but I didn't have a clue where. Or why.

After the OSS was disbanded, I'd thought I was going to have to go back to the States and try to get a job. Maybe as a cop. Merylo had told me back then that I'd have been a good one. A few nights in taverns without anyone to talk to about the Torso Killer case and the Black Dahlia, that career switch even sounded good to me.

Instead, I ended up using all that knowledge I'd gained by setting myself up as a Nazi hunter. All the SS officers were in hiding, trying to sneak off to South America and other countries. The hours were long and the pay was short, but I found a way to stay in Europe. I just couldn't give up hoping that, somehow, the Black Dahlia would find its way back into my hands.

We seemed fated for each other.

Then in the fall, an old friend of mine from the war years told me about several former high-ranking SS officers who'd been meeting at an abandoned monastery near the Austrian-Swiss border. He went on to tell me that the monastery had been an elite SS ceremonial center, and that it had probably been prepared for such an event even as the war turned against Germany.

That started me thinking about the monastery where Dr. Strauss had found the stained glass window that had the names of the officers of the Brotherhood of Thule on it.

What really caught my attention was when he mentioned the village near the monastery. A series of dismembered corpses had been found in the surrounding lakes. After that, I put aside the other cases I was working on and got out to that monastery.

Slipping and sliding through the debris, scudding in from the hole blown in the side of the monastery, you get to your feet and switch on your flashlight. The narrow beam doesn't give you much light.

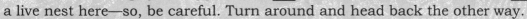

Turn to the left, sweeping your flashlight across the boxes with the Wermacht insignias until you find the steps leading up. Go up the steps to the wooden door at the top.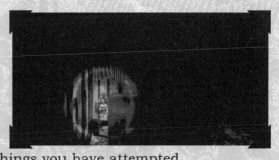

See the keyhole on the door? Yeah— well, old habits die hard. Take a peek.

It looks as though you stepped into a live nest here—so, be careful. Turn around and head back the other way.

Looking around from up here, you can see what looks like a deep hole in the ground between the stacks of crates. Your friend also told you about the tunnels that run for long distances under the monastery. Maybe this is a way down to them.

When you get to the hole, though, you discover that it's just a well. Perhaps it could provide you with a way into the underground tunnels, but given the facts that your flashlight won't penetrate the darkness very far and that the sides of the well look smooth, climbing down into the well could be one of the most dangerous things you have attempted.

Return to the crates, stepping between the two stacks of crates to your right. There's a winch that will help you work the well.

TIP

Walk up to the steps. Look over to the winch by moving the mouse until you can see it. Walk back through the crates to get to the winch. Then, left-click on the winch to bring it into closer view. The solution is to pull the left handle down and then pull the right handle up by left-clicking on the levers. This action lowers the rope.

If you fail to lower the right handle down after the rope is let down, when you step onto the rope you will fall straight down through the well to your death.

*To get down the well safely, **both levers** have to be in the **down** position.*

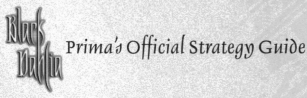
Wine Cellar

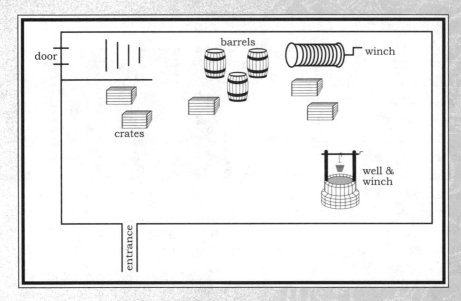

At the winch, pull the left lever down and then pull the right lever up, releasing the rope. Once that's done, lower the right lever again to engage the ratcheting pawl, allowing the rope to peel off slowly.

Walk back to the well and use the rope to descend through the well. You drop your flashlight along the way, but you still have the lighter Merylo gave you at the Raven Room the night you found the old man's body...so many years ago.

TIP   *After working the winch, left-click on the well to take it down.*

At the bottom of the well, you find a torch. Once you light it with your lighter, things immediately seem to look better. The tunnel looks as though it

Central Chamber Map

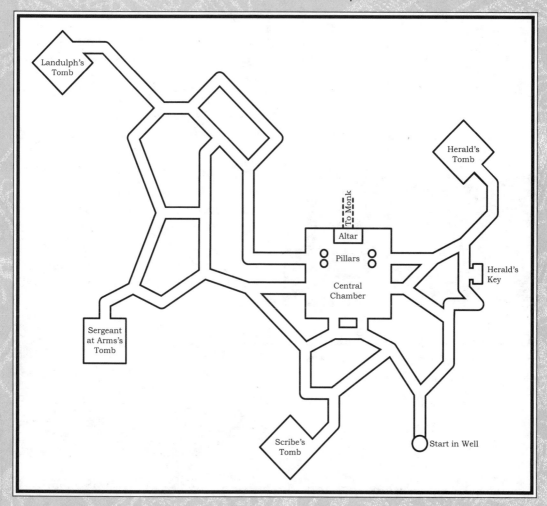

stretches on forever in front of you. Better get started. From looking around, you know that the Germans are still poking around.

And there's no going back up that well winch.

NOTE   *Change to Disk #5.*

The Herald's Tomb

TIP

To get to the Herald's Key area, left-click the mouse once and then take the right fork when you're offered a choice.

Left-click three times; then take the right fork when you're offered a choice.

Left-click three times and then immediately turn right to find the hidden area where the Herald's Key is located.

After wandering through the dark tunnels for what seems like hours, you find a small alcove to your right. Inside the alcove is a small altar covered with candles, skulls, and pottery.

Move closer and inspect the pottery. In the box at the bottom right side of the altar, you will find a brass oval. Take it and walk back to the tunnel. Keep following the tunnel.

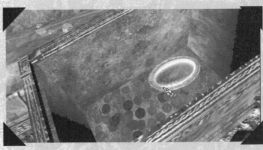

TIP

Once you have the brass oval (actually a key), walk back out into the tunnel. When you exit from the alcove, the game has you facing in the wrong direction. Turn right to head in the direction you need to go.

Left-click once and choose the right tunnel when you're offered a choice.

Left-click three more times to get to the Herald's room.

At the end of this tunnel is a dank, quiet room with a number of lit torches around it. A sarcophagus is across from you against the wall.

The walls to the left and to the right hold the bodies of the dead. It's funny when you think of it, but looking at all the designs, you recognize the family crest on the wall above the sarcophagus. This was the Herald's

room, and these collections of bones were old Louie the Fish's ancestors.

When you walk over to the sarcophagus, look up. You will notice that the ceiling in this area is impossible to see. It makes you wonder what might be hidden there, doesn't it?

Now study the sarcophagus itself. Look at the round indentation on the front of it. It reminds you of the flip side of the brass oval you found back in the alcove.

TIP

If you haven't taken a look at the brass oval's other side, right-click and go to Inventory to do so. Simply flip it over to see that the same design on the back of the oval is on the front of the sarcophagus.

To use the brass oval (listed as Artifact in your Inventory) on the sarcophagus, be sure that you have clicked on the sarcophagus's keyhole, bringing it into close view. Then left-click on Use.

When you fit the brass oval onto the sarcophagus, it lifts the sarcophagus's lid. Inside is a *very* dead body, but notice how shiny the lid's inside is. The runes on the ceiling are reflected on the lid.

Some of these same runes are on that bag of tiles you have kept all these years! Write the runes down in your notebook.

TIP

To write the runes in your notebook, simply left-click on the reflection on the lid. When you go to use them later, however, remember that you have to reverse their order. Remember that you have copied the mirror image of the runes.

Be sure you left-click on the reflection of the runes to add them to your notebook!

That's the only secret in this room. Time to get moving. Wander back into the tunnels.

TIP

Leave this room by left-clicking on the doorway. In the tunnel, left-click twice and then turn right at the Y.

Left-click once and then turn right at the second Y.

Left-click twice. This puts you into the area marked as CENTRAL CHAMBER on the map.

As you enter the large central chamber of the labyrinth, turn to the right to see the altar area.

Approach the altar. You will discover that the four pillars around the altar each have four rings. Each ring has 16 runes, totaling 64 runes altogether at the altar. A little experimentation shows you that all the rings

revolve, giving you an incredible number of combinations.

For now, leave the pillars alone. You need more information before you can solve this puzzle. Turn 180 degrees to face the doors on the wall opposite the altar. Walk out of the Central Chamber through the door on the *left* to return to the tunnels.

TIP

You're now headed for the Scribe's Tomb. The following list is a set of directions that takes you there:

Turn left at the Y you face as you leave the Central Chamber.

Left-click twice and then turn right at the second Y.

Left-click three times and then turn left at the third Y.

Left-click three times to enter the Scribe's Tomb.

The Scribe's Tomb

Twisting and turning through more of the dust-lined tunnels—your torch cleaving the darkness—you soon find yourself in another tomb.

The sarcophagus in this room is on the left side. There's no lock holding this one shut. Evidently, the lid was shattered years ago.

On the wall opposite the sarcophagus, there is a statue of a man carrying a rolled parchment; a small pool rests at its feet.

Peering into the pool, you don't see anything. The water does not appear poisonous. Enough poking around for now. You're a trained investigator, so investigate the broken sarcophagus.

Sure enough. When you look inside the sarcophagus, you see pieces of a broken tablet among the scattering of bones. Gather the tablet pieces and see if you can put them together.

TIP

Left-clicking on the tablet pieces puts them into your Inventory as Stone Pieces. You will discover that, although you can manipulate them in the Inventory, you have no clue as to what they do.

To solve this puzzle, take the Stone Pieces over to the small pool at the foot of the statue. Next, Use them on the water. This action drops them into the water; the runes written on them are then revealed.

This is the correct assembly pattern, complete with a Before and After picture.

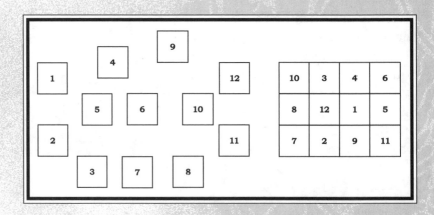

Putting the runes together will be tough if you can't see what's on them. Take the tablet pieces back to the small pool behind you and see if you can clean them up.

Yeah, that's a lot better—now you can see the pieces. Looking at them, you realize that these tablet pieces are more runes, which are on the parchment Helen Strauss gave you. It only takes a few minutes to piece the stone tablet together. Copy the runes into your notebook.

Now that you have the runes, you're finished here. Remember from Chapter 3 that there were four officers of the Brotherhood of Thule. Hopefully, there will be more runes in the other two tombs elsewhere in these tunnels. Get to hunting.

TIP

After walking through the door, follow the procedure below:
Left-click two times and then turn left at the Y.
Left-click two times and then turn left at the second Y.
Left-click three times and then turn left at the third Y.
Left-click one time and then turn left at the fourth Y.
Left-click four times and then turn left at the fifth Y.
Left-click two times to arrive in the Sergeant at Arms's Tomb.

The Sergeant at Arms's Tomb

Take a look around this room. You don't need your investigative skills and deductive reasoning to realize that you have arrived in the Sergeant

at Arms's Tomb. All the swords and weapons lying around the room give *that* away at once. If you need further convincing, however, turn around and look at the ceiling above the doorway.

After searching the dead lying in the walls and the other items scattered about the floor, you don't find much of interest. When you approach the sarcophagus, however, you find another puzzle-lock that will test your mental abilities.

Set to work on the sliding block to figure out the combination in order to open the sarcophagus.

TIP

Getting to the puzzle-lock on top of the sarcophagus requires clicking on top of the coffin.

To open the slider puzzle on the sarcophagus:

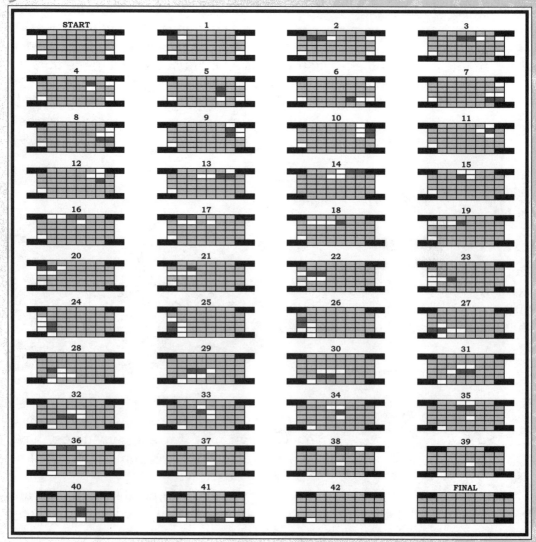

Inside the sarcophagus, you find the last remains of a particular Sergeant at Arms. Clasped in the skeleton's bony hands is a sword that you should inspect more closely. Along the spine of the sword blade are four runes that you need to copy.

After you have copied the runes, turn and walk out the door. There's one last tomb to raid.

TIP

After you walk through the door, follow the following directions to reach Landulph's Tomb:

Left-click one time and then turn left at the Y.
Left-click two times and then turn left at the Y.
Left-click three times and then turn left at the Y.
Left-click three times to arrive at Landulph's Tomb.

Landulph's Tomb

As soon as you step through the doorway, the underground tunnels you've been following break away into a large smoke-filled cavern; the glow of hot magma comes from below. A bridge lies ahead of you and leads to the fourth sarcophagus.

The bodies in the iron cages on either side of the bridge don't exactly promise a vacation in getting across the bridge. Still, you have to see what's in the sarcophagus if you want to solve this mystery.

Stepping on the first step up the stairway leading to the sarcophagus proves you've got trouble. An arrow narrowly misses you, thunking into the torch you're carrying. Look down at the steps in front of you. Several runes are carved into the front part of the steps.

From your studies of the Nordic runes over the years, you know that the rune ᚱ means travel, while the rune ᚦ means pain. That's got to be the clue you were looking for. As you ascend the stairs, only place your feet on the steps marked with the rune for travel.

TIP

The path up the stairs can be tricky, especially when you discover that you have to come back down the steps without being able to see the runes. Number the three sections of steps 1–3 from left to right. Then left-click on the steps in the following order to reach the sarcophagus:

1

3

1 or 3

2

3

1

3

Be sure to Save before you start up the steps. If you left-click on the wrong section, you will be shot with an arrow and will fall over the side of the bridge to your death.

At the top of the stairs, turn your attention immediately to the sarcophagus.

Notice that the lid has been broken. Examine the lid anyway to get the four runes written across it.

TIP

Be sure to left-click on the lid again to write the runes in your notebook. You will need them if you are going to solve the puzzle of the Central Chamber.

Next, take a look inside to see what's left of Landulph. Someone has taken his skull, which lets you know that someone is already working on the ritual.

With the runes copied into your notebook, go back and count all the runes you have copied since this case began. There are 24, exactly the same number as the tiles in the bag of runes Pensky got from Santini. Take the opportunity now to put it together.

TIP

Below is a list of the runes and the order in which they should go (from top to bottom).

Also, take time now to reread the papers you took from Angelo Santini's room.

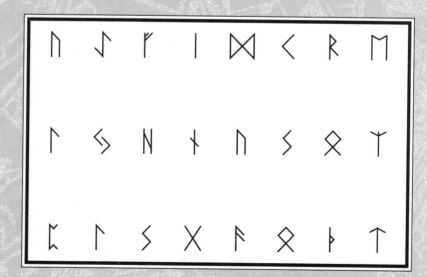

Time to return to the Central Chamber to try your luck with the four stone pillars around the altar. Remember to watch your step when you go back down the stairs.

TIP

Left-click on the bridge to start back down. To take the correct path back down the steps, renumber the sections 1–3 from left to right. Go down them in the following order:

> *1*
>
> *3*
>
> *1*
>
> *2*
>
> *1 or 3*
>
> *1*
>
> *3*

At the bottom, left-click on the doorway twice to return to the tunnels. To get to the Central Chamber:
Left-click twice and then turn left at the first Y.
Left-click once and then turn left at the second Y.
Left-click four times and then turn left at the third Y.
Left-click four times and then step out into the Central Chamber.

The Pillars in Runes

Upon entering the Central Chamber, turn left and walk to the altar. Thinking about the runes you have copied, you realize that there were four groups—four groups of runes and four pillars with turning rings that each bear runes.

Coincidence? Not very likely. Turn to the pillar to your left and start rotating the rings of runes. Each officer in the Brotherhood of Thule probably had a pass code to open the altar. Do you remember the papers in Angelo Santini's hiding place concerning the burial place of the dead abbot? If your geography's right—and you haven't lost your way—you must be somewhere underneath it.

Go to work on the pillars, trying the combinations of runes you found in each sarcophagus.

TIP

We will solve the pillars in the following order:

1. *The left front pillar.*
2. *The left back pillar.*
3. *The right front pillar.*
4. *The right back pillar.*

Take a moment to copy the runes from the game notebook to a piece of paper. This will make things easier.

Left-click on the first pillar to your left. Dial in the combination you got from the Herald's Tomb by left-clicking and holding the mouse button down. Drag the cursor to spin the ring, and line the runes up in the center between the two metal clasps above and below the rings. (Remember to reverse the rune list, because you copied the runes from a reflection on the sarcophagus's lid. If you don't reverse the whole order, you'll be able to put the Herald and Scribe runes on the wrong pillars.)

Next, back off and left-click on the second pillar to your left. Dial in the rune combination you got from the Scribe's Tomb.

Back off and left-click on the first pillar to the right. Dial in the rune combination you got from the Sergeant at Arms's Tomb.

Back off and left-click on the second pillar to the right. Dial in the rune combination you got from Landulph's Tomb.

Once you have all the pillars set properly, the secret door against the back wall opens behind the altar.

With a grinding roar, a concealed door opens behind the altar. Knowing you're very close to your goal, you go through it.

NOTE

Change to Disk #7

Hey, Abbot!

Daylight breaks softly against the ornate crypt in front of you. The effigy of an aged monk is embossed on the lid.

Approach the sarcophagus to take a peek. While you're looking at him,

recall the prophecy in Santini's papers that mentioned Estefan, the man who fooled the evil archbishop. The legend reads that, if the casing that once housed the Black Dahlia is returned to him, his soul will be freed to seek

Monk's Sarcophagus

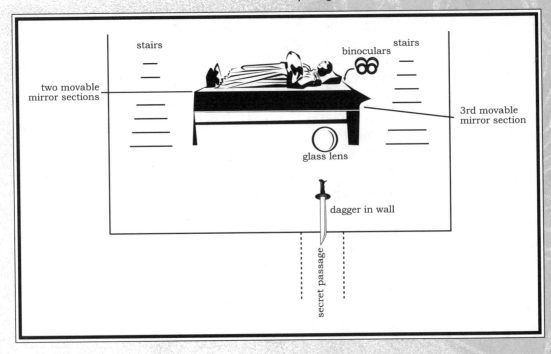

eternal rest. And look—the effigy's hands are cupped...kind of in the shape and the size of the casing.

Curious, huh?

Maybe it's time to put the fable to the test. Walk up to the sarcophagus and put the Black Dahlia casing into the effigy's hands.

TIP   *To put the Black Dahlia casing into the effigy's hands, left-click on the effigy to get as close as you can. Next, go to your Inventory and select the Bag of Runes. Left-click on Use.*

As soon as the casing sits in the effigy's hands, smoke curls and rises, filling the room. As you choke and gasp for air, visions of Odin and the Brotherhood of Thule fill your mind. Also, there are images of demons and foul things.

The smoke clears from the room, but you notice the way the effigy's eyes start to glow red. Something is causing this; try to find out what it is.

You briefly check the door in front of you and discover that it's locked tight. You have to find another way out of this room.

Dropping down into the trench to your right, follow the stairs down. Turn left immediately and look at the end of the sarcophagus. Two checkerboard patterns draw your attention. When you reach out to touch them, you discover they revolve, revealing other surfaces.

TIP   *Left-click on the checkerboard sections to move them around. The left checkerboard turns counterclockwise, while the one on the right turns clockwise.*

With a little experimentation, you discover that these revolving sections have three sides. One of the sides appears to be a mirror.

Walk around the sarcophagus. There are more checkerboard sections here, but none of them are mobile. Look at the round glass surface near the far end on your left—that's definitely interesting.

Around the corner, you find two other curiosities. One is another mobile checkerboard section, which turns clockwise. To its right, what appears to be binoculars jut from the wall.

Take a look through the binoculars. Smoky, red-hot magma seethes below the sarcophagus's lid. It looks as though there may be something at the other end, where the other two moving sections are, but it's hard to tell.

Pondering the possibilities of the mirrored sides of the moving pieces and the glass on the other side of the sarcophagus, you think that you can do something about your limited vision. Adjust the mirrored side to your left first, fixing it so that the mirror points toward the glass in the sarcophagus's side.

TIP

To solve the puzzle with the sarcophagus and the mirrors, you need to line up the mirrors so that you can see through the glass lens in the side. You will be able to see a secret through the binoculars at that time.

Adjust the mirror beside the binoculars by turning it until it faces you. Then, left-click on it one more time.

At the other end of the sarcophagus, adjust the left mirror so that this mirror faces you. Then, left-click on it one more time, too.

Turn the mirror on the right until it faces you, too. Then, left-click on it once.

When you return to the binoculars at the other end of the sarcophagus, you will see the secret.

Once you have adjusted the mirrors to the angles that you think you'll need, return to the binoculars. Peer through. You can see an image now, but you don't know where it is.

Logic suggests that it has to be somewhere on the side where you found the glass lens. Return to that side of the coffin and look at the wall. It only takes you a moment to find it.

TIP

If you have trouble finding the secret image, get in front of the wall where the glass lens is. Turn so that the lens is in front of you. Then run the cursor along the wall opposite the glass lens. The secret item lights up when you run the cursor over it.

Approach the secret area cautiously. Checking it with your fingers, you find that a dagger is embedded in the wall. Pull it out carefully, and you reveal the hidden door.

The Price of Failure
From the Journal of James R. Pearson

I pocketed the dagger I pulled out of the wall. It surprised me when the hidden door opened up in front of me in spite of all that I've been through. Even being predisposed to all the events that have unfolded around me, I guess that I maintained some doubts.

I took out the lighter and my pistol. Then I stepped into the darkness. I found a door at the other end and let myself through into a room that was filled with Nazi paraphernalia and the all too familiar red, white, and black flag. I stood there for a moment, having a harder time believing a Nazi stronghold had been overlooked in the monastery than I did in believing I'd just released the soul of a good man who'd given up his life in the fight against the darkest evil.

Then footsteps sounded behind the other door, getting closer. I stepped back behind my door just in time. Peering through the crack that I left by not closing the door all the way, I saw a man enter the room.

He acted totally unconcerned as he hung up his hat and his coat. It took me a moment to recognize him. But when I did, I had no doubts about what I was going to do. I rolled the hammer back on my .45 and advanced into the room.

"Well, well, well," I said, trying to sound as if I'd just arrived with a group of Marines instead of showing up by myself. "If it isn't Von Hess. Fancy meeting you here." I prodded him between the shoulder blades with the .45, not letting him turn around, letting him know I had it there.

Startled, Von Hess put his hands up. "Who?"

"What's the matter? You don't remember me? Well, I guess it has been a while since my days at the COI in Cleveland."

"Ah, Mr. Pearson if I'm not mistaken." Suddenly confident, Von Hess turned around.

"Uh uh uh." I waggled the pistol in his face. "No sudden moves. It would be a shame to have to use this."

"Don't be a fool! You're hopelessly outnumbered! You won't get out of here alive!"

"You don't suppose I was dumb enough to come in here without any backup, do you?" And I tried to sound like I wasn't. Moving out of cover like that wasn't one of my brightest moves. But seeing Von Hess again after all these years hit a red-hot nerve in my brain that temporarily snuffed out all thoughts of survival.

"You're bluffing."

"Just go ahead and try me." I grabbed him by the lapels and shook him hard enough to make his confidence go away. "Besides, your men aren't going to be doing any shooting as long as I've got you here."

"It seems that you have me at a disadvantage then."

"You're damned right I do," I told him vehemently, grabbing him by the lapels. "And now you're going to answer a few questions."

"As you wish."

"What's going on out there?" I asked, referring to the activity I'd spotted in the monastery.

"They are sanctifying the ritual items."

"What items?"

"You know, it would be better for you if you let me go. You are in an impossible situation here."

"Yeah, yeah. I appreciate the concern. Now I'm not going to ask you again: What ritual items?"

"The skull and the chalice."

"They won't do you any good without the Dahlia." It felt good saying that, letting him know I was playing his game as close as he was. It felt even better watching that calm exterior come apart.

"How did you know?"

"I spent five years trying to figure out what that gem's secret was."

"Then you know whoever controls the Dahlia can control the world."

"What?" I couldn't believe what he'd just said. "What is it with you Krauts and ruling the world anyway?"

"You realize you have no hope here. Your situation is hopeless. You are surrounded by a force of men who were once the elite officers of the SS. I can assure you, however, if you surrender you'll be treated most considerably."

"I know what your idea of consideration is: a bullet in the back of the head. I don't think so."

Von Hess didn't look happy about my decision.

I shifted gears, getting back to the past that had led us here to this moment. "I want to know what really happened back in Cleveland in '41. How did you get to Dr. Eisenstadt?"

"But I didn't get to anyone. I was held for questioning. I was in your custody the entire time. When war broke out, I was sent back to my native land."

"Then who killed Eisenstadt? Who took the Dahlia?"

"I have no idea what you're talking about."

I pushed the .45 up under his chin, hard. "Don't play me for an idiot. You were in the Raven Room for a reason. Who killed Eisenstadt?"

With the .45 at his throat, Von Hess's perfect English lost its polish. "I swear, I did not kill this man."

"Then who did?"

"I do not know." Von Hess hesitated before answering, and his eyes cut away from mine.

I knew I wasn't getting the truth. "You're lying! Spill it!"

"Do what you must. There are fates worse than death."

My anger took over then, spilling out of me before I could stop it. I swung at Von Hess, hitting him full in the mouth.

He looked stunned, but he took it.

"You've been playing me for a sap ever since Cleveland," I grated. "I've had about enough of it. Tell me who's behind all this!"

"I don't—"

"Tell me!" I hit him again, turning his head around.

"So like a boy. Playing at cops and robbers! You have no idea when you're in over your head!"

"Maybe I should just hand you straight over to the Nuremberg tribunal. We'll see how you like to talk when you're staring at the gas chamber."

Before he could answer, I heard footsteps behind me. I turned, bringing my gun up. I couldn't believe it when I saw FBI agent Dick Winslow step into the room. Four hard-looking men with guns flanked him.

"Winslow! What the hell are you doing here?" I asked.

"I can't let you get all the glory, old sport."

"But how did you..."

"My informants must have gotten the same tip as you. We came to investigate the monastery. We saw you bumbling around back here. Looked like you might be in a spot of trouble. So I thought we should lend a hand." Winslow turned his attention to Von Hess. "Who's your prisoner?"

"He's an acquaintance of ours from the old days. You remember the Nazi we arrested in Cleveland? His name's Von Hess."

Winslow looked at the German. "Why, it is Von Hess." He turned back to me, a smile on his face. "Mind if I have a word with him?"

"I guess not."

Getting close to Von Hess, Winslow quietly asked, "Where is it?"

Von Hess acted more nervous than he had at any time with me. Honest fear lit fires in his eyes. "There wasn't time. We couldn't get them all out. You must understand the lock mechanisms were difficult. But don't worry. My men are on it. We'll have it back soon."

"What's going on?" I demanded, moving in closer. Things weren't making any sense at all, but I was catching up quick. My stomach churned sickeningly.

"Not now, Jimbo," Winslow said, not taking his eyes off Von Hess.

I stood my ground, looking for an opening, aware that his men were flanking me with guns in their hands.

"You left it behind?" Winslow asked in a disbelieving voice.

"The Americans were everywhere!" Von Hess protested.

"You bungling idiot!" In an eye blink, Winslow ripped his gun free of its holster and fired pointblank into Von Hess's chest.

"What the hell are you doing?" I asked, starting forward.

Winslow ignored me, emptying the pistol's whole clip into Von Hess. The man's body jerked on the ground. "Never could abide incompetence."

I decided not to say a word, hoping to get my pistol up before anyone noticed.

Winslow didn't miss it. "No. I think it best if you drop that gun, sport. Nasty thing could go off at any second."

Not having any choice, I gently laid the pistol on the ground. I looked back at him. "I don't get it. What's your game, Winslow?"

"Oh, you always were rather naive, Jimbo. I thought we'd just got lucky when you led us to the Brotherhood's messenger. But really...Dr. Eisenstadt, the Torso Killer himself. It's almost too much to ask. And you led me right to his back door where he wouldn't suspect a thing."

It all came together for me in a rush. "You! You're the one who killed Eisenstadt!"

"Why, yes." Winslow tipped his hat to acknowledge the feat. "Guilty as charged. Not as smart as you thought you were, eh, sport?"

"Smart enough to get to the Black Dahlia before you."

That announcement set him back, but he worked quickly to cover his surprise. "You have it?"

"Yeah, that's right I have it. But you tell me, if this thing is so important, why'd you ever let it go?"

"It was that fool, Hitler. What a pathetic little man. We thought of him as a god, but what did he do when we handed him the means to control the world? He buried it underground."

"Where the damn thing belongs," I assured him.

"Ah, Jimbo, you disappoint me. I thought you of all people would appreciate its...grandeur."

"There's nothing grand about it. That gem's brought this world nothing but evil."

"Sacrifices have been made." Winslow took his hat off and handed it to one of his men. "But isn't that the truth behind all of man's glorious endeavors? The pyramids were built on the backs of a thousand slaves. The Coliseum on the blood of its gladiators. Empires on the lives of their soldiers."

"All testaments to madmen. Pencil dicks like you."

Winslow moved before I expected it, driving home a solid right hook to my stomach. I collapsed, going down to my knees.

"Where is it?" Winslow demanded. "Where's the Dahlia?"

I struggled to get the words out. "I...I sold it. To a five-dollar prostitute. How's your mother these days, Dick?"

Winslow only grinned at me. "Clever, Jimbo." Then he hit me, driving me down to the ground. "Where is it?"

"Shove it up your ass."

"Ah, well. I didn't expect you to cooperate. You shan't deter me for long. We'll find the Dahlia."

"Not if I can help it."

"Jimbo, really. You're in no position to stop me from doing anything."

"As long as I have the Dahlia——"

"But you don't, do you? You were quite good there for a moment, sport." Winslow turned and shot a grin at his men. "I really did believe that he had it." His eyes came back to mine. "But if you really did have it, you never would have told me, now would you?"

"So now what?" I asked.

"I could spend a few hours torturing you just for fun. But I'm afraid I really don't have time for that now. The only thing to do...is to kill you. It's a shame really. I always did like you, Jimbo."

"I can see you're all busted up."

"Good-bye, old sport." Winslow raised his pistol.

I waited for it to come, staring down the barrel of that pistol. The seconds dragged on.

Without warning, Winslow's gun snapped. But it didn't fire. He tried it again, but it was empty, all of the bullets spent on Von Hess. He pulled the pistol off me, then spoke in German to one of the men. Winslow left the room without another look at me.

All of them but the man he'd talked to followed him. The guy waited about a heartbeat after they'd left, then he started kicking me. I grabbed his leg. Before he could shoot me, I flipped him to the ground and buried that ceremonial dagger I'd found into his chest.

He struggled for a moment, then went limp. I grabbed the pistol and hurried after Winslow.

But it was too late. By the time I got outside, they were all gone.

I couldn't believe Winslow had been operating behind my back so well in Cleveland. Maybe I was naive, but I wasn't going to stay that way.

And he was wrong about one thing. I did know where the Black Dahlia was. Now it remained to be seen if I could talk Uncle Sam's military out of it. Turning Winslow in as a German spy would earn me some bonus points.

I hoped.

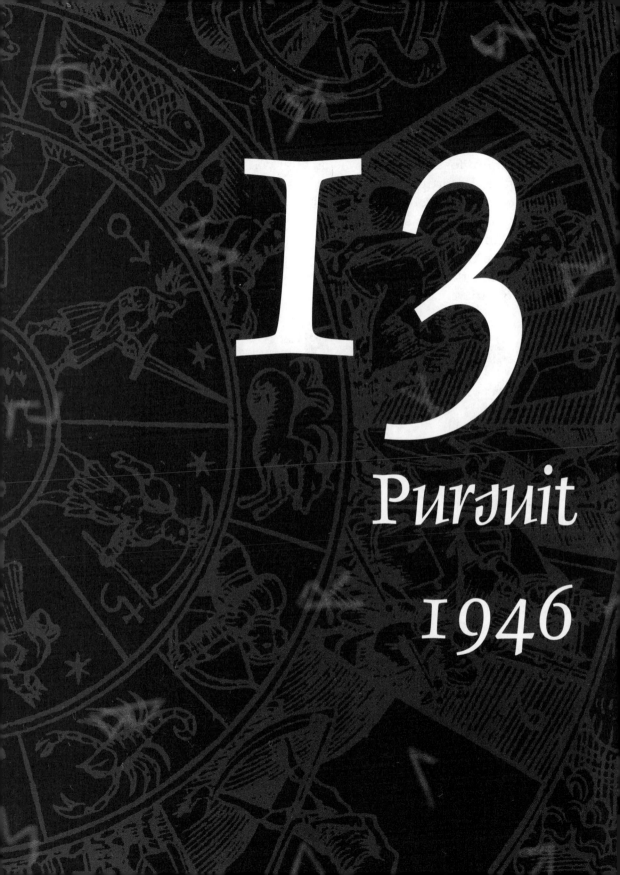

13

Pursuit

1946

The Mystery of Matt Collins

The manhunt for Dick Winslow is on after you make your report to the proper authorities. Unfortunately, you also discover that the Black Dahlia is missing, too. It takes you some time, but you find out that a member of the quartermaster corps swiped it and then sold it to a young airman named Matt Collins.

Once you find out where Matt Collins is billeted, you head there immediately. One of the airmen in the billet, however, has some bad news for you when you arrive.

According to the airman, Matt Collins has been killed in a training exercise. As you listen, you realize that the young man is right in thinking that something strange is going on. It sounds as though someone deliberately killed Collins.

When you ask him about Collins in detail, you find out that Collins sent the Black Dahlia home to his girlfriend.

Ask him where Collins's bunk was and then go search the footlocker.

TIP

To search the footlocker, left-click on it. Once you're inside, shift the contents around by left-clicking on them and scooting them. There are a number of things to look at, but what you want are the letters Collins received from his girl back in LA. You find them under the drawer on the left side of the locker.

Left-click on the drawer and drag it to the right side of the locker. Left-click through the contents to get the picture of Elizabeth Short and the letters with her address.

Left-click on the letters to get the address added to your notebook.

Over the last few years, searching has become one of your best skills. The young airman was right about only a few things being in the locker. Your best finds are the photograph of Elizabeth Short and the letters Collins kept with her return address on them.

Inside one of the letters is another picture. You talk to the young airman and ask if it's okay to take the picture. He says sure and that Elizabeth is becoming a popular girl.

When you ask about his response, the young airman describes the other man, who asked about Elizabeth, well enough for you to know that it's Winslow. Winslow even went on to tell the young airman that he was going to see Elizabeth in LA.

A cold chill runs through you when you realize that Winslow has picked up the trail, too, and that he's ahead of you.

Making Tracks

Trying to catch up to Winslow, you end up back in the States aboard a railroad train going from New York to Los Angeles. While you're eating, you notice the ashtray in front of you has cigarette butts in it. Inspecting them more closely, you recognize them as the Turkish cigarettes Winslow is so fond of.

TIP

Left-click on the ashtray in front of you to get the Turkish cigarettes clue.

Since the cigarettes are there, it means that Winslow must be on the train, too. Call out to the porter and ask him if he saw who was sitting at the table before you.

He can't remember the name of the person, but he's sure it wasn't Dick Winslow. He promises to check the dining car seating chart when he has the time. At the present moment, he's busy.

Impatient about getting to Winslow if he's on the train, you go to the porter's station to take a look at the seating chart yourself. It's on the podium where the porter was standing when you called him.

TIP  *To get to the podium, left-click on the doors, but don't go through them. Turn to the right and left-click twice on the paper on the podium to get a good look at it.*

Dick Winslow's name isn't on the dining room chart, but look at line 4, shift 2. Matt Collins is definitely a name you recognize—and the Matt Collins you know of isn't in any shape to be traveling across the country.

You know from experience that the chief conductor has an office at the back of the train. Skip the meal and get back to the conductor's office.

TIP  *To get to the conductor's office, you have to go through six passenger cars and the baggage car. It's a long trip, but you're about to find a map that will cut your travel time down.*

Pulling Out All the Stops

The conductor is in his office when you arrive. He's the epitome of a professional, and you get the feeling that you're not going to be able to shuck and hustle him easily to get the information you need.

Ask him about room assignments. Knowing that Winslow is traveling under the name of Matt Collins, ask for him by that name.

TIP

Type in MATT COLLINS when the conductor asks you for the name of the party you want to contact.

The conductor checks his list, but tells you that Collins left specific instructions that he didn't want to be bothered by anyone.

Stonewalled for the moment, go back out into the baggage car and think. Undoubtedly, Winslow brought luggage on board the train. Maybe you can get his room number from the luggage.

As you search through the luggage, you notice the big brown suitcase near the crate in the center of the baggage car. You pick it up to search around it better, sitting it on the crate. The train is vibrating so much, though, that the suitcase falls to the floor.

The train's brake cord is above the crate. One good pull on that and you could stop the train and call in security. Winslow probably would get away in all the confusion, though—*if* you could get the train security people to listen to you, that is. Getting the man one-on-one would be a better solution.

NOTE

Do not pull the brake cord. *Doing so will get you thrown off the train immediately and will end your game. If you haven't Saved the game in a long time, now is the time to do so.*

Although you have searched diligently, you realize that this effort may all be in vain. Winslow has buried himself into the train; he'll be difficult to find if you don't get a look at the passenger list.

On your way back to the conductor's office to make another attempt on the conductor's sympathetic side, you notice the map on the door you just came through. Take it up because you'll need it.

TIP

You couldn't have gotten the train map the first time you went through the door to the conductor's office. It wasn't active at that time. When you unfold the train map, though,

you see that it maps out all the cars, though none of the sleeper cars by number.

Left-click on the folded map in the slot to add it to your World Map function.

Left-click on the String to the right of the door to add it to your Inventory.

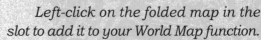

While you're taking the map, you also notice a roll of string on the shelves to your right. Seeing the string gives you an idea; pick it up.

Take the string back to the suitcase that fell off the crate. Pick the suitcase up and put it on the crate

again. This time, though, tie the string to the suitcase and to the brake cord. When the suitcase vibrates off the crate, it pulls the brake cord. After you have tied the string to the suitcase and the brake cord, head back to the conductor's office. After the train comes to a grinding, screeching halt, the conductor goes to investigate. Maybe you can get a look at the passenger list then.

TIP

Pick the suitcase up and put it on the crate. Go to your Inventory and select the String. Left-click Use to make all the necessary arrangements. Then get back to the conductor's office as quickly as you can.

Note: *If you don't leave the baggage car before the tied suitcase falls, you'll be kicked off the train.*

As you leave the baggage car, the brakes lock up. He hurries past you to see what the problem is. Now get back to his office and search the list.

NOTE

Right-click on the mouse and then left-click to bring up the supplemental list. Left-click on the World Map and then left-click on the Caboose to go there.

Knock on the conductor's office door to be sure that no one is inside. Then show yourself on in. The passenger list is in the desk drawer on the left side.

Scanning down the passenger list, you find Matt Collins listed on the first page. His car and room are #283 and #7, respectively. Your train map, how-ever, doesn't list the cars by number.

Being the *trained* investigator that you are, you note that a couple in Car #823 needed a cradle for their baby and that a woman on Car #238 needs wheelchair assistance.

The next thing that catches your eye is a repair list for all the sleeper cars. You make a note of the repairs supposed to be done to each car. Car #283 is supposed to have a light fixture replaced, carpet stains cleaned, shellac for a chipped railing, and a broken number plate replaced. The broken number plate has been checked off, indicating that it's been finished.

Leave the conductor's office and get ready to search the sleeper cars.

Runed!

After walking through the baggage car, you start taking stock of the sleeper car, matching it against the list of information you have compiled. In a short time, you find the car you're looking for. Through a process of elimination, you figure out that Car #283 is three cars up from the baggage car. Left-click to go there immediately.

You ease into the compartment behind door #7, expecting to catch Winslow in the room. But he's not there. After looking around the room and finding

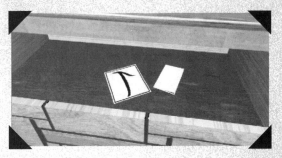

the cigarette case filled with black Turkish cigarettes on the nightstand next to the bed on your left, you know that you have the right room.

To the right of the door as you enter is a chest of drawers. Inside the top drawer, you find a piece of paper with a rune drawn on it.

Curious about it, you pick up the paper. Ink smears across your fingers. Without warning, you start to feel woozy and sick. Almost out of control, you stumble over to the bed and lie down, hoping the feeling will pass quickly. Instead, a powerful hallucination sweeps over you. Images of you falling long distances, of Winslow's voice chanting insanity, and of laughter fill your mind.

A young woman's voice brings you back to the present. When you open your eyes, you see a beautiful young woman standing over you; a look of irritation fills her face.

She tells you that you're in her sleeper. Still under the influence of the drug, you make the connection that Winslow/Collins is no longer there. You also discover that you're in Chicago already and that you've been asleep for hours.

The young woman thinks that you got drunk and that you're sleeping it off. You tell her about Winslow, though, not wanting her to run and get train security.

For some reason, no matter how strange it must sound to her, she believes you. She also tells you that her name is Alice Casey.

Your hurried departure upsets her again. You've got to get back to the conductor's office to find out about Winslow. If he's changed sleeper cars, where is he now?

TIP

Right-click on the mouse to bring up the supplemental list. Left-click on the World Map and then left-click on the Caboose.

The conductor sits at his desk when you arrive. You ask about Matt Collins.

He tells you that Collins got off at Chicago and took the Express, which will reach Los Angeles at least 20 hours ahead of you. But you also find out that Collins left his baggage behind.

Return to the baggage car and conduct a search for Winslow's baggage. After some digging, you find a file on a shelf to the right of the door where you got the train map.

 **TIP**   *Left-click on the baggage chart twice to take a look at it.*

The tag number for Matt Collins's luggage is 0100AA. Knowing that, you begin to search through the suitcases and crates in earnest.

You find the trunk in the center section of the baggage car.

Opening the trunk proves difficult, though. Winslow has safeguarded it with a trick lock. It takes some doing, but you can open the trunk.

Trunk Puzzle

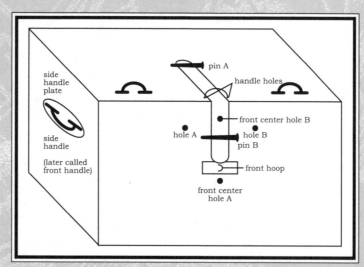

TIP

Here is the solution to the lock on Winslow's trunk:

1.   Remove small pin "A" from the top loop and place it in front hole "A" to the left of the long hasp.

2.   Remove large pin "B" from the front loop and place it in front hole "B" to the right of the long hasp.

3.   Flip the top hasp down and open the lid. You will hear a click as the side handle loosens partially.

4.   Close the lid; the side handle is now unlatched and free.

5.   Flip up the top hasp and the front hasp.

6.   Remove pin "B" from front hole "B" and place in the front center hole "B" that was formerly covered by the front hasp.

7.   Slide the front hoop up.

8.   Remove pin "A" from the front left hole and place in center hole "A" that was formerly hidden by the front hoop.

9.   Remove the handle from the side and place in the top pair of holes over the top and front hasps.

10. Remove the side handle plate and place it on the front, fitting the newly opened notch over the raised front hoop and putting the four pins into the four small front holes.

11. Remove the handle from the top and place it into the holes in the plate that has just been placed there. (Note: There is not enough clearance for the handle to fit over the front hoop in its upper position without the added thickness provided by the plate.)

12. Slide the secret front panel up.

Peering inside the opened trunk, you notice a slab of intricately carved black stone. It looks a lot like the missing piece of the sarcophagus lid from Landulph's tomb in the crypts beneath the monastery.

Wanting to foil Winslow's plans for delivering the trunk, you switch papers with the box next to it.

With Winslow off the train, there's only one resource left for finding out what he may possibly be up to. You have got to get back to his compartment—and that means charming the young woman who's in there now.

TIP

Right-click on the mouse to bring up the supplemental list. Left-click on the World Map and then left-click on Sleeper #283 (the third sleeper up from the baggage car).

Alice Casey, Budding Actress

Alice isn't in the compartment when you get there. Thinking that she may have wanted to get a bite to eat or a drink, you go to the dining car. Getting caught in her compartment this time is a bad idea.

TIP

Right-click on the mouse to bring up the supplemental list. Left-click on the World Map and then left-click on the Dining Car.

In the dining car, you see Alice seated at a table. Go over to her and strike up a conversation.

From the Journal of James R. Pearson

I hated the idea of losing Winslow when I was so close to him. I felt angry at him and myself, but I shelved it all temporarily as I took a seat opposite Alice Casey in the dining car.

She still didn't look happy to see me, and I was, frankly, surprised when she told me I could sit down.

"You still sore about this morning?" I asked.

Her eyes flashed. "It's not every day I find a strange man in my sleeping compartment." She smiled, and I liked what I saw. "I might not mind it all that much if you weren't so smug about it."

"I was just trying to get a little rise out of you."

"Men! You think awfully highly of yourself, don't you?" She leaned in to light her cigarette.

I held the lighter while she got her smoke going. "Not particularly," I answered. "What do you think about me?"

"I don't think much of you at all."

I liked the way she held her head when she told me that. I figured then and there she'd be a tough cookie to handle. "I don't think I introduced myself properly. I'm Jim. Pearson."

"I'd like to say it's a pleasure to meet you, Mr. Pearson."

"Well then, Miss Casey, I'll just have to make sure that it is. Let's say I apologize and we start over fresh?"

"All right. But there won't be any third chances."

"So you really didn't see the man who had the sleeping compartment before you?"

"No I didn't. It was empty when I got on in Chicago. Except for you. Are you really a cop?"

"Well, not exactly. I used to work for the OSS."

Her eyes go wide, and I knew she'd been to the picture shows or read spy novels that glamorized the work I used to do. I didn't have that high of an opinion about it. Not any more.

"The OSS?" she asked. "Really? Were you a spy?"

"Of sorts."

"And this man you're after, what's he done?"

"Well, he's a murderer and a traitor for starters. That's enough right there to send him to the chair. It's probably not even half of what he's done." Suddenly I regretted sitting down and asking her about Winslow. Looking at her, all blond hair and blue eyes, I couldn't help thinking how nice it would have been to be having any other conversation than the one we were having now.

"And what about you, Jim? What have you done?"

"I'm not sure I get what you're after."

"You must have seen and done things the rest of us can only imagine. How thrilling it must have been."

It was none of those things, and I knew it. But I didn't want to get too detailed with the reasons why I felt that way. Death was something a soldier had to leave on the battlefield. If he could. "Well, it's not like in the books or the picture shows, Alice. It's not thrilling, it's not any fun at all. It's nerve-wracking and gruesome and tragic. And when my man's finally behind bars, I want to give it all a long rest."

"Well, I'm sure it beats the heck out of being a waitress in Skokie, Illinois."

"Oh, I don't know. I think a guy could learn to like a quiet life in a place like Skokie." I gave her a smile, hoping to lighten up the mood. But she was already up, talking to someone who'd lived part of some fantasy life she'd read about or saw in a movie house. "So where are you headed?"

"Los Angeles."

"You don't say. I'm headed to Los Angeles myself."

"You, too? Well, what do you know? Here I haven't even so much as set foot in Los Angeles and already I've made a new friend.

"So what's out there for you?"

"Why Hollywood, of course. I'm going to be a movie star." She said it with conviction.

"Blondes are a dime a dozen out there, I hear," I said.

"You said you'd play nice." She frowned at me.

"I know how to play nice. It's just teasing is more fun."

"Why, if a girl knew you any better, Mr. Pearson, she might think you were flirting with her."

"Well, if a girl knew me any better, Miss Casey, she might know it." I watched her smile.

"We'll be in Los Angeles in the morning," Alice said. "What will you do when you get there?"

"I'll start looking for my man. You?"

"I suppose I'll look for a place and try and find a job. You won't forget about me, will you?"

"When you're a big star, I'll say I knew you when."

She laughed at me, and I decided I really liked that sound. "Now you know that's not what I meant."

"When all this nastiness is over and done with, I'll be sure to look you up. I promise." I pushed myself up from the table. "In the meanwhile, I've got to try to get some sleep."

"Good night, Jim, and good luck with your search."

"Thanks. Good night, Alice."

"Jim?"

"Yes?"

"Don't forget your promise."

I looked at her, and I meant every word I said. "Don't worry, Alice. A guy's not very likely to forget a pretty girl like you." Then I took myself off to my compartment, trying not to think about that lead Winslow had on me.

NOTE

Change to Disk #6.

14

City of Angels

January 10, 1947

The Skeptical Sergeant

Once you're in Los Angeles, you don't waste any time booking a room at a cheap motel. Winslow has a head start, and you need to figure out a way to cut that lead down. In your room, pick up the phone and call the Police.

TIP *Left-click on the phone beside the bed to pull up the menu. Then left-click on The Police. Matt Collins and Elizabeth Short are listed too, but there's no connection.*

When you get an LAPD detective on the phone, you tell him that Elizabeth Short is in danger. The detective doesn't sound real enthusiastic about what you have to say, but he agrees to meet with you at the diner across the street. Hang up the phone and go meet Detective Maxwell.

TIP *Right-click to bring up the supplemental list. Left-click on the World Map, and then left-click on Gabe's Diner to go there.*

Gabe's Diner is a small place, and a big man like Detective Maxwell makes it seem even smaller. The man may as well wear a sign that reads Homicide Bull.

Tell him about Elizabeth Short, and follow it up with the story you've put together on Winslow. Detective Maxwell doesn't buy it at all but reluctantly agrees to look into the matter. Talking to him further only seems to irritate him and he leaves.

The one bright spot is that you run into Alice, who's gotten a room at the Sunset Arms Hotel, where you're staying.

Maxwell's attitude is a bit depressing, and he has a certain lack of professional courtesy. Don't brood over it. Once you get your things stored at your hotel room, get off your duff and get down to the train station. It's time to find out what's become of Winslow's trunk.

TIP *Right-click to bring up the supplemental list. Left-click on the World Map, and then left-click on Train Station Shipping Office to go there.*

Mail Service

The train station isn't too busy when you get there. Study the two windows in front of you, and you'll see that one window is the Outgoing Parcels window, the other the Incoming Parcels window.

Since Winslow's trunk is an incoming parcel, try that window first. When you ring the bell, a fastidious clerk bounces up to the counter.

Ask him about Winslow's package. He immediately asks you about your receipt. You can only tell him that you don't have a receipt. He confidently tells you that you can't pick up the package without the receipt. When

you tell him you just want to find out if the package has arrived, his explanation gets complicated in a hurry.

Ask him if you can see the shipping manifests, thinking maybe you can just look for yourself.

His refusal is firm. If you don't have a package coming in, you can't look at the manifests.

Rather than battle the futility of bureaucracy, think for a moment. All you need is a package addressed to you, and you'll be able to look at the lists. Look in the trash can to the left.

You're in luck! There's an empty box inside. Just retrieve it and address it to yourself. When you're finished, take it to the Outgoing Parcels clerk.

TIP *The Box shows up in your Inventory. Simply go to the Outgoing Parcels clerk. Send the Box by selecting it from the Inventory and left-clicking on Use.*

Send the Box Express so that it arrives quickly. The clerk can't believe he heard you right. Once you're finished at the Train Station Shipping Office, follow up on the lead you had to the boarding house where Elizabeth Short lived when she wrote her letters to Collins.

TIP *Right-click to bring up the supplemental list. Left-click on World Map and then left-click on Boarding House.*

The Boarding House

The lady who runs the boarding house is Mrs. Underhill, a woman investigators learn to love because she gossips. As she shows you around the room, ask her about Elizabeth Short.

She says that she doesn't know where Elizabeth is, but she's willing to bet that she's with a man or in a bar waiting to meet men. Ask her about the Black Dahlia.

Mrs. Underhill waxes on eloquently about Elizabeth's boyfriend dying. She also remembers a weird black gem with strange carvings on it.

You know Elizabeth has the gem, but where to find her? With Mrs. Underhill watching on in obvious adoration, search the room.

The chest of drawers yields nothing except a used lipstick and a pack of gum. The closet has been stripped bare. Checking under the bed turns up one shoe. But you're not looking for Cinderella, so toss it back under there.

Growing desperate, you turn your attention to the nightstand beside the bed. The top drawer has a hairbrush and a letter.

Dear Mrs. U.

I'm real sorry about last month's rent. I promise to make it up to you. Trust me, I've got some real hot prospects this week with a friend of a producer from Prometheus Pictures. He has promised me that I will be an extra in their next picture!

Isn't it exciting? So if you could wait a few more days, as soon as my advance comes in, I'll turn it over to you, I promise. Thanks so much for your patience. You have been such a darling about everything so far.

XoXoXo

E.S.

The second drawer is empty, but the third drawer has a Harlequin romance novel and a cocktail napkin from a place called the Biltmore Hotel Bar.

Well, since that's your most solid clue, ankle it over to the Biltmore and see if Elizabeth is there.

TIP

Right-click to bring up the supplemental list. Left-click on the World Map and then left-click on Biltmore Hotel.

The Biltmore proves to be a dive, a place you could imagine the Elizabeth Short you're getting to know would hang out during the evening hours. Walk over to the bartender and show him Elizabeth's photo.

TIP

Right-click to bring up the supplemental list and left-click on Inventory. Left-click on Photo and then left-click on Use.

The bartender recognizes the photo at once. He asks if you're a cop. When you tell him "no," he tells you that she's a regular. You tell him that you'll try back later.

Okay, you've got a couple of leads working here, but now it's time to get back to the train station to see if your train has come in—or at least the package you sent.

TIP

Right-click to bring up the supplemental list. Left-click on the World Map and then left-click on Train Station Shipping Office.

Special Delivery

At the train station, approach the Incoming Parcels window. Ask the clerk about the status of your package.

When he asks for your receipt, you give it to him, and he goes back to get the package. While you're signing for the package, you spot the entry for the Matt Collins shipment, noting that it was picked up by the ABC Moving Company.

This is shaping up nicely. If an individual had picked up the package, you might not have found the trail so easily. But a company would be listed with the phone company. Head back over to your hotel room, and let your fingers do the walking.

TIP *Right-click to bring up the supplemental list. Left-click on the World Map. Left-click on the Sunset Arms Hotel to go there.*

Use the phone and ask the operator for the ABC Moving Company. Once you have the movers on the line, you are connected with a secretary named Amy. She tells you that you have to talk to Steve about the package you're interested in. She also tells you that they're locking up even as you speak and that you'll have to wait until Monday.

Monday isn't going to cut it. If the package is still in transit, you have a chance of getting to it before Winslow. Head over to the ABC Moving Company. Breaking and entering isn't new to you, and the stakes could well be Elizabeth Short's life.

TIP *Right-click to bring up the supplemental list. Left-click on the World Map and then left-click on ABC Moving Company to go there.*

It's As Easy As ABC

You search the ABC offices by flashlight after jimmying the lock. The first thing that draws your attention is the file on the desk. It proves to be nothing, but the middle left drawer gives you a list of drivers and trucks for the last week.

On the wall behind the desk and above the filing cabinet, you find a note that helps you understand the company's system for handling deliveries.

ABC
Moving Co.
January 9, 1947

Dear Amy,

You're such a dear, filling in for me while Jack and I
honeymoon at Laguna Beach. I don't have to tell you what
a relief it'll be to get this wedding over with and
finally get away from the office. I just wish the timing
of it had been a little better. Darn those state
auditors! You'd think they'd have better things to do
than to harass a little company like ABC Moving. Don't
think I won't remember this come election time!

I managed to take care of everything except for this
week's pickup log. I've already filed the shipping
receipts, so all you need to do is write down the I.D.
numbers. We wouldn't want the auditors to be unable to
find a file, now would we? Don't worry, it should be a
snap, as long as you get the guys to fill the log out.
Don't be afraid to nag them. They can be as stubborn as
six-year-olds some days. My I.D. system is as simple as
ABC (ha ha—boy, let me tell you, you'll get tired of
saying that all week!). First of all, every I.D. number
starts with the initials of the driver who delivers the
package. Every I.D. ends with a number for the week of
the year following the number for the day of the week.
(Starting with Monday, of course!)

The client's initials immediately precede the numbers
for the day and week. We have some drivers with the same
last initial, so I also use the truck number for them.
Each driver uses the same truck every day, except on
Fridays. Friday is our maintenance day, so one truck
gets serviced every week. They rotate which one every
week in numerical order. Ken likes his truck and

complained all last Friday when he had to use old #10, but none of the other guys complain that much.

Oh, before I forget, following the driver's initial, you need to put in the zone code for the point of origin.

Now, according to union regulations, drivers must stay within their assigned zones. Packages that are picked up in one zone that are to be delivered to another zone must be transferred to the driver for that zone. Unless, of course, the package is too bulky. Then another union regulation prohibits the transfer and the original driver has to deliver it. The guys always complain about it, but they're the ones who voted for it! I guess it's easier for them if the zones were divided a little differently. Zone II has downtown LA at its north border and includes the East LA area. If only Florence were a little further west. Then it'd be in Zone III instead of II. And with Glendale split down the middle with the east side in Zone I, the guys don't know whether they're coming or going sometimes.

Oh, before I forget, Ken drives truck 1, Owens truck 4, O. Greene #7, and Marty #5. I don't know how star-struck you are, but if you ever want a tour of the stars's homes, Marty really knows his way around Hollywood. Why, just the other month he delivered a package to Cary Grant. Boy, how I wish I'd been along for that delivery! I'm just glad I don't have Steve's route. He complains about the guy at the train station all the time. He's even more of a stickler for regulations than the state's auditors. It takes Steve forever to pick up a package from that guy.

Oh, and if you're not sure where to put something, just file it under miscellaneous.

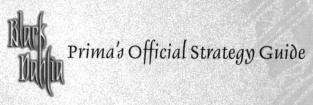

If anything unusual comes up, don't panic. The world
isn't going to end. I'll just straighten it out when I'm
back. Good luck. I'll see you in two weeks!

Love,

Marge

Some system, huh? Well, let's see how well it works. You know immediately that Steve is the driver who picks up at the train station. The girl on the phone told you that you'd have to talk to Steve about the package. Go back to the desk and take out the delivery list.

According to the information in the letter, the delivery I.D. number starts with the driver's initials and proceeds as follows: truck number, point of origin code, the client's initials, the number for the day of the week, and a number for the week of the year.

Going over the delivery sheet, you find that Steve made a pickup at Union Station on January 10. His initials are evidently S.O. The package was signed for by AKP.

That gives you part of the number you're searching for: SO? AKP??

The delivery was made on January 10, a Friday. Using the moving company's numbering system for the days of the week, we know that one of the numbers is a five. (Friday is the fifth day of the week according to the moving company's system.) Also, we're in the second week (week #2) of the year. Our number is

now SO?AKP52, leaving only the zone number to be found.

On page one, you'll find a package delivered on January 6 by S.O. Reading the number according to the moving company's system, you discover that Union Station is in Zone I. You're looking for delivery number SOIAKP52.

Open the third drawer of the filing cabinet under the note on the wall; SOIAKP52 is toward the back. When you find it, take it out and look it over.

It looks as though Winslow sent a crate of champagne to King Productions at RKO Studios. Yeah, well, you know that was no champagne. Close up the file and put it away. It's time to go to the movies.

 **TIP**   *Right-click to bring up the supplemental list. Left-click on the World Map and then left-click on Movie Studio to go there.*

There's no joy at the studios, though. There's a big gorilla who guards the door. He doesn't mince his words and tells you that what you're looking for is a closed set. Without a pass, you're not getting in.

Elizabeth Short
From the Journal of James R. Pearson

I went back to my room and waited for evening, figuring if Elizabeth Short was running true to her current form, she'd show up at the Biltmore then. When it was time, I flagged a cab and rode over to the bar.

 **TIP**   *Right-click to bring up the supplemental list. Left-click on the World Map and then left-click on Biltmore Hotel.*

When I got to the bar, I started to ask Ike the bartender about the woman. Then I spotted Elizabeth Short sitting at a nearby stool. I reined in my excitement and tried to approach her casually.

"Excuse me," I said.

She turned to look at me, and I saw how that look could take a man's breath away. She was stunning, long black hair and limpid pools for eyes.

"Are you Elizabeth Short?"

"Who are you?"

I wondered about how best to frame the lie I was about to tell. Still, I needed her trust, even if I had to steal it from her. Seeing her like that, busted up over her boyfriend, I knew I wasn't going to feel good about lying to her. "I was an acquaintance of Captain Collins."

"Oh. Mattie." She broke eye contact and looked away from me. Her voice dropped. "Mattie's dead."

"Yes, I know. I'm sorry, Miss Short."

"Thanks, mister." She gave me a bright smile that showed the hurt she was carrying around. "And call me Lizzie."

"Thanks, Lizzie. My name is Jim."

"Did you——you know Mattie very well?"

"Not as well as I would have liked. Everybody makes him out to be a real hero."

"My Mattie. The war hero. Were you a hero, Jim?" She didn't look at me, but I could hear the taunt in her voice.

"Oh, I don't know. No more than anybody else."

"Well how about the hero buys a girl a drink?" She glanced up at me again, knowing she was pushing the situation to a critical point. Either I wanted to talk to her enough to pay for the privilege or I was history.

"Sure, Lizzie," I answered. Getting her a little more drunk was going to make questioning her easier, but what she was doing to herself wasn't something I wanted to be part of. But if it hadn't been me, it would have been someone else. And I needed the Black Dahlia. I turned to the bartender. "One bourbon. And a——what do you have?"

"Gin."

"Gin and——?" When there was no response, I ordered it straight, just the way she called it. "Gin for the lady."

The bartender poured the drinks and set them before us.

"A girl could get to like you, Jim, you keep treating her this way."

I got back to the reason I was there, hoping I didn't come across as sounding too eager. "Did Matt send you a black gem when he was stationed in Europe?"

Suspicion flared in her black gaze. "Matt sent me a lot of things."

"The way I hear it from Mrs. Underhill, is you weren't very shy about showing that gem off."

"Mrs. Underhill is a cheap gossip." She turned away from me.

"Did he send you a gem?"

"Yeah, he sent it. He knew how to treat a girl like a real lady." Looking back at me, her words were full of promise, but underscored with challenge. "You know how to treat a girl like a real lady, Jim?"

"I guess that depends on which girls you talk to," I said. "Can I see the gem Matt sent you?"

"It's someplace safe."

"Can you take me there?"

"Are you trying to feed a girl a line, Jim?" She smiled, like she was laughing at what she saw as my inept come-on.

"I'm trying to help you. I've got reason to believe that you're in some real danger."

"Who'd want to hurt me? I don't have an enemy in the world. All I got is friends. Right, Ike?"

"You said it, Lizzie," the bartender replied.

"A man named Winslow is after that gem of yours. He's killed a lot of people trying to get it. I think he might have been responsible for Matt's death."

That got her attention, shaking her hard girl image. "Mattie? But—but the army said it was an accident."

"I don't think so."

She finished the drink in front of her and put her empty glass back down. "Buy me another drink."

"Don't you think you've—"

"I said buy me another drink." Her voice hardened and got louder, assuming control of the situation. She was used to taking control of guys who wanted something from her, and in her view, I'd just joined those ranks. "If you won't, there's plenty of other guys in here who will."

"All right." I turned my attention to the bartender. "Another round for us, Ike."

"Coming right up." The bartender came over and built the drinks.

I peeled off a single from my roll to pay for the drinks. Ike went away. "This won't help, Lizzie," I said.

"It helps just fine."

"Hey, c'mon, let's get out of here."

"What for?"

"I don't like it here." That was the age-old litany of the young, the insecure, and the passive aggressive. "Let's go someplace where we can talk in private about Matt and that gem he sent you."

"Mattie? Mattie's dead. What more is there to talk about?"

"I'm sorry, Lizzie. I'm just trying to help."

"You're too late. Now go away. You're giving me the blues." She looked away from me, dismissing me.

"It's never too late." Her glare cut short my protest, making me realize how empty it sounded. No matter what, Collins was dead. It was too late. "All right. How about tomorrow?"

The bartender scooped up the ringing phone. "Yeah, I think so. Hold on a second. Your name Pearson?"

"Yeah."

"It's for you." Ike handed me the phone.

"Hello."

"Evening, Mr. Pearson. Ramsey, LAPD. Detective Maxwell needs to see you."

"I'm kind of busy right now, detective. Can it wait till tomorrow. Say, how did you know—"

"We found a body. It's been cut up pretty bad. Are you still there? Pearson?"

"Yeah—yeah, I'm still here. I'll be right down to the station house."

"We're at Manhattan Beach."

"Manhattan Beach?"

"At the crime scene. Next to the marina. Hurry your ass over here."

"I'll be right there." I hung up the phone and took a paper and pencil from my pocket. "I've got to go, Lizzie. Meet me—" I wrote quickly, putting down the address of the Sunset Arms Hotel, "meet me here. Tomorrow afternoon. I'll buy you lunch."

"All right, Jim, I'll meet you. Maybe you ain't so bad after all."

"Oh, I don't know. Maybe I'm worse. You'll just have to get to know me." The sad part was, I knew that was true. I felt bad about stirring up all that hurt she was carrying around, being part of it eroding away what was left of her and whatever dreams she'd had.

"Story of my life. Every guy I meet seems to turn out to be a louse."

"I'll see you tomorrow, then? Don't forget."
"Tomorrow. I'll see you tomorrow."
Her voice drifted off. I didn't know then that that was the last time I was going to hear it. At least, the last time I'd hear it outside of a nightmare.

After you leave, Winslow comes calling, offering to buy Elizabeth Short a drink.

15

A Fresh Corpse

January 15, 1947

Breaking and Entering

The phone call from Maxwell proves to be a hoax, so you know that something's gone sour. When you get back to the Biltmore, it's closed, and you never did learn where Elizabeth Short called home.

The next day, she misses your lunch engagement, and you get the impression that maybe things have gone worse than you could have imagined. After a little thought, you realize that your only tie to Elizabeth Short is Ike, the bartender at the Biltmore.

So go on. Invest a little shoe leather, and go see if Ike has heard anything.

 **TIP**

Right-click on the mouse to bring up the supplemental list. Left-click on the World Map and then left-click on the Biltmore Hotel to go there.

Ike's shift has started when you arrive, but the afternoon clientele is slack. A lot of empty chairs surrounds the tables. Walk up to him and ask about Elizabeth Short.

He says that the woman hasn't been in since the night she was with you. On that night, though, she left with another guy. He goes on to say that she generally leaves every night with a guy. He's surprised that she didn't leave you a key.

Ask about the guy she left with. Question his information, trying to make him angry.

Ask him about the key comment.

He asks you what kind of keys do women leave for guys in hotel bars.

Obviously, that would be a hotel key, but play along with this guy anyway. Ask him if she gives out keys often.

Ike says she gives out plenty of keys and, when he's asked, says maybe she left one with him.

This guy's full of ego, so pop his balloon by telling him you think that he's lying about getting a key himself.

Ike becomes upset immediately and bellows out that Elizabeth is staying at Room 201.

Ask him again about the guy Elizabeth Short left with.

Ike suddenly develops a form of amnesia, a condition curable with money. Bribe him until you get all the answers you need. At the end, he says that he'll see about getting a key for you.

Leave him there and go explore on your own. This is a hotel after all— Room 201 can't hide from you.

TIP

To reach the hotel corridor and the steps to the second floor, turn left at the bar and left-click to walk forward. Turn right and left-click again to go upstairs.

A minute later, you're beating feet up the stairs to the hotel's second floor. The rooms up here are all numbered. Room 201 is at the end on the right near the window overlooking the alley.

When you knock on the door, though, there's no answer. Turn your attention to the window on the left. Through the glass, you can see a fire escape, which seems to lead to Elizabeth Short's room.

TIP

To crawl through the window, you have to knock on #201's door first! After you knock, left-click on the window to open it and then left-click on it again to go through.

Climb through the window and go down to Elizabeth's room. Peer through the window. You can see that her home wouldn't ever have graced the pages of *Homes Beautiful.* When

you try the window, you find that it's stuck, held fast by a board that runs along the frame.

TIP

Left-click on the window to get a closer look at the window. Then drag the cursor up to see the board that blocks the window's lower section from raising on the window's right side.

Left-click on the window frame above the glass to pull the glass pane down. Then left-click on the board to knock it out of the way.

Move down to the lower section of the bottom window frame and left-click on it to open it. Left-click on the window frame again to go inside.

During the war, you learned a number of ways to break and enter different buildings. This window with its board jammed against the window frame is no problem at all.

Once you're inside the room, the scattered whiskey bottles and clothing tell you the story of Elizabeth Short's life. A brief check through the chest of drawers shows that the woman is traveling light these days.

After tossing the room thoroughly, you're about to give up hope of finding anything. Then you spot something on the trim molding around the room's door.

TIP

Left-click on the top of the trim molding to get a closer look. Left-click on the Key to pick it up. Left-click again to add it to the Inventory.

You recognize the key's design at once; it belongs to a train station. But the number's been filed off. You have already been to the closest station in Los Angeles. It's possible that Elizabeth stashed the Black Dahlia in one of the train station lockers.

As you think this over, you also realize that the woman is still missing. Recovering the Black Dahlia is important, but so is making sure that nothing happened to Elizabeth Short. Maybe the two of you just missed each other. Maybe she's waiting for you at your hotel room by now. It's worth a look.

TIP   *Right-click on the mouse to bring up the supplemental list. Left-click on the World Map and then left-click on Sunset Arms Hotel.*

Busted!

You've got company when you return to the hotel—only it's not Elizabeth Short. It's Detective Maxwell and a friend, and the visit is definitely *business*.

Maxwell takes the lead, introducing his partner, Vernon. Then he starts hammering you with questions about where you were and about Elizabeth Short. You don't know what's going on, but you don't like being grilled.

Maxwell goes on to tell you that Elizabeth Short has turned up dead, and you're the prime suspect. You recognize the work from the description of her death.

When Maxwell asks you again where you were last night, blame the murder on Winslow.

Even with the corpse on his hands, Maxwell doesn't like the idea of having you tell him how to do his job. He pins the murder squarely back on your shoulders.

Not holding back now and angry yourself, you tell him you've been tracking down leads on his case.

That goes over like a lead balloon. Maxwell has decided that he doesn't like you at all. He leans on you harder and then lets Vernon attack you.

While you're trying to catch your breath, Alice steps in through the door and tells the detectives that you were with her all night—and that what you were doing is none of their business.

Still not liking the story, Maxwell and Vernon issue a few last threats and then leave.

Alice asks if she did okay, and you can't help but agree. At least she got those two big gorillas off you. When you ask her why she helped you, she says she couldn't stand by and watch you get beat up. Besides, she's sure you're innocent of whatever they think you've done.

Feeling as though you owe her something, you tell her more about Winslow and the case. She offers to help; reluctantly, you take it. Maybe she can be of some assistance…as long as you can keep her out of harm's way.

You mention the crate that you had shipped to the movie studio. You also tell her that you can't get in to see it.

Smiling, she tells you that you're looking at the newest script girl for RKO Studios. You recognize the name at once, knowing that's where King Productions is filming. Alice says that she'll drop a studio pass by your room later.

Then she rushes off, not wanting to be late for her first day. She blows you a kiss on her way out the door.

Well, it's obvious the little gal has a crush on you, but get your head out of the clouds—you've got work to do. Maxwell didn't get around to making you cough up the train station locker key you found at Elizabeth Short's. It's time to make the most of that key—get on over to the train station.

TIP

Right-click on the mouse to bring up the supplemental list. Left-click on the World Map and then left-click on Train Station.

Eisenstadt's Cane

At the train station, you're stuck with the immense task of trying the key on every locker. Even if you got away with it and the station security didn't throw

you out, you would draw a lot of unwanted attention.

It's time to parley what you learned about Elizabeth Short into a winning hand. You knew she had a locker here because you have the key in your hand. But do you remember the letter she wrote to Matt Collins, the one you found in the dead airman's locker? In that letter, she told Collins that she would come up with a foolproof way of remembering her locker number.

Thinking about the condition of her hotel room, you figure Elizabeth wasn't big on personal responsibility. Whatever method she found for remembering the locker number must have been simple.

Spotting the pay phone on the nearby wall gets you to thinking about the way Elizabeth Short signed all her letters to Collins. Always "ES." Just her initials. Looking at the dial on the front of the pay phone, you find that the initials "ES" translate into "37" on the telephone dial.

Not believing it could be that simple, you make your way through the lockers and find #37. Sure enough, when you put your key in the lock, it opens.

TIP   *When you approach the locker, you don't have to get into your Inventory for the key to open the locker. Since you have the key, just left-click on the locker door to open it.*

There's quite a collection inside the locker. In the back is an umbrella and a wrap. Two small suitcases and a jewelry box occupy the front, as well as a bundle of letters rubber-banded together.

The letters are all from Matt Collins, making plans for the future he didn't live to see. In one of the letters, he mentions buying the Black Dahlia from a quartermaster. The letter gives no indication that he might have known what the Dahlia was.

The jewelry is mostly junk—cheap knock-offs and inexpensive pieces. But in the front, you hit pay dirt. It's in the form of a yellow piece of paper that turns out to be a receipt from Willington's Antiques. The store appears to have an address right here in Los Angeles. It states that a large piece of black sapphire was sold to the store for $250.

TIP   *You need to take the Willington's Antiques receipt with you. Double left-click on the receipt to add it to your Inventory.*

Get moving. If you're in luck, the antique store will still have the Dahlia.

TIP

Right-click on the mouse to bring up the supplemental list. Left-click on the World Map and then left-click on Antique Shop to go there.

A man greets you on the other side of the counter at Willington's Antiques. Ask him about the Black Dahlia.

He tells you he was very impressed with the Dahlia. Even though you offer to buy it back, he tells you he can't because he sold it to someone else that morning.

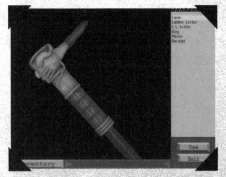

Disappointed? Yeah, but you still may be able to trail the gem. Ask him who purchased the Black Dahlia, confirming that the buyer was indeed Winslow.

The man also tells you about the cane Winslow traded in for the Dahlia. The mention of that cane makes you immediately think of Eisenstadt's cane. With everything you've been through, you could hardly forget about that.

Ask him to see the cane. He readily agrees, showing you the flaws in it. You recognize it as Eisenstadt's cane for sure. You also know that you have to have it. The antique store owner drives a hard bargain, asking $100 for it and leaving you nearly destitute.

The man was correct about the frontispiece on the cane. It is interesting, but he might not have known what that collection of runes signifies. You do, though. You find that the four wheels turn, allowing you to lock in different combinations of runes. After some consideration, you decide to try the series of four runes you recovered from the tombs under the monastery.

To solve this riddle, you need to dial in the series of four runes carefully. Some of the combinations will set up some of the rune sequences; others will not. Always check to see that all four rune sequences are being filled.

If you've forgotten the sequences for the Scribe, Herald, Sergeant at Arms, and Landulph, bring up your Notepad and copy them from that.

Get the cane in the Inventory. Notice that three runes on each dial are immediately available to you. Number the rows 1–4 from left to right, angling down the cane from the hand piece. Do you see the M and the 1 on the first row? Start with these because they are beginning runes for Landulph's combination and the Scribe's combination, respectively.

Solve the puzzle by rotating the second row of runes one rune to the right. Rotate the third row of runes two runes to the left. Rotate the fourth row of runes seven runes to the right.

Once all the runes are lined up, take off the top of the cane and remove the sheet of semitransparent velum inside. The velum is marked with what looks like a child's scribbles. Only the simple map compass in the lower right hand corner gives you any clue as to what this sheet is: a Treasure Map.

The compass in the corner indicates that this sheet may be a map. But a map to what?

For the moment, put the map and cane away. It's time to move again. The crate should have made its way to the movie studio by now. Get back to your hotel room and see if Alice was able to get you a pass.

Right-click on the mouse to bring up the supplemental list. Left-click on the World Map and then left-click on Sunset Arms Hotel.

Talking Pictures

When you get back to your hotel room, take a look around. Alice has left your studio pass on the pillow on the bed. Pick it up and get over to the movie studio.

Left-click on the studio pass to pick it up from the bed. Left-click on it again to add it to your Inventory.

Right-click on the mouse to bring up the supplemental list. Left-click on the World Map and then left-click on Movie Studio to go there.

The studio pass gets you onto the lot without a problem. You arrive in the middle of a scene from one of the productions now underway. Some

sort of space picture, judging from the costumes.

In the middle of the scene, the overhead lights explode, showering sparks down onto the cast. The director flies out of his seat, going into

hysterics. He clears the set, demanding to know where Al King is. He's told that King is sick and isn't there.

Since no one's paying any particular attention to you, why don't you take a look around for the crate? It isn't hard to find, tucked away in the shadows to the right of the motion picture screen.

Walking over to it, you discover that the crate is filled with toys. Dozens of jack-in-the-boxes. You can bet that when Winslow received those, he wasn't a happy guy.

Notice the paper taped to the boxes? Why don't you take a closer look at it.

TIP

Left-click on the paper inside the crate. This lets you talk to Alice, which adds Al King's address to the World Map. If you forget to left-click on the paper, you won't be able to proceed with gameplay.

Now that you know where King is, why don't you go rescue Alice from that shaggy dog/alien actor that's hitting on her.

From the Journal of James R. Pearson

Watching the Shaggy Dog, or whatever he was, putting the moves all over Alice, I decided to intercede on her behalf. After what she'd done to clear me with the homicide dicks, it was the least I could do. Besides, I wanted to ask her about the possible connection between Winslow and King.

When I joined them, the Shaggy Dog was in the middle of his spiel.

"So anyways, I been getting all the best jobs since I got a new agent. I can hook you up with him if you want." Then he noticed me standing there and decided to scram. Probably remembered a fire hydrant in need of attention. "I'll catch you later."

Alice smiled up at me after the actor left.

I decided not to cast any disparaging remarks about her latest encounter, although the temptation was there. "So how's the new script girl doing?"

"Oh it's far busier and far less glamorous than I could have imagined. But otherwise it's simply perfect. I'm loving every minute of it."

She sounded so positive about the experience, I hated bringing up the faults I'd seen so far. "Set seems a little chaotic here."

"From what I've been told, everything that could go wrong with this production has gone wrong."

"What's the story with the guy who's about to put a gun to his head?"

"Who? Simon?" She looked at the director slumped in his chair. "Oh, he's under a lot of pressure to make sure this film gets done right. I've talked with the crew. He's an absolute dictator, but at least they don't blame him for the problems with the film."

"Who do they blame?"

"Al King. The producer. They say he's been away from the set when the production has needed him most."

That brought me back to the discovery I'd just made concerning the crate. Al King's signature on the crate meant he was the guy it was shipped to. So what was it about King that had him so busy he couldn't be on hand for a film he was producing? I turned my attention back to Alice. "I found the crate from the train with Winslow's tags on it. Al King signed for it. Could he possibly be the connection between Winslow and the studio?"

"Oh you don't think he could—" She looked me in the eyes and decided I was serious. "No, he couldn't possibly be connected with your killer. Mr. King is a big, cuddly teddy bear of a man. He's the sweetest thing. If you were ever to meet him, you'd know."

"Yeah, I wish I could. Why isn't he on the set?"

"He's home sick." She paused, then looked at me, her positive attitude and smile totally recovered. "Say, why don't you come around to the house later?"

"What house?"

"Mr. King's house. I'll be spending the afternoon there helping him with his work. You can meet him yourself. Then I'm sure you'll see he couldn't possibly be the type of man to help that Winslow."

"You know, that sounds like it might not be a bad idea. You sure Mr. King wouldn't mind you inviting visitors around his place?"

"Oh, he won't even know. People come in and out of his house all the time. We can say you're there to pitch an idea. This manhunt of yours is a perfect story.

"I should be going. Mr. King will be expecting me soon. Stop around later. His house is the last one on Pacific Shore Road. You can't miss it."

"Okay. I will."

She started to leave, then turned around and kissed me on the cheek.

I watched her go, feeling a smile spread across my face that a sandblaster couldn't have removed.

I killed time in the hotel room, catching up on all the journal entries I'd made and reviewing the facts. The tie between Winslow and King might be circumstantial. But it was all I had going for me. I showered, shaved and changed clothes, then I caught a cab out to Pacific Shore Road.

 **TIP**

Right-click on the mouse to bring up the supplemental list. Left-click on the World Map and then left-click on Al King's House to go there.

King's beach house turns out to be even more than you ever expected. One look at it tells you the guy is rolling in dough.

After meeting you, Alice takes you into the living room, equipped with a wet bar. Al King comes over to give you a soft soap job, telling you he's going to make Alice into a big star.

Al King's Home

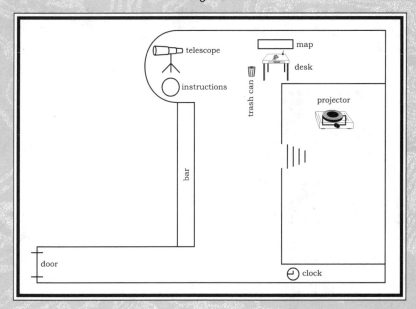

King isn't even interested in your cover. He leaves you and Alice alone. For a guy who's supposed to be sick, he's getting around pretty well, isn't he? Now it's time to shake down the room.

Turn your attention back to the foyer. You passed a number of framed photographs on the wall as you entered. Photographs often tell a lot about the people who keep them.

There are a number of pictures there, including signed ones by Richy Star, Groucho Marx, and other celebrities. Searching through the book shelves nets you your biggest prize—a photograph of King and Winslow!

The picture looks like it was taken in college, so maybe King and Winslow were buddies back in some fraternity.

Either way, it definitely ties the two men together. Behind it is a picture of what looks like the two boys and their fathers. They're posed in front of some game they'd brought down, and they're all cradling shotguns. Evidently, Winslow acquired a taste for killing a long time ago.

Ask Alice to see what she knows about the fraternity picture.

She says that she's never seen it, but she's willing to go ask King about it.

The living room overlooks a back patio above the sea. A projection screen hangs on the wall beside the patio.

On the other side of the living room's sunken area, there is a desk against the wall underneath a topographical map.

Landscapes and Deadscapes

Turning your attention to the desk, you discover a small notebook lying open on top of it. Upon further examination of the notebook, you see some cryptic comments with a drawing of the telescope in it. You've been around long enough to read through the words on the pages: King has been using the telescope to spy on some women in the neighborhood. But you're not quite certain what the numbers below the entries mean.

Shift your attention to the topographical map on the wall above the desk. The compass in the lower right corner reminds you of the Treasure Map you found in Eisenstadt's cane. Taking the Treasure Map out, you align its compass over the wall map's compass. Notice the marked spots on the topographical map. Two arrows mark King's home, while the "X" marks a spot on the map that is at an elevation of 250 feet. The target area is at an elevation of 250 feet. You're standing at an elevation of 100 feet. By subtracting the two, the difference of elevation is 150 feet. To exit the map, hit (Esc).

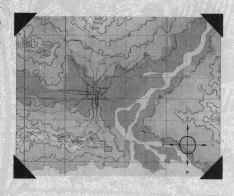

Pursuing this line of thought, walk over to the telescope facing the bay windows.

The first thing you notice about the telescope is the box on its side. Judging from the Saturn Telescope's markings, the box allows the telescope to be finely adjusted horizontally and vertically by coordinates. You realize now what the numbers in King's notebook mean. These are coordinates to houses he frequently watches.

Peering through the telescope becomes an exercise in futility.

TIP

Left-click on the telescope to use it. Left-click and drag to go from side to side and up and down.

Back away from the telescope for now and go check out the trash bin beside the desk. It holds a treasure trove of possibilities.

First, there's a collection of torn papers that turn out to be telegrams. This is a definite clue. Piece them back together to find out what the original messages were.

NOTE

After you left-click on the torn telegrams to place them in your Inventory, right-click to bring up the supplemental list and then go to the Inventory. Select Telegram to put them on the user screen.

Piecing the telegrams back together takes time, patience, and an eye for detail. Though not drawn to scale or shape, the diagram below will help guide you through putting the telegrams together.

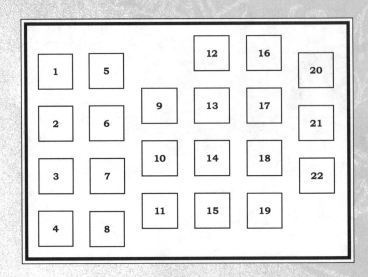

As you reconstruct the telegrams, start all the way in the upper left-hand corner; you'll need the room. Follow the following list of instructions:

Put #6 in the upper left corner of your working screen.

Put #1 in #6's place.

Put #9 beside #6.

Put #5 in #9's place.

Put #11 beside #9.

Put #18 beside #11.

Put #17 under #6.

Put #2 in #17's place.

Put #12 under #6.

Put #1 (now occupying #6's original place) in #12's place.

Put #16 under #9.

Put #5 in #11's place.

Put #4 under #18.

Put #1 (now occupying #12's original space) beside #4.

Put #3 beside #1.

Put #22 beside #3.

This series of moves completes the first telegram from Dick Winslow to King regarding the shipment. For the second telegram, follow this set of instructions:

Place #20 as far up in the right-hand corner as you can while keeping it on the viewing screen.

Put #19 beside #20.

Put #13 beside #19.

Put #21 beside #13.

Put #14 under #21.

Put #2 (now occupying #17's place) under #20.

Put #15 beside #2.

Put #7 beside #15.

Put #8 beside #7.

Put #5 (now occupying #11's place) under #2.

Put #15 beside #5.

Now you have both telegrams together, although the second one is of a more personal nature. Once you reconstruct the telegram, exit the Inventory screen and then return to it to find the telegram taped back together.

When you finish with this paper puzzle, you find that there are actually *two* telegrams, not one. The first is from someone named Dorothy, who is obviously upset with King.

```
AL MERRY CHRISTMAS YOU PIG STOP WHERE'S MY MONEY STOP
YOU'RE WAY BEHIND ON YOUR PAYMENTS AGAIN STOP YOU DON'T
EXPECT ME TO GO TO LOS ANGELES TO GET IT DO YOU STOP I
DON'T CARE HOW WARM IT IS IN JANUARY ON THE WEST COAST
I'M NOT PUTTING ONE LOUSY FOOT IN THAT GODFORSAKEN TOWN
AGAIN STOP IF YOU DON'T TAKE CARE OF THIS RIGHT AWAY I'M
GOING TO HAVE A SUMMONS DELIVERED TO YOUR STUDIO STOP
WHAT WOULD THE BOYS THINK IF MY LAWYER SHOWED UP WITH IT
WHILE YOU WERE SHOOTING STOP HOPE I NEVER SEE YOU AGAIN
CHUMP STOP


    DOROTHY
```

The second note is much more promising...and puzzling.

```
AL I'M HEADING TO THE WEST COAST STOP SHOULD GET TO LOS
ANGELES SOMETIME IN JANUARY STOP I'M HAVING A PACKAGE
DELIVERED TO YOUR STUDIO STOP SEE THAT IT GETS TO THE
```

OLD SHOOTING LODGE STOP I'LL HANDLE IT FROM THERE STOP I
TRUST YOU WILL TAKE CARE OF THIS RIGHT AWAY STOP SEE YOU
LATER CHUM STOP

DICK

Old shooting lodge? Now that sets your investigative mind tingling, doesn't it? Does the old shooting lodge refer to a place where movies are made, or does it refer to the hunting picture? These locations could be vastly different.

Prowling through the trash, you find a newspaper folded back to a particular story that catches your eye. You read through it briefly, realizing that the sarcophagus in the story could very well be made from the same stone as the one in Landulph's tomb.

VANDALS DESECRATE CEMETERY

The county sheriff's department reported that a mausoleum at the Ferrin's Hill cemetery was defaced by vandals last night. The ornate tomb of Victor Von Klaus, renowned actor and pioneer of the silent picture era, was apparently broken into some time between midnight and 6:30 a.m. on January 13. Von Klaus, whose remains had rested peacefully in the mausoleum since his death in 1913, was a known Germanophile and eccentric. The beautiful nouveau style architecture of his ornate tomb has been covered with bizarre graffiti, and the sarcophagus in which his casket had been interred was broken open. Damage from the vandalism was estimated to reach into the thousands of dollars with the value of the shattered sarcophagus alone be set at well over $5,000. This last item was reported to be of German origin and made of a rare and valuable black marble. The stone can be identified by peculiar defects that only occur in the marble unearthed at one particular quarry located in the Giant Mountains of Eastern Germany. A large section of the sarcophagus lid was apparently removed by the vandals.

The mausoleum certainly bears investigating, but finish going through the trash can first. You also find a pair of gloves and a chisel inside. That's definitely proof enough to go have a look at the mausoleum.

TIP

Right-click on the mouse to bring up the supplemental list. Left-click on the World Map and then left-click on Ferrin Hill Cemetery to go there.

16
Final Gambit

Ferrin's Hill Mausoleum

When you arrive at the mausoleum, no one's there but everything's still a mess. Pictures adorn the walls on the sides of the sarcophagus.

Writing on the wall to your right draws your attention. After inspecting it, most of the writing appears to be quotes.

TIP   *Left-click on the walls to read the quotes.*

EVERYTHING'S GOT A MORAL, IF ONLY YOU CAN FIND IT.

WHEN ALL THE BLANDISHMENTS
 OF LIFE ARE GONE,
 THE COWARD SNEAKS TO DEATH
 THE BRAVE LIVE ON!

WHEN YOU LOOK LONG
 INTO AN ABYSS
 THE ABYSS ALSO
 LOOKS INTO YOU

I AM BECOME DEATH
 THE DESTROYER OF WORLDS

VIRTUOUS AND VICIOUS
 EVERY MAN MUST BE
 FEW IN TH'EXTREME
 BUT ALL IN THE DEGREE

One quote looks stranger than all the others. It reminds you of something you could have found in the tombs. Evidently, you're supposed to figure out the mathematical riddle that's been painted in blood on the wall.

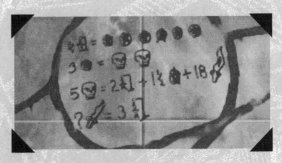

If you just want the answer, skip to the next page. But if you need help working the problem out, read on.

You start by knowing that **4 Hanged Men = 6 Stars**.

You also know that **3 Stars = 2 Skulls**.

Since **4 Hanged Men = 6 Stars**, then **2 Hanged Men = 3 Stars** (divide both sides by 2).

We just figured out that **3 Stars = 2 Skulls**. So, since **3 Stars = 2 Hanged Men**, then **2 Skulls = 2 Hanged Men**.

Next you find that **5 Skulls = 2 Hanged Men + 1 and a half Stars + 18 Flames**.

We already figured out that **2 Skulls = 2 Hanged Men**. Since **3 stars = 2 Skulls**, then **1 and a half Stars = 1 Skull**.

Now that we know the value of each item in terms of Skulls, substitute for what you know. You know that:

> **1 and a half Stars = 1 Skull**

> **1 Hanged Man = 1 Skull**

The problem should now read like this:

> Original Equation: **5 Skulls = 2 Hanged Men + 1 and a half Stars + 18 Flames**

> Substituted Equation: **5 Skulls = 2 Skulls + 1 Skull + 18 Flames**

Now, work the problem algebraically. (You want all the Skulls on one side of the equation; all Flames on the other):

> **5 Skulls = 3 Skulls + 18 Flames**

> **5 Skulls – 3 Skulls = 3 Skulls – 3 Skulls + 18 Flames** (subtract 3 Skulls from each side)

2 Skulls = 18 Flames

2 Skulls ÷ 2 = 18 Flames ÷ 2 (divide both sides by 2)

1 Skull = 9 Flames

Since **1 Skull = 1 Hanged Man**, **1 Hanged Man = 9 Flames**. So, now all that is left to figure out is how many Flames equal 3 Hanged Men.

1 Hanged Man = 9 Flames

3 × 1 Hanged Men = 9 Flames × 3 (multiply both sides by 3)

3 Hanged Men = 27 Skulls

All that work and what do you have? An answer of 27. But what are you supposed to do with that number?

Continue searching the room. One of the small jars on the floor has a note in it. Take it out and read it.

JIMBO,

HERE'S A HINT THAT YOU CAN SPOT FROM MILES AWAY! THOUGH I'LL BET YOU HAVE TO LOOK AT IT 100 TIMES BEFORE YOU GET IT.

You recognize the piece of paper that Winslow's note is written on. It's from a book of Nietzsche's work. While you were in Germany, you studied it. But why is the page number 165 circled?

And why is Winslow taunting you? Is he trying to lead you to him? If so, he's feeling really confident.

There's nothing else in the mausoleum, so return to King's house. Winslow's taunting note suggests that there's something else at King's house if you can find it.

TIP

Right-click on the mouse to bring up the supplemental list. Left-click on the World Map and then left-click on Al King's House to go there.

Back at the beach house, you set yourself to working out the problem of the telescope's coordinates. After reading Winslow's note, you're sure that he left you instructions on how to get to him.

Return to the topographical map and get the elevation of King's house. Subtract it from the elevation indicated by the velum overlay and then cross-reference it with the distance on the chart next to the telescope. When you start to think about the cryptic note Winslow left for you, it makes you think that the page number 165 is supposed to be multiplied by 100, giving you the distance coordinate. You get an answer of +0.5. That's one of the numbers you need.

Assuming the answer to the riddle, 27, is the number you need for the other coordinate, use the box on the telescope's side and dial it in. Look through the telescope.

TIP

To use the telescope properly, enter the number +0.5 and 27. Bring the view into focus by left-clicking on the triangles on the horizontal and vertical lines; even them up. When you have them matched, you see Winslow in the shooting lodge.

REMEMBER: You have to line the two sets of triangle arrows exactly to trigger the video sequence.

Bingo! You got it. There's the shooting lodge, and there's Dick Winslow—looking back at you with a pair of binoculars! After he knows you've seen him, he waves as though he doesn't have a care in the world.

Shaken, you back away from the telescope. As you make your way over to the topographical map of the area, Alice calls out to you. You tell her that she's got to leave, that Winslow is onto you, and that he's playing some kind of game with you. She protests, saying she can't leave now because of her job.

Finally, your argument wins out, and she agrees to go back to the hotel room and wait for you. Once you have the location of the shooting lodge, you call a cab and go there. You're excited but fearful. You finally ran Winslow to ground, but that appears to be *exactly* what he wanted you to do.

The Shooting Lodge

Arriving at the shooting lodge, you find the front door locked. To your left, there is a window that looks as though it would be easy to get through.

When you try to push the window up, you crash through the floor instead. You land in the basement under the shooting lodge—in a pool of blood. As you look around at the torture tools and at the blood, you realize that you have found Elizabeth Short's murder scene.

Getting to your feet, you cross the room to the ladder against a wall.

As you near the ladder, you find a picture tacked to it. The picture has been dipped in blood. When you look at it, you realize that it's a picture of Alice. Winslow *has* been spying on you longer than you had thought. It comes to you in a sudden cold rush that, perhaps, you've put Alice in danger— and you have no one but yourself to blame....

When you turn the picture over, you see the writing on the back: *THE NINTH VICTIM HAS BEEN CHOSEN.* Save your game now.

Frantic now, you start up the ladder, but one of the rungs breaks when you pull on it. As you plunge down, you hear a familiar hissing sound— the sound of fuses burning.

Flames break out all around you, and a section of the wall goes down to your left. Behind the wall are three lockers and a door.

The door's locked, and if you don't get out soon, you're going to burn down with the shooting lodge. Approach the locker on the left and search it. Inside are three jack-in-the-boxes with cryptic messages.

You immediately identify the toys as part of the load shipped to the movie

studio in the trunk you diverted on the train. Winslow's games haven't ended yet. The messages are, as follows:

THE WORLD IS BUT A STAGE, JIMBO; WHERE EVERY MAN MUST PLAY A PART, AND YOURS A SAD ONE.

FAIR IS FOUL, AND FOUL IS FAIR: HOW DO YOU ESCAPE THE FIRE AND SMOKY AIR?

IS THIS A JACK-IN-THE-BOX I SEE BEFORE ME, THE HANDLE IN MY HAND.

The second locker has more jack-in-the-boxes with the following messages:

SOON IT SHALL BE HER TIME TO DIE, AND GO WE KNOW NOT WHERE; TO LIE IN COLD OBSTRUCTION AND TO ROT.

WHEN YOU LOOK LONG INTO THE EYES OF THE CLOWN, DO NOT THE EYES OF THE CLOWN ALSO LOOK INTO YOURS?

ALACK, POOR ELIZABETH, SHE'S GONE THE WAY OF ALL FLESH. SHE MADE A LOVELY CORPSE.

The third locker is a surprise. When you put your hand on the handle to drag it open, a painful burning shoots across your hand. When you snatch your hand back, pulling open the door, you look down at your hand and realize that you've been badly burnt. A fresh burn in the shape of ⚧ is on your hand. Inside the locker, there's a car battery hooked up to the door. That's what hurt you.

Hanging behind the car battery is a single key. Take it and hope that it opens the basement door. With your hand throbbing, you manage to open the door and plunge out into the woods beyond.

Covered with blood and scared to death, you still manage to drive back to your hotel.

Where's Alice?

Back at the hotel, Alice is gone, but she left a message.

Dear Jim,

I know I promised I would stay right here until you returned, but Mr. King called me in to work this evening. Poor Al is feeling rather under the weather. I've never heard someone sound so sick! As it turns out, none of the other girls are available tonight to take care of him, so I guess the new girl gets to take her turn. I tried to back out gracefully, but Al wasn't taking no for an answer. I don't really have a say in the matter, not if I want to keep the job. I'll be careful, I promise, although I'm sure there's nothing to worry about. I'll see you later tonight.

Love,

Alice

Move! You know things are bad, and Alice is caught smack dab in the middle of them.

Back at King's house, everything is in disarray. It looks as if an earthquake or a tornado has swept through the place. Broken glass and overturned furniture are everywhere. The books have been knocked off their shelves.

Notes written in blood are all over the walls, quotes taken from Shakespeare and Lewis Carroll.

MY MISTRESS, MY SALVATION

BLACK DAHLIA

YET WHO WOULD HAVE THOUGHT THE OLD MAN TO HAVE HAD SO MUCH BLOOD IN HIM?

As you make your way through the house, you see a large pool of blood in the center of the sunken living room area. Take a look at the table to the left. Someone has left a movie projector sitting there.

You know it was Winslow, and you can't begin to imagine what might be on that film. Still, you have no choice but to watch it. As you approach the projector, you see a note taped to its side.

CURIOUSER AND CURIOUSER! CRIED ALICE

Below the note is an ON switch.

TIP

You have to pull back from the note one click to get to the ON switch at the base of the projector. Left-click on the switch to activate the projector and start the film.

You turn the projector on and watch the film. Winslow hams it up for the camera, beating King down to the ground with a riding crop. Alice is tied up in the background.

Winslow taunts you and then goes to get a meat cleaver. Still talking to you, his face in the camera, he chops King to pieces.

The film ends abruptly, not letting you see what has happened to Alice. As you look around the room, you wonder whether all the blood you see be-longed to one man...or if it belonged to King *and* Alice?

Still, even in this moment of hysteria, your keen investigative mind nudges your attention. There was something in the film, something that didn't be-long. As you watch it again, you see the big clock on the wall behind Alice. It's set at five minutes to five.

Given the amount of time you've been gone, there was no way that that film was shot at 4:55. Looking over to the right, the clock now reads 9:00.

Run over to the study doors and try to open them. Every effort, though, goes wasted as the doors are locked tightly. Turn your attention to the clock on the wall. Move the hour hand to 5. Then move the minute hand to the 11 and sweep it clockwise to the

1. When the hula dancer comes out, move the minute hand quickly back to the 11. A door behind the bookshelves to your right opens up, revealing darkness and a long flight of steps.

There's no choice now. Alice is in trouble—if she's even alive.

The AɈtral Portal

Deep in the underground caverns under Al King's home, you wander through the smoky mist rising from the sandy ground. Everything looks eerie, as if it's been carved from another world, another time.

Only the thought of Alice being somewhere out in all that drives you

forward. Winslow has gone completely crazy.

Then, in the distance on your right, you believe you can see Alice. As you close on her, you see that she's hanging suspended from a rope, her wrists tied together.

Fearing for her safety, you rush up. Locating a knife, you cut her free, both of you moaning. As you start to recover, she thanks you, then her voice deepens—becoming Winslow's voice.

Before you can move, Winslow appears before you, seemingly shedding Alice's appearance like a snake shedding its skin. He hits you, knocking you down. Then he taunts you while you're dazed.

Calling out to Alice, he brings her toward you. Your heart sinks when you see the way she automatically obeys him. Like an automaton, completely in Winslow's thrall. He commands her to kill you, then he takes up the dagger and plunges it into the cave wall. As he draws the blade down, a door opens in the solid rock.

Alice keeps guard over you. Pleading with her, you try to get her to give you the pistol. Then, unexpectedly, she turns the pistol on herself and pulls the trigger. She collapses, dead by the time she hits the ground.

Resolutely, worn out by everything you've been through, you pick up the pistol and continue the chase. It's all that you have left.

As you step through the portal, you realize that you've been here before. This is the same pool where you viewed all of the visions that led you to the Torso Killer.

Peering through the darkness ahead, you spot Winslow at a dark altar. Already, he has the items he needs to complete the ritual. He begins speaking in a loud voice, loud enough to wake the dead around you.

TIP

To view the game's Good Ending, wait until your weapon's Cross Hairs appear, then shoot the Black Dahlia out of Winslow's hand.

To view the game's Bad Ending, wait and do nothing. Or simply shoot Winslow. Both versions are a delight and should be pursued.

17

Quick Trip Walkthrough

Chapter 1

The Pensky Questions

LEFT-CLICK to go behind the desk in your office.
DRAG the cursor down, and LEFT-CLICK on the right drawer.
LEFT-CLICK on the To Do List.
LEFT-CLICK on the To Do List again to put it back.
LEFT-CLICK on the To Do List a second time, and then hold the *left* mouse button to move the To Do List up and reveal the Revolver.
LEFT-CLICK on the Revolver to take it.
LEFT-CLICK on the down arrow to close the drawer.
LEFT-CLICK to go around in front of the desk.
TURN RIGHT, and face the Locked Cabinet.
LEFT-CLICK on the Locked Cabinet to approach it.
RIGHT-CLICK to bring up the supplemental list.
LEFT-CLICK on the Inventory.
LEFT-CLICK on the Revolver in the list.
LEFT-CLICK on the Revolver's butt and hold the *left* mouse button down while dragging the cursor to the right.
LEFT-CLICK on the Key in the Revolver.
LEFT-CLICK on the Key again to place it in the Inventory.
LEFT-CLICK on the Key from Revolver to look at it.
LEFT-CLICK on USE to open the Locked Cabinet.
LEFT-CLICK on the Message (in the upper left area).
LEFT-CLICK on the down arrow to put it back.
LEFT-CLICK on the Letter from Sullivan.
RIGHT-CLICK to bring up the supplemental list.
LEFT-CLICK on the World Map.
LEFT-CLICK on Sullivan's Office.
LEFT-CLICK on Sullivan.
LEFT-CLICK on *Ask about Your Predecessor*.
LEFT-CLICK on *Ask about The Case File*.
LEFT-CLICK on the Initial Crime Report.
LEFT-CLICK on *Ask about Finster* (under Victim).
LEFT-CLICK on *Tell Him It Looks Like Fascist Propaganda*.
LEFT-CLICK on *Ask about Detective*.
RIGHT-CLICK to bring up the supplemental list.
LEFT-CLICK on the World Map.
LEFT-CLICK on Detective Merylo's Office.

Chapter 2

Get A Clue, Get A Bigger Puzzle

LEFT-CLICK on Detective Merylo.
LEFT-CLICK on *Ask about the Torso Murders*.
LEFT-CLICK on *Ask If the FBI Is Helping with the Torso Murders Case*.
LEFT-CLICK on *Ask about Mr. Finster's Complaint*.
LEFT-CLICK and hold the *left* mouse button down, dragging the cursor to the Mug Book.
LEFT-CLICK on the Mug Book.
LEFT-CLICK on the Finster Stationery.
RIGHT-CLICK to bring up the supplemental list.
LEFT-CLICK on the World Map.
LEFT-CLICK on Hank Finster's Office.
LEFT-CLICK on Finster.
LEFT-CLICK on *Ask about the Man Who Gave Him the Invitation*.
LEFT-CLICK on *Ask for the Messenger's Description*.
LEFT-CLICK on *Ask Where He Can Find the Messenger*.
LEFT-CLICK on *Ask about the Brotherhood of Thule*.
RIGHT-CLICK to bring up the supplemental list.
LEFT-CLICK on the World Map.
LEFT-CLICK on McGinty's Bar.
LEFT-CLICK to walk toward the Bartender.
TURN RIGHT and LEFT-CLICK on the Bartender.
LEFT-CLICK on *Ask about the Foreman*.
TURN RIGHT and LEFT-CLICK to go toward the FBI Agent.
TURN LEFT and LEFT-CLICK to go toward the FBI Agent again.
LEFT-CLICK on the FBI Agent.
LEFT-CLICK on *Ask about the Foreman*.
LEFT-CLICK on *Ask Who He Is*.
RIGHT-CLICK to bring up the supplemental list.
LEFT-CLICK on World Map.
LEFT-CLICK on Sullivan's Office.
LEFT-CLICK on Sullivan.
LEFT-CLICK on *Ask about the Blacklist*.
RIGHT-CLICK to bring up the supplemental list.
LEFT-CLICK on the World Map.
LEFT-CLICK on My Office.
Blacklist Puzzle: For a detailed solution on obtaining Dr. Strauss's number, see page 27.
LEFT-CLICK to go behind the desk.
LEFT-CLICK on the Phone.

LEFT-CLICK the following numbers: 267-404.
RIGHT-CLICK to bring up the supplemental list.
LEFT-CLICK on the World Map.
LEFT-CLICK on Detective Merylo's Office.
LEFT-CLICK on *Ask about Special Agent Winslow.*
RIGHT-CLICK to pull up the supplemental list.
LEFT-CLICK on the World Map.
LEFT-CLICK on My Office.
LEFT-CLICK on the down arrow on the Message.

CHANGE TO DISK #2

Chapter 3
Puzzling Encounters

LEFT-CLICK on Helen Strauss.
LEFT-CLICK on *Ask about Her Father, Professor Strauss.*
LEFT-CLICK on *Ask about Her Field of Expertise.*
RIGHT-CLICK to bring up the supplemental list.
LEFT-CLICK on the World Map.
LEFT-CLICK on My Office.
TURN RIGHT and LEFT-CLICK on the Light Switch.
LEFT-CLICK and hold the *left* mouse button down, dragging the cursor up to the ceiling Light Fixture.
LEFT-CLICK on the Light Fixture.
RIGHT-CLICK to bring up the supplemental list.
LEFT-CLICK on the World Map.
LEFT-CLICK on McGinty's Bar.
LEFT-CLICK to go forward past the Bartender.
LEFT-CLICK to go forward again.
TURN LEFT and LEFT-CLICK on the Bald Man (Hansen).
LEFT-CLICK on Hansen.
LEFT-CLICK on *Ask about the Foreman.*
RIGHT-CLICK to bring up the supplemental list.
LEFT-CLICK on the World Map.
LEFT-CLICK on the Museum of Natural History.
RIGHT-CLICK to bring up the supplemental list.
LEFT-CLICK on the Inventory.
LEFT-CLICK on the Case File.
LEFT-CLICK on Use.
LEFT-CLICK on the down arrow to back away from the Book.
RIGHT-CLICK to bring up the supplemental list.
LEFT-CLICK on the Inventory.
LEFT-CLICK on the Finster Stationery.
LEFT-CLICK on Use.

LEFT-CLICK on the down arrow to move away from the Book.
RIGHT-CLICK to bring up the supplemental list.
LEFT-CLICK on the Inventory.
LEFT-CLICK on the Bag of Runes.
LEFT-CLICK on Use.
LEFT-CLICK on Helen Strauss.
LEFT-CLICK on *Ask about the Stained Glass Window.*
LEFT-CLICK on the Stained Glass Window.
Stained Glass Window Puzzle: For a solution to the Stained Glass Window Puzzle, see page 44.
LEFT-CLICK on the down arrow on Solved Puzzle to back away.
LEFT-CLICK on the Light above Work Table to turn it on.
LEFT-CLICK on the List of Names to back away.
RIGHT-CLICK to bring up the supplemental list.
LEFT-CLICK on the World Map.
LEFT-CLICK on McGinty's Bar.
LEFT-CLICK to walk by the Bartender.
LEFT-CLICK again to walk forward.
TURN RIGHT and LEFT-CLICK on the Phone on the wall three times to use it. LEFT-CLICK to dial 267-259.
TYPE "Louie Fischterwald" and press [Enter].
RIGHT-CLICK to bring up the supplemental list.
LEFT-CLICK on the World Map.
LEFT-CLICK on the Raven Room.

Chapter 4
Death Takes a Hand

TURN RIGHT and LEFT-CLICK on the Intercom.
LEFT-CLICK on the Intercom again.
LEFT-CLICK on *Tell Him Finster Sent You.*
LEFT-CLICK to back away from the Door.
TURN RIGHT and LEFT-CLICK on the Card by the desk leg.
LEFT-CLICK on the Card.
LEFT-CLICK on the Card again to put it in the Inventory.
RIGHT-CLICK to bring up the supplemental list.
LEFT-CLICK on the Inventory.
LEFT-CLICK on the Holy Card.
LEFT-CLICK on the Card to turn it over and read its other side.
LEFT-CLICK on Exit to get out of Inventory.
RIGHT-CLICK to bring up the supplemental list.
LEFT-CLICK on the World Map.
LEFT-CLICK on St. Bartholomew's Mission.

LEFT-CLICK on the Deskman (Ernie).
LEFT-CLICK on *Ask about Louie*.
LEFT-CLICK on *Ask Him How He Knows Louie*.
LEFT-CLICK on *Ask Him What He Does*.
LEFT-CLICK on *Ask If The Mission Has Been Busy*.
RIGHT-CLICK to bring up the supplemental list.
LEFT-CLICK on the World Map.
LEFT-CLICK on the Museum of Natural History.
LEFT-CLICK on Helen Strauss.
LEFT-CLICK on *Ask If She's Figured Out How the Pieces of Runes Assemble*.
RIGHT-CLICK to bring up the supplemental list.
LEFT-CLICK on the World Map.
LEFT-CLICK on the Raven Room.
LEFT-CLICK on Louie.
LEFT-CLICK on *Confront Louie about the Invitation*.
RIGHT-CLICK to bring up the supplemental list.
LEFT-CLICK on the World Map.
LEFT-CLICK on St. Bartholomew's Mission.
LEFT-CLICK on Ernie.
LEFT-CLICK on *Trick Ernie into Leaving*.
LEFT-CLICK and drag the cursor under the desk. Then, LEFT-CLICK again to look under the desk.
LEFT-CLICK on the Black Suitcase.
Ernie's Suitcase Puzzle: See page 56 for Ernie's Suitcase Puzzle Solution.
LEFT-CLICK on the Picture to take it.
LEFT-CLICK on the Picture again to put it in Inventory.
LEFT-CLICK on the down arrow to back away from the Suitcase.
RIGHT-CLICK to bring up the supplemental list.
LEFT-CLICK on the World Map.
LEFT-CLICK on Detective Merylo's Office.
LEFT-CLICK on Detective Merylo.
LEFT-CLICK on *Show Him Ernie's Photo*.
RIGHT-CLICK to bring up the supplemental list.
LEFT-CLICK on the World Map.
LEFT-CLICK on the Raven Room.
LEFT-CLICK on the Inventory.
LEFT-CLICK on Ernie's Photo.
LEFT-CLICK on Use to use Ernie's Photo on Louie.
TURN RIGHT and LEFT-CLICK to go forward. (Or TURN LEFT and LEFT-CLICK to go forward.)
LEFT-CLICK on the Bottle to throw it. (Or LEFT-CLICK and shoot the Pipes near the gunman's hiding place.)
LEFT-CLICK to shoot the Gunman.

CHANGE TO DISK #3

Chapter 5
There Is a Crooked Man

LEFT-CLICK on Detective Merylo.
LEFT-CLICK on *Ask Him about the Warehouse Gunman*.
LEFT-CLICK on *Tell Him What You Know*.
LEFT-CLICK on the Newspaper.
LEFT-CLICK on the story, *Rest of Torso Victim's Remains Found*.
LEFT-CLICK on the down arrow to back away from the Newspaper.
LEFT-CLICK on the story, *I Survived the Torso Killer*.
LEFT-CLICK on the down arrow to back away from the Newspaper.
RIGHT-CLICK to bring up the supplemental list.
LEFT-CLICK on the World Map.
LEFT-CLICK on Sullivan's Office.
LEFT-CLICK on Sullivan.
LEFT-CLICK on *Update Your Boss on Your Case*.
LEFT-CLICK on *Ask about Mr. Pensky*.
RIGHT-CLICK to bring up the supplemental list.
LEFT-CLICK on the Inventory.
LEFT-CLICK on the Matchbook in list.
LEFT-CLICK on the right arrow on the Matchbook to turn it over and to get a phone number.
LEFT-CLICK on the front of the Matchbook to open it and get the name Muhlhaven.
LEFT-CLICK on Exit.
RIGHT-CLICK to bring up the supplemental list.
LEFT-CLICK on the World Map.
LEFT-CLICK on Hotel Cleveland.
LEFT-CLICK on the Hotel Clerk.
LEFT-CLICK on *Ask If Muhlhaven Is in*.
LEFT-CLICK on *Ask More about Muhlhaven*.
LEFT-CLICK on *Ask for Muhlhaven's Room Number*.
LEFT-CLICK on *Threaten Him* or *Bribe Him*; either action ends the same way.
TURN RIGHT and LEFT-CLICK on the Phone on the wall.
LEFT-CLICK on the Phone again.
LEFT-CLICK to dial 425-637.
TURN RIGHT and LEFT-CLICK on the Maid's Cart.
LEFT-CLICK on the Maid's Cart again.
LEFT-CLICK on the Butter Knife.
LEFT-CLICK on the down arrow to back away from the Cart.

LEFT-CLICK and drag the cursor up to the
  Transom above the door.
LEFT-CLICK on the Transom.
TURN RIGHT and LEFT-CLICK on the Bed.
TURN RIGHT and LEFT-CLICK on the Nightstand
  to the right of the Bed.
LEFT-CLICK on the Vase on the Nightstand.
LEFT-CLICK on the Key in the Vase.
LEFT-CLICK on the down arrow to add it to the
  Inventory.
LEFT-CLICK on the Invitation in the Vase.
TURN RIGHT and LEFT-CLICK on the Armoire
  against the wall.
LEFT-CLICK on the Armoire's Handles.
LEFT-CLICK two times on the down arrow to
  back away.
TURN LEFT and LEFT-CLICK on the Bed.
LEFT-CLICK two times on the Vase.
LEFT-CLICK two times on the Photo in the Vase.
RIGHT-CLICK to bring up supplemental list.
LEFT-CLICK on Inventory.
LEFT-CLICK on Photo from 23G.
LEFT-CLICK to turn over and read message.
LEFT-CLICK to exit.
LEFT-CLICK on the down arrow to step away
  from the Photo.
RIGHT-CLICK to bring up the supplemental list.
LEFT-CLICK on the World Map.
LEFT-CLICK on Louie's Loft.
LEFT-CLICK to go forward into Louie's Loft.
TURN RIGHT and LEFT-CLICK on the stove.
LEFT-CLICK on the small Broom beside the stove.
LEFT-CLICK on the down arrow to back away.
TURN RIGHT and LEFT-CLICK on the Floor in the
  walkway straight from the door; this is the
  only interactive section here. Refer to the
  screen capture in Chapter 5 if you are having
  difficulty with this action.
LEFT-CLICK two times on the Lockbox hidden
  beneath the flooring.
Lockbox Puzzle: For the Lockbox Puzzle
  Solution, see page 75.
LEFT-CLICK on the down arrow to step away
  from the hiding place.
RIGHT-CLICK to bring up the supplemental list.
LEFT-CLICK on the World Map.
LEFT-CLICK on Sullivan's Office.
LEFT-CLICK on Sullivan.
LEFT-CLICK on *Ask about Joseph Muhlhaven.*
LEFT-CLICK on *Ask about Blackmailer.*
LEFT-CLICK on *Ask about Photo.*
LEFT-CLICK on *Ask about Pensky's Last Case.*

RIGHT-CLICK to bring up the supplemental list.
LEFT-CLICK on the World Map.
LEFT-CLICK on Flanagan's.
RIGHT-CLICK to bring up the supplemental list.
LEFT-CLICK on the World Map.
LEFT-CLICK on FBI Office.
LEFT-CLICK on Winslow.
LEFT-CLICK on *Ask about the Warehouse
  Gunman.*
LEFT-CLICK on *Ask about Joseph Muhlhaven.*
LEFT-CLICK on *Ask about the Blackmailer.*
LEFT-CLICK on *Ask about Pensky's Files.*
RIGHT-CLICK to bring up the supplemental list.
LEFT-CLICK on the World Map.
LEFT-CLICK on Hotel Cleveland.
TURN LEFT and LEFT-CLICK on the Armoire.
LEFT-CLICK on the Armoire Handle.
RIGHT-CLICK to bring up the supplemental list.
LEFT-CLICK on the Inventory.
LEFT-CLICK on the Signet Ring.
LEFT-CLICK on Use.

Chapter 6
Feather and Fang

LEFT-CLICK on the Invitation four times (the
  folded black papers under the ties).
RIGHT-CLICK to bring up the supplemental list.
LEFT-CLICK on the World Map.
LEFT-CLICK on the FBI Office.
TURN LEFT and LEFT-CLICK two times on the
  Picture to the right of the adjoining door.
LEFT-CLICK on the left side of the Picture.
Winslow's Safe Puzzle: For the solution to
  Winslow's Safe Puzzle, see page 87.
LEFT-CLICK on the File on the top shelf.
LEFT-CLICK through All papers (until you find
  out that Pensky is at the Sunnyvale Rest
  Home, which requires a Level 3 Security
  Clearance in order to see him).
LEFT-CLICK on the down arrow to get out of
  the File.
LEFT-CLICK on the ID Card on the second shelf.
LEFT-CLICK on the down arrow to back away
  from the Safe.
RIGHT-CLICK to bring up the supplemental list.
LEFT-CLICK on the World Map.
LEFT-CLICK on the Sunnyvale Rest Home.

Chapter 7
The Pensky Interviews

LEFT-CLICK on Pensky.
LEFT-CLICK on *Ask about His Case*.
LEFT-CLICK on *Ask about the Torso Killings*.
LEFT-CLICK on *Ask about the Raven Room*.
LEFT-CLICK on *Ask about the Dreams That Have Troubled Him*.
RIGHT-CLICK to pull up the supplemental list.
LEFT-CLICK on the World Map.
LEFT-CLICK on My Office.
TURN RIGHT and LEFT-CLICK on the Books to the right of the Locked Cabinet.
LEFT-CLICK on *The Crusades*.
LEFT-CLICK two times on the Raven's Feather.
RIGHT-CLICK to pull up the supplemental list.
LEFT-CLICK on the World Map.
LEFT-CLICK on Louie's Loft.
LEFT-CLICK to walk forward.
TURN LEFT and LEFT-CLICK on the Dresser.
RIGHT-CLICK to bring up the supplemental list.
LEFT-CLICK on the Inventory.
LEFT-CLICK on the Lockbox Key.
LEFT-CLICK on Use.
Dresser Lock Puzzle: For the solution to Louie's Dresser Lock Puzzle, see page 100.
LEFT-CLICK on the Fang hidden in the locking mechanism.
LEFT-CLICK on the Fang again to add it to the Inventory.
RIGHT-CLICK to bring up the supplemental list.
LEFT-CLICK on the World Map.
LEFT-CLICK on Flanagan's.
LEFT-CLICK on Muhlhaven.
LEFT-CLICK on *Ask Why He's Being Blackmailed*.
LEFT-CLICK on *Ask about the Raven Room*.
LEFT-CLICK on *Ask How to Get in to the Party*.
RIGHT-CLICK to pull up the supplemental list.
LEFT-CLICK on the Inventory.
LEFT-CLICK on the Invitation.
LEFT-CLICK on Use.
RIGHT-CLICK to pull up the supplemental list.
LEFT-CLICK on the World Map.
LEFT-CLICK on Sunnyvale Rest Home.
LEFT-CLICK on Pensky.
LEFT-CLICK on *Ask about the Party at the Raven Room* .
RIGHT-CLICK to bring up the supplemental list.
LEFT-CLICK on the World Map.

LEFT-CLICK on the Museum of Natural History.
TURN RIGHT and LEFT-CLICK on the Display Case.
LEFT-CLICK on paper in case.
LEFT-CLICK on the down arrow to pull back from the Seals.
LEFT-CLICK on the Seal.
LEFT-CLICK on the Seal again to open it.
Seal Puzzle: For the solution to the Seal Puzzle, see page 105.

CHANGE TO DISK #4

Chapter 8
Party Crashing the Raven Room

TURN LEFT and LEFT-CLICK on the Door by the Bouncer.
TURN LEFT and LEFT-CLICK on the Dish (an upside-down bowl)on the Table.
LEFT-CLICK on the Wait Station Entrance beside the Table.
TURN RIGHT and RIGHT-CLICK to bring up the supplemental list.
LEFT-CLICK on the Inventory.
LEFT-CLICK on the Dish.
LEFT-CLICK on Use.
LEFT-CLICK on the Tray of Glasses.
TURN LEFT and LEFT-CLICK to pull the chain on the light above the table.
LEFT-CLICK on the Table.
Brotherhood of Thule Table Puzzle: To solve the Brotherhood of Thule Table Puzzle, see page 113.
LEFT-CLICK on the down arrow to back away from the Letter.

Chapter 9
Murder Written in the Stars

LEFT-CLICK on Cassandra.
LEFT-CLICK on *Ask about Mr. Pensky*.
LEFT-CLICK on *Tell Her about Your Nightmares*.
LEFT-CLICK on *Yes*.
Dream Door Puzzle: For the solution to the Dream Door Puzzle, see page 122.
PRESS [Esc] to return to Cassandra.
LEFT-CLICK on Cassandra.
LEFT-CLICK on *Tell Her about the Crystal Spheres*.
LEFT-CLICK on the Book to turn the page.

LEFT-CLICK on the down arrow to move away from the Book.
RIGHT-CLICK to bring up the supplemental list.
LEFT-CLICK on the World Map.
LEFT-CLICK on Sullivan's Office.
LEFT-CLICK on Sullivan.
LEFT-CLICK on *Mention Link between Brotherhood of Thule and Torso Killings*.
LEFT-CLICK on *Ask about Von Hess*.
RIGHT-CLICK to bring up the supplemental list.
LEFT-CLICK on the World Map.
LEFT-CLICK on Detective Merylo's Office.
LEFT-CLICK on Merylo.
LEFT-CLICK on *Ask to See Evidence on Torso Case* .
LEFT-CLICK on Item #1.
LEFT-CLICK to turn through all the Pages. (The arrow *must* be placed to the right to get through all the pages).
LEFT-CLICK on the Victim's Address on the third page to open the Santini House location.
LEFT-CLICK on the top of Page #1 to talk to Merylo.
LEFT-CLICK on the down arrow to return to the Evidence Tracking Log.
LEFT-CLICK on Item #2.
LEFT-CLICK on the Victim Photo.
LEFT-CLICK on the down arrow to return to the Evidence Tracking Log.
LEFT-CLICK on Item #3.
LEFT-CLICK on the Newspaper.
LEFT-CLICK on the down arrow to return to the Evidence Tracking Log.
LEFT-CLICK on Items #4–#18 in order to take a look at them.
LEFT-CLICK on Item 19 to talk to Merylo about the FBI confiscation.
LEFT-CLICK on the down arrow to exit from the Evidence Tracking Log.
LEFT-CLICK on Merylo.
LEFT-CLICK on *Ask about Von Hess*.
LEFT-CLICK on *Ask about Von Hess's Medallion*.
RIGHT-CLICK to bring up the supplemental list.
LEFT-CLICK on the World Map.
LEFT-CLICK on the FBI Office.
LEFT-CLICK on Winslow.
LEFT-CLICK on *Ask about Von Hess*.
LEFT-CLICK on *Ask about Von Hess's Medallion*.
LEFT-CLICK on *Ask to See Torso Case Evidence*.
LEFT-CLICK on *Ask If He Has Any of Detective Merylo's Evidence*.
LEFT-CLICK on *Ask about Pensky*.

RIGHT-CLICK to bring up the supplemental list.
LEFT-CLICK on the World Map.
LEFT-CLICK on Kingsbury Run.
RIGHT-CLICK to bring up the supplemental list.
LEFT-CLICK on the World Map.
LEFT-CLICK on the Santini House.
LEFT-CLICK on Mrs. Santini to *Ask about Killer's Motives*.
LEFT-CLICK on Mrs. Santini to get her to leave.
TURN RIGHT and LEFT-CLICK on the Light Switch.
TURN LEFT and LEFT-CLICK on the window to the right of the Bed.
LEFT-CLICK on the bottom of the Window Shade, hold it down, and pull the shade down ALL THE WAY! Then release the *left* mouse button.
RIGHT-CLICK to bring up the supplemental list.
LEFT-CLICK on the World Map.
LEFT-CLICK on the Raven Room.
TURN RIGHT and LEFT-CLICK on the Back Room Door.
Raven Room Back Door Puzzle: For the solution to the Raven Room Back Door Puzzle, see page 135.
RIGHT-CLICK to bring up the supplemental list.
LEFT-CLICK on the World Map.
LEFT-CLICK on Detective Merylo's Office.
LEFT-CLICK on Merylo.
LEFT-CLICK on *Ask If Winslow Returned the Evidence*.
LEFT-CLICK on Item # 19.
RIGHT-CLICK to bring up the supplemental list.
LEFT-CLICK on the World Map.
LEFT-CLICK on the Psychic Parlor.
LEFT-CLICK on Cassandra.
LEFT-CLICK on *Ask to Be Put into Trance*.
Sphere Puzzle: To solve the Sphere Puzzle, see page 137.
LEFT-CLICK to go forward.
LEFT-CLICK on Odin Pool.
LEFT-CLICK on *ALL* of the Stones to have visions.
LEFT-CLICK on the down arrow to back away from Odin Pool.
PRESS [Esc] to get back to Cassandra.
LEFT-CLICK on Cassandra.
LEFT-CLICK on *Tell Her about the Stones and the Pool* .
LEFT-CLICK on *Tell Her You Saw Yourself in the Pool*.
RIGHT-CLICK to bring up the supplemental list.
LEFT-CLICK on the World Map.
LEFT-CLICK on the Santini House.

TURN LEFT and LEFT-CLICK to walk by the Desk.
LEFT-CLICK on the Baseboard.
LEFT-CLICK on the papers.
LEFT-CLICK on the Runes.
LEFT-CLICK on Kingsbury Run.

CHANGE TO DISK #5

Chapter 10
Track Down

LEFT-CLICK to go forward.
TURN RIGHT and LEFT-CLICK forward four times.
TURN LEFT and LEFT-CLICK forward six times.
TURN RIGHT to find the Valves.
Valve Puzzle: To solve the Valve Puzzle, see page 156.
LEFT-CLICK on the Door.
LEFT-CLICK on the Keyhole.
RIGHT-CLICK to bring up the supplemental list.
LEFT-CLICK on the World Map.
LEFT-CLICK on the FBI Office.
LEFT-CLICK on Winslow.
LEFT-CLICK on *Ask for Von Hess's Medallion*.
LEFT-CLICK on the Door Keyhole.
LEFT-CLICK on the Door.
Sliding Lever Puzzle: To solve the Sliding Lever Puzzle, see page 159.
TURN LEFT and drag the cursor up.
LEFT-CLICK on the Ledge.
RIGHT-CLICK to bring up the supplemental list.
LEFT-CLICK on the World Map.
LEFT-CLICK on the Raven Room.
LEFT-CLICK on the Robe Closet.
LEFT-CLICK on the Table to the right of the Robe Closet.
LEFT-CLICK on the left Candleholder.
Candleholder Puzzle: For the solution to the Candleholder Puzzle, see page 163.
LEFT-CLICK on the green Talisman.
LEFT-CLICK on the green Talisman again to put it in the Inventory.
RIGHT-CLICK to bring up the supplemental list.
LEFT-CLICK on the World Map.
LEFT-CLICK on the Psychic Parlor.
LEFT-CLICK on Cassandra.
LEFT-CLICK on *Ask To Be Put into Trance*.
LEFT-CLICK to go forward to the pool.
LEFT-CLICK on the Odin Pool.
LEFT-CLICK on the Talisman Icon.
PRESS [Esc] to return to Cassandra.

TURN RIGHT and LEFT-CLICK to move toward the Bookshelves.
LEFT-CLICK on the Book on the second shelf down and to the right.

Chapter 11
Recovery of the Black Dahlia

LEFT-CLICK on the Sun Door.
Sun Door Puzzle: To solve the Sun Door Puzzle, see page 172.
LEFT-CLICK on the Left Vault.
Retracting Bars Puzzle: For the solution to the Retracting Bars Puzzle, see page 174.
LEFT-CLICK on the down arrow to back away from vault.
TURN RIGHT and LEFT-CLICK on the Middle Vault.
Multiple Key Puzzle: For the solution to the Multiple Key Puzzle, see page 175.
LEFT-CLICK on the down arrow to back away from the vault.
TURN RIGHT and LEFT-CLICK on the Right Vault.
Gear Lock Puzzle: For the solution to the Gear Lock Puzzle, see page 176.
LEFT-CLICK on the Black Dahlia.

CHANGE TO DISK #6

Chapter 12
The Monastery

TURN LEFT and LEFT-CLICK on the Steps.
LEFT-CLICK on the Peephole.
LEFT-CLICK on the crates to move forward.
TURN LEFT and LEFT-CLICK to move forward again.
TURN LEFT and LEFT-CLICK to make your way through the crates.
LEFT-CLICK on the Winch.
LEFT-CLICK on the Left Lever.
LEFT-CLICK on the Right Lever.
LEFT-CLICK on the Right Lever again after the rope uncoils.
LEFT-CLICK on the down arrow to back away from the Winch.
TURN RIGHT and LEFT-CLICK on the path through the crates.
TURN LEFT and LEFT-CLICK on the Well Pulley.

CHANGE TO DISK #5

LEFT-CLICK forward.

TURN RIGHT and LEFT-CLICK forward three times.

TURN RIGHT and LEFT-CLICK forward three times.

TURN RIGHT and LEFT-CLICK forward.

LEFT-CLICK on the Altar.

LEFT-CLICK on the Box to right of the Altar.

LEFT-CLICK on the Oval two times. (Herald's Key: check screen capture in this chapter if necessary.)

LEFT-CLICK on the down arrow two times to back away from the Altar.

TURN RIGHT and LEFT-CLICK on the Tunnel.

TURN 180 degrees and LEFT-CLICK on the Tunnel.

TURN RIGHT and LEFT-CLICK forward three times.

LEFT-CLICK on the Sarcophagus.

LEFT-CLICK on the Sarcophagus Lock.

RIGHT-CLICK to bring up the supplemental list.

LEFT-CLICK on the Inventory.

LEFT-CLICK on the Artifact.

LEFT-CLICK on Use.

LEFT-CLICK on the top of the Sarcophagus. (Inside the lid is where the Runes are.)

LEFT-CLICK on the down arrow to back away from the Sarcophagus.

TURN AROUND and LEFT-CLICK to exit from the Herald's Tomb.

LEFT-CLICK forward two times.

TURN RIGHT and LEFT-CLICK forward.

TURN RIGHT again and LEFT-CLICK forward two times to enter the Central Chamber.

LEFT-CLICK on altar and turn around 180 degrees.

LEFT-CLICK on the Tunnel to the left in front of you (exiting from the Central Chamber).

TURN RIGHT and LEFT-CLICK forward two times.

TURN LEFT and LEFT-CLICK forward.

TURN LEFT and LEFT-CLICK forward two times.

TURN RIGHT and LEFT-CLICK forward three times to arrive in the Scribe's Tomb.

TURN LEFT and LEFT-CLICK on the Scribe's Sarcophagus two times.

LEFT-CLICK on the Stone Pieces.

TURN RIGHT and LEFT-CLICK on the Pool opposite the Sarcophagus.

RIGHT-CLICK to bring up the supplemental list.

LEFT-CLICK on the Inventory.

LEFT-CLICK on the Stone Pieces.

LEFT-CLICK on Use.

Stone Pieces Puzzle: For the solution to the Stone Pieces Puzzle, see page 188.

TURN RIGHT and LEFT-CLICK on the Door.

LEFT-CLICK forward two times.

TURN LEFT and LEFT-CLICK forward two times.

TURN LEFT and LEFT-CLICK forward three times.

TURN LEFT and LEFT-CLICK forward.

TURN LEFT and LEFT-CLICK forward four times.

TURN LEFT and LEFT-CLICK forward two times to enter the Sergeant At Arms's Tomb.

LEFT-CLICK on the Sarcophagus.

LEFT-CLICK on the top of the Sarcophagus.

Slider Lock Puzzle: For the solution to the Slider Lock Puzzle, see page 190.

LEFT-CLICK on the Sword Blade to copy the Runes.

LEFT-CLICK on the down arrow two times to back away from the Sarcophagus.

TURN RIGHT and LEFT-CLICK on the Door.

LEFT-CLICK forward.

TURN LEFT and LEFT-CLICK forward two times.

TURN LEFT and LEFT-CLICK forward three times.

TURN LEFT and LEFT-CLICK forward three times to enter Landulph's Tomb.

LEFT-CLICK forward to approach the Bridge.

LEFT-CLICK on the Bridge.

Bridge Steps Puzzle: For the detailed solution to the Bridge Steps Puzzle, see page 192–194.

LEFT-CLICK on the Left Section of the Bridge Step.

LEFT-CLICK on the Right Section of the Bridge Step.

LEFT-CLICK on the Left or Right Section of the Bridge Step.

LEFT-CLICK on the Middle Section of the Bridge Step.

LEFT-CLICK on the Right Section of the Bridge Step.

LEFT-CLICK on the Left Section of the Bridge Step.

LEFT-CLICK on the Right Section of the Bridge Step to get to the top.

LEFT-CLICK on Landulph's Sarcophagus.

LEFT-CLICK on the Broken Lid of the Sarcophagus.

LEFT-CLICK on the Runes to copy them, making a complete set of the Runes in order to put the Black Dahlia case back together.

Black Dahlia Casing Puzzle: For the solution to the Black Dahlia Casing Puzzle, see page 193.

LEFT-CLICK on the down arrow to back away from the Sarcophagus.

LEFT-CLICK on the Open Section of the
  Sarcophagus Lid to peer inside.
LEFT-CLICK on the down arrow two times to
  back away from the Sarcophagus.
TURN RIGHT and LEFT-CLICK on the Bridge.
LEFT-CLICK on the Left Section of the
  Bridge Step.
LEFT-CLICK on the Right Section of the
  Bridge Step.
LEFT-CLICK on the Left Section of the
  Bridge Step.
LEFT-CLICK on the Middle Section of the
  Bridge Step.
LEFT-CLICK on the Left or Right Section of the
  Bridge Step.
LEFT-CLICK on the Left Section of the
  Bridge Step.
LEFT-CLICK on the Right Section of the
  Bridge Step.
LEFT-CLICK on the Bridge to cross it.
LEFT-CLICK on the Entrance to go back out.
LEFT-CLICK forward two times.
TURN LEFT and LEFT-CLICK forward.
TURN LEFT and LEFT-CLICK forward four times.
TURN LEFT and LEFT-CLICK forward four times
  to arrive in the Central Chamber.
TURN RIGHT and LEFT-CLICK on the Altar.
TURN LEFT and LEFT-CLICK on the First
  Left Pillar.
Altar Pillar Puzzle: For the solution to the Altar
  Pillar Puzzle, see page 195.

CHANGE TO DISK #7

Chapter 13

Pursuit

LEFT-CLICK on the Abbot's Sarcophagus.
LEFT-CLICK on the Abbot's Sarcophagus again.
RIGHT-CLICK to bring up the supplemental list.
LEFT-CLICK on the Inventory.
LEFT-CLICK on the Bag of Runes.
LEFT-CLICK on Use.
TURN RIGHT and LEFT-CLICK onto the Trench
  around the Sarcophagus.
TURN LEFT and LEFT-CLICK on the Left Square
  Section three times at the foot of the
  Sarcophagus.
LEFT-CLICK on the Right Square Section two
  times at the foot of the Sarcophagus.
TURN RIGHT and LEFT-CLICK deeper into trench.

LEFT-CLICK forward.
TURN LEFT and LEFT-CLICK on the Square
  Section two times.
LEFT-CLICK on the Binoculars.
LEFT-CLICK on the down arrow to step away
  from the Binoculars.
TURN LEFT and LEFT-CLICK forward.
TURN LEFT and search the Wall on the right for a
  Hot Spot. (The cursor becomes active).
LEFT-CLICK on the Hot Spot to pull the
  Dagger out.
LEFT-CLICK on *Ask about Ritual in Monastery.*
LEFT-CLICK on *Ask How He Got to the Torso
  Killer in Cleveland.*
LEFT-CLICK on Von Hess.
LEFT-CLICK on Airman.
LEFT-CLICK on *Ask about Collins.*
LEFT-CLICK on *Ask Where Collins' Bunk Was.*
TURN LEFT and LEFT-CLICK on Collins's
  Footlocker.
LEFT-CLICK and hold on the Drawer to slide it to
  the right.
LEFT-CLICK on the Letters.
LEFT-CLICK on the down arrow to select a Letter.
  (This takes you directly to the Train.)
LEFT-CLICK on the Ashtray on the Table.
LEFT-CLICK forward to go to the Porter's Station.
TURN RIGHT and LEFT-CLICK on the Dining
  Car List.
LEFT-CLICK on the Dining Car List again.
LEFT-CLICK on the down arrow to step away
  from the Dining Car List.
LEFT-CLICK on the down arrow again to step
  away from the Porter's Station.
TURN LEFT and LEFT-CLICK on the Door.
LEFT-CLICK three times and then LEFT-CLICK
  on the Door.
LEFT-CLICK three times and then LEFT-CLICK
  on the Door.
LEFT-CLICK three times and then LEFT-CLICK
  on the Door.
LEFT-CLICK three times and then LEFT-CLICK
  on the Door.
LEFT-CLICK three times and then LEFT-CLICK
  on the Door.
LEFT-CLICK three times and then LEFT-CLICK
  on the Door.
LEFT-CLICK three times to get through the
  Baggage Car. Then LEFT-CLICK on the
  Conductor's Office Door.
LEFT-CLICK on the Conductor.
LEFT-CLICK on *Ask about Room Assignments.*

TYPE "Matt Collins".
TURN RIGHT and LEFT-CLICK on the Door.
LEFT-CLICK on the Door.
LEFT-CLICK two times to cross the Baggage Car.
LEFT-CLICK on the Map Holder on the Door.
LEFT-CLICK on the Map two times to add it to
  the Inventory.
LEFT-CLICK on the down arrow to step back from
  the Door.
TURN RIGHT and LEFT-CLICK on the Spool of
  String on Shelf 2 to add it to the Inventory.
TURN RIGHT and LEFT-CLICK to go to the
  middle of the Baggage Car.
TURN RIGHT and LEFT-CLICK on the Emergency
  Brake Wire. **ONLY DO THIS ONCE!**
TURN LEFT, LEFT-CLICK, and drag the cursor
  down. Then LEFT-CLICK on the Brown
  Suitcase on the right side of the Car.
TURN RIGHT so that both the Suitcase and the
  Emergency Brake are in your view
  (**IMPORTANT:** the trick won't work any other
  way! Definitely Save to ensure success!)
RIGHT-CLICK to bring up the supplemental list.
LEFT-CLICK on the Inventory.
LEFT-CLICK on String.
LEFT-CLICK on Use.
LEFT-CLICK two times on the Conductor's Door
  immediately!
LEFT-CLICK on the Conductor's Desk.
LEFT-CLICK on the Left Drawer of the Desk.
LEFT-CLICK on the Clipboard.
LEFT-CLICK through three pages.
LEFT-CLICK on the down arrow to close the
  Drawer.
LEFT-CLICK on the Clipboard on the Desk to get
  the Repair List.
LEFT-CLICK on the down arrow to put the
  Clipboard down.
LEFT-CLICK on the down arrow to back away
  from the Desk.
RIGHT-CLICK to bring up the supplemental list.
LEFT-CLICK on the World Map.
LEFT-CLICK on the third Sleeper Car up from the
  Baggage Car.
LEFT-CLICK two times and then LEFT-CLICK on
  Door #7.
TURN RIGHT and LEFT-CLICK on the Top Drawer
  of the Chest of Drawers.
LEFT-CLICK on the Paper With Rune.
RIGHT-CLICK to bring up the supplemental list.
LEFT-CLICK on the World Map.
LEFT-CLICK on the Caboose.

LEFT-CLICK on the Caboose Door.
LEFT-CLICK on the Conductor.
LEFT-CLICK on *Ask about Collins*.
TURN RIGHT and LEFT-CLICK on the Door.
LEFT-CLICK on the Baggage Car Door.
LEFT-CLICK two times to get to the other end of
  the Baggage Car.
TURN RIGHT and LEFT-CLICK on the Clipboard
  on the top shelf. (You have to search carefully
  for it.)
LEFT-CLICK on the Clipboard.
LEFT-CLICK on the down arrow to step back from
  the Baggage List.
LEFT-CLICK on the down arrow to step back from
  the Shelves.
TURN RIGHT and LEFT-CLICK forward.
LEFT-CLICK on Winslow's Trunk on the left side
  of the Baggage Car.
Winslow's Trunk Puzzle: To solve Winslow's
  Trunk Puzzle, see page 213.
RIGHT-CLICK to bring up the supplemental list.
LEFT-CLICK on the World Map.
LEFT-CLICK on the third Sleeper Car up from the
  Baggage Car.
LEFT-CLICK forward two times.
LEFT-CLICK on Door #7.
RIGHT-CLICK to bring up the supplemental list.
LEFT-CLICK on the World Map.
LEFT-CLICK on the Dining Car.
LEFT-CLICK forward.
LEFT-CLICK on Alice.
LEFT-CLICK on *Apologize to Her*.
LEFT-CLICK on *Ask If She Saw Winslow*.
LEFT-CLICK on *Ask Her Where She's Going*.
LEFT-CLICK on Alice again.

CHANGE TO DISK #6

Chapter 14
City of Angels

LEFT-CLICK and drag the cursor down to
  the Phone.
LEFT-CLICK on the Phone.
LEFT-CLICK on The Police.
LEFT-CLICK on Hang Up.
RIGHT-CLICK to bring up the supplemental list.
LEFT-CLICK on the World Map.
LEFT-CLICK on Gabe's Diner.
LEFT-CLICK on Detective Maxwell.
LEFT-CLICK on *Tell Him about Elizabeth Short*.

LEFT-CLICK on *Tell Him about Winslow.*
LEFT-CLICK on Detective Maxwell.
RIGHT-CLICK to pull up the supplemental list.
LEFT-CLICK on the World Map.
LEFT-CLICK on the Train Station Shipping Office.
LEFT-CLICK on the Incoming Parcels Office.
LEFT-CLICK on the Incoming Parcels Clerk.
LEFT-CLICK on *Ask about Winslow's Package.*
LEFT-CLICK on *Ask to See Shipping Manifests.*
LEFT-CLICK on the down arrow to back away
   from the Window.
TURN LEFT and LEFT-CLICK on the Trash Can.
LEFT-CLICK on the Box.
LEFT-CLICK on the Outgoing Parcels Window.
LEFT-CLICK on the Outgoing Parcels Clerk.
LEFT-CLICK on *Ask about Winslow's Package.*
RIGHT-CLICK to pull up the supplemental list.
LEFT-CLICK on the Inventory.
LEFT-CLICK on the Box.
LEFT-CLICK on Use.
LEFT-CLICK on *Choose Express Delivery.*
RIGHT-CLICK to pull up the supplemental list.
LEFT-CLICK on the World Map.
LEFT-CLICK on the Boarding House.
LEFT-CLICK on Mrs. Underhill.
LEFT-CLICK on *Ask about Elizabeth Short.*
LEFT-CLICK on *Ask about the Black Dahlia.*
TURN RIGHT and LEFT-CLICK on the Dresser
   Drawers. Then LEFT-CLICK on the down
   arrow to push them back.
LEFT-CLICK on the down arrow to step back from
   the Dresser.
TURN RIGHT and LEFT-CLICK on the Closet.
LEFT-CLICK on the down arrow to step back from
   the Closet.
TURN RIGHT and LEFT-CLICK on the Bed.
TURN RIGHT and LEFT-CLICK on the
   Nightstand.
LEFT-CLICK on the Top Drawer of the
   Nightstand.
LEFT-CLICK on the Note in the Top Drawer
   two times.
LEFT-CLICK on the down arrow to close the
   Drawer.
LEFT-CLICK on the Middle Drawer of the Dresser.
LEFT-CLICK on the down arrow to close the
   Drawer.
LEFT-CLICK on the Bottom Drawer of the
   Nightstand.
LEFT-CLICK on the Romance Novel.
LEFT-CLICK on the down arrow to put the
   Romance Novel back.

LEFT-CLICK on the Note under the
   Romance Novel.
LEFT-CLICK on the Note again.
LEFT-CLICK on the down arrow to close the
   Drawer.
LEFT-CLICK on the down arrow to step back from
   the Nightstand.
RIGHT-CLICK to pull up the supplemental list.
LEFT-CLICK on the World Map.
LEFT-CLICK on the Biltmore Hotel.
LEFT-CLICK on Ike, the Bartender.
RIGHT-CLICK to pull up the supplemental list.
LEFT-CLICK on the Inventory.
LEFT-CLICK on the Photo.
LEFT-CLICK on Use.
RIGHT-CLICK to pull up the supplemental list.
LEFT-CLICK on the World Map.
LEFT-CLICK on the Train Station Shipping Office.
LEFT-CLICK on the Incoming Parcels Window.
LEFT-CLICK on the Incoming Parcels Clerk.
LEFT-CLICK on *Ask about Status of Package.*
LEFT-CLICK on the down arrow to back away
   from the Manifest.
RIGHT-CLICK to pull up the supplemental list.
LEFT-CLICK on the World Map.
LEFT-CLICK on Sunset Arms Hotel.
LEFT-CLICK on the Phone.
LEFT-CLICK on the ABC Moving, Co.
LEFT-CLICK on Hang Up.
RIGHT-CLICK to pull up the supplemental list.
LEFT-CLICK on the World Map.
LEFT-CLICK on the ABC Moving Company.
LEFT-CLICK on the Desk.
LEFT-CLICK on the Middle Left Desk Drawer.
LEFT-CLICK on the Delivery Sheets and then
   LEFT-CLICK to go through the pages.
LEFT-CLICK on the down arrow to put the
   Clipboard back.
LEFT-CLICK on the down arrow to close the
   Drawer.
LEFT-CLICK on the down arrow to back away
   from the Desk.
TURN RIGHT and LEFT-CLICK on the Note above
   the Filing Cabinet.
LEFT-CLICK through the three pages.
LEFT-CLICK on the down arrow to back away
   from the Note.
TURN RIGHT and LEFT-CLICK on the File
   Cabinet.
LEFT-CLICK on the Bottom Drawer of the File
   Cabinet.

ABC MOVING Delivery Puzzle: For the solution to the ABC Moving Delivery Puzzle, see page 228.

LEFT-CLICK on SOIAKP52.

LEFT-CLICK on the File to flip through the pages.

LEFT-CLICK on the down arrow to close the File.

RIGHT-CLICK to pull up the supplemental list.

LEFT-CLICK on the World Map.

LEFT-CLICK on the Movie Studio.

RIGHT-CLICK to pull up the supplemental list.

LEFT-CLICK on the World Map.

LEFT-CLICK on the Biltmore Hotel.

LEFT-CLICK on Elizabeth Short.

LEFT-CLICK on *Ask about Black Dahlia.*

LEFT-CLICK on *Ask to See the Black Dahlia.*

CHANGE TO DISK #8

Chapter 15
A Fresh Corpse

RIGHT-CLICK to pull up the supplemental list.

LEFT-CLICK on the World Map.

LEFT-CLICK on the Biltmore Hotel.

LEFT-CLICK on Ike.

LEFT-CLICK on *Ask about Elizabeth Short.*

LEFT-CLICK on *Ask about Guy She Left with.*

LEFT-CLICK on *Bribe Him.*

LEFT-CLICK on *Question His Information.*

TURN LEFT and LEFT-CLICK forward.

TURN RIGHT and LEFT-CLICK on the Stairs.

LEFT-CLICK forward two times.

TURN RIGHT and LEFT-CLICK on Door #201.

TURN LEFT and LEFT-CLICK on the bottom of the Window to go to the Fire Escape.

LEFT-CLICK on the open Window.

TURN RIGHT and LEFT-CLICK on #201's Window.

LEFT-CLICK and drag the cursor to the top of the Window.

LEFT-CLICK on the top of the Window.

LEFT-CLICK on the Stick holding the Window closed.

LEFT-CLICK and drag the cursor to the bottom of the Window.

LEFT-CLICK on the bottom of the Window.

LEFT-CLICK on the open Window to go inside.

TURN LEFT and LEFT-CLICK on the top of the Door.

LEFT-CLICK on the Key on the top of the Door Trim two times to add it to the Inventory.

RIGHT-CLICK to pull up the supplemental list.

LEFT-CLICK on the World Map.

LEFT-CLICK on the Sunset Arms Hotel.

LEFT-CLICK on *Blame Murder on Winslow.*

LEFT-CLICK on *Tell Him You've Been Tracking Down Leads on Your Case.*

LEFT-CLICK on Alice.

LEFT-CLICK on *Ask Her Why She Helped Him.*

LEFT-CLICK on Alice again.

RIGHT-CLICK to pull up the supplemental list.

LEFT-CLICK on the World Map.

LEFT-CLICK on the Train Station Lockers.

TURN RIGHT and LEFT-CLICK on the First Row of Lockers.

TURN RIGHT and LEFT-CLICK on the section of Lockers 033–038.

LEFT-CLICK on Locker 37.

LEFT-CLICK on the Yellow Receipt two times.

RIGHT-CLICK to pull up the supplemental list.

LEFT-CLICK on the World Map.

LEFT-CLICK on Willington's Antiques.

LEFT-CLICK on the antique Clerk.

LEFT-CLICK on *Ask about the Black Dahlia.*

LEFT-CLICK on *Ask Him Who Purchased the Black Dahlia.*

LEFT-CLICK on *Ask to See the Cane.*

RIGHT-CLICK to pull up the supplemental list.

LEFT-CLICK on the Inventory.

LEFT-CLICK on the Cane.

Eisenstadt's Cane Puzzle: For the solution to the Eisenstadt's Cane Puzzle, see page 243.

LEFT-CLICK on the Treasure Map to take it out of the Cane.

LEFT-CLICK on Exit.

RIGHT-CLICK to pull up the supplemental list.

LEFT-CLICK on the World Map.

LEFT-CLICK on the Sunset Arms Hotel.

TURN LEFT and LEFT-CLICK on the Studio Pass on the Bed.

LEFT-CLICK on the Studio Pass again.

LEFT-CLICK on the Sunset Arms Note to back away from it.

RIGHT-CLICK to pull up the supplemental list.

LEFT-CLICK on the World Map.

LEFT-CLICK on the Movie Studio.

TURN RIGHT and LEFT-CLICK on the open Trunk in the shadows.

LEFT-CLICK on the Note in the Trunk two times.

LEFT-CLICK on the down arrow to step back from the Trunk.

TURN RIGHT and LEFT-CLICK on Alice two times.

LEFT-CLICK on *Ask How Her New Job Is.*

LEFT-CLICK on *Ask Her If Al King Is Connected to Winslow.*
LEFT-CLICK on Alice.
RIGHT-CLICK to pull up the supplemental list.
LEFT-CLICK on the World Map.
LEFT-CLICK on Al King's House.
LEFT-CLICK on Alice.
LEFT-CLICK on *Ask Her Why She Came to Hollywood.*
LEFT-CLICK on the Pictures Behind Alice.
LEFT-CLICK on the down arrow to step back.
TURN RIGHT and LEFT-CLICK on the third Book Shelf down.
LEFT-CLICK on the Pictures.
LEFT-CLICK on the down arrow to put the Pictures back.
TURN LEFT and LEFT-CLICK forward.
LEFT-CLICK on the Desk.
LEFT-CLICK on the Book on the Desk.
LEFT-CLICK on the down arrow to put the Book back.
LEFT-CLICK on the down arrow again to step back from the Desk.
LEFT-CLICK on the Topographical Map above the Desk.
RIGHT-CLICK to pull up the supplemental list.
LEFT-CLICK on the Inventory.
LEFT-CLICK on the Treasure Map.
LEFT-CLICK on Use.
ALIGN Compass Roses.
PRESS [Esc] to step back from the Maps.
LEFT-CLICK on the Trash Can beside the Desk.
LEFT-CLICK on the Telegram Pieces twice.
Telegram Pieces Puzzle: For the solution to the Telegram Pieces Puzzle, see page 250.
LEFT-CLICK on the Newspaper.
LEFT-CLICK on the down arrow to put the Newspaper down.
LEFT-CLICK on the Gloves twice.
LEFT-CLICK on the chisel twice.
RIGHT-CLICK to pull up the supplemental list.
LEFT-CLICK on the World Map.
LEFT-CLICK on Ferrin's Hill Cemetery.

Chapter 16
Final Gambit

TURN RIGHT and LEFT-CLICK on the Puzzle circled in red.
Winslow's Algebra Puzzle: For the solution to Winslow's Algebra Puzzle, see page 257.

LEFT-CLICK on the down arrow to step back from the Puzzle.
TURN LEFT and LEFT-CLICK on the Gold Vase.
LEFT-CLICK on the Note inside the Vase two times.
RIGHT-CLICK to pull up the supplemental list.
LEFT-CLICK on the World Map.
LEFT-CLICK on Al King's House.
TURN RIGHT and LEFT-CLICK forward toward the Telescope.
TURN LEFT and LEFT-CLICK on the Telescope Control Box.
LEFT-CLICK First Dial to +0.5 and Second Dial to 27.
LEFT-CLICK on the down arrow to back away from the Telescope Control Box.
LEFT-CLICK on the Telescope.
LEFT-CLICK and drag to match up both sets of Cross Hair Triangles.
TURN RIGHT and LEFT-CLICK on the Ladder.
LEFT-CLICK on Alice's Photo on the Ladder.
LEFT-CLICK on the down arrow.
TURN LEFT and LEFT-CLICK on the first Locker.
LEFT-CLICK on EACH Jack-In-The-Box **AND** their messages.
LEFT-CLICK on the down arrow to get out of each message.
LEFT-CLICK on the down arrow to get out of the first Locker.
LEFT-CLICK on the second Locker.
LEFT-CLICK on EACH Jack-In-The-Box **AND** their messages.
LEFT-CLICK on the down arrow to get out of each message.
LEFT-CLICK on the down arrow to get out of the second Locker.
LEFT-CLICK on the third Locker.
LEFT-CLICK on the Key in the third Locker.
LEFT-CLICK forward.
TURN RIGHT and LEFT-CLICK forward into a sunken area of Al King's Living Room.
TURN LEFT and LEFT-CLICK on the Movie Projector.
LEFT-CLICK on the Note.
LEFT-CLICK on the down arrow to back away.
LEFT-CLICK on the Projector's On/Off Switch.
LEFT-CLICK on the down arrow to back away from the Projector.
TURN LEFT and LEFT-CLICK forward toward the Bar.
TURN LEFT and LEFT-CLICK toward the Clock on the wall.

TURN LEFT and LEFT-CLICK on the Clock.

LEFT-CLICK to move the Hour Hand to 5.

LEFT-CLICK to move the Minute Hand to 11 and
then back to the 1.

LEFT-CLICK on the Minute Hand while the Hula
Girl is OUT and move it to the 11 again to
open the Secret Door.

Change to Disk #1

TURN RIGHT and LEFT-CLICK forward.

LEFT-CLICK on Alice.

LEFT-CLICK on the Black Dahlia to shoot it.

To get the alternate, evil ending: Don't
shoot at all, shoot Winslow, or shoot and
completely miss.

COMING SOON...

MULTIPLAYER SUPPORT. TWO-SIDED ACTION. DYNAMIC STORY. THE ALL-NEW *JETFIGHTER*.

JETFIGHTER
FULLBURN

TEEN
T
ESRB

Interplay
AFFILIATE PARTNERSHIP

MISSION
STUDIOS

PC CD-ROM

MISSION
STUDIOS CORPORATION

www.missionstudios.com

Interplay

AFFILIATE PARTNERSHIP

www.interplay.com